Land, Rights and the Politics of Investments in Africa

Land, Rights and the Politics of Investments in Africa

Ruling Elites, Investors and Populations in Natural Resource Investments

Edited by

Lars Buur

Professor in the Political Economy of Development, Roskilde University, Denmark

José Jaime Macuane

Associate Professor of Political Science and Public Administration, University Eduardo Mondlane, Mozambique

Faustin Peter Maganga

Associate Professor, Directorate of Research, Innovation and Consultancy (DRIC), St. John's University of Tanzania, Tanzania

Rasmus H. Pedersen

Senior Researcher, Danish Institute for International Studies, Denmark

Edward Elgar
PUBLISHING

Cheltenham, UK • Northampton, MA, USA

Cover image: Leandre Chastagnier on Unsplash

Published by
Edward Elgar Publishing Limited
The Lypiatts
15 Lansdown Road
Cheltenham
Glos GL50 2JA
UK

Edward Elgar Publishing, Inc.
William Pratt House
9 Dewey Court
Northampton
Massachusetts 01060
USA

A catalogue record for this book
is available from the British Library

Library of Congress Control Number: 2023930302

This book is available electronically in the **Elgar**online
Political Science and Public Policy subject collection
http://dx.doi.org/10.4337/9781800377264

Printed on elemental chlorine free (ECF)
recycled paper containing 30% Post-Consumer Waste

ISBN 978 1 80037 725 7 (cased)
ISBN 978 1 80037 726 4 (eBook)

Printed and bound in the USA

Contents

Contributors

Kathrin Beykirch has a Master's Degree in Global Studies and International Development Studies from Roskilde University, where she graduated in 2017. Since 2019 Kathrin has worked for GIZ – the German Corporation for International Cooperation for a Good Governance Programme in Mozambique.

Evans Boadu is an Associate Lecturer with the School of Government and a Postdoctoral Research Fellow at the School of Public Health, at the University of the Western Cape. Evans' research interests are in social policies, monitoring and evaluation, indigenous knowledge, culturally responsive evaluation, governance and political history of Africa and community-based development and their overarching implications on socio-economic issues in Ghana, South Africa and Africa at large. He has published articles in *Evaluation and Program Planning*, *Extractive Industries and Society*, among others.

Lars Buur is Professor in the Political Economy of Development at Roskilde University. He has a PhD in Ethnography and Social Anthropology from Aarhus University. His key research interests include state formation and sovereignty, natural resource investments, industrial policy in Africa and social cash transfers. His key publications can be found in *Extractive Industries and Society*, *Third World Quarterly*, *Geoforum*, among others. He has also co-authored with Lindsay Whitfield, Ole Therkildsen and Mette Kjær *The Politics of African Industrial Policy* (Cambridge University Press 2015) and has edited several books and journal special issues on traditional authorities, security and sovereignty.

Thabit Jacob is a former Postdoctoral Researcher at the Danish Institute for International Studies and presently a Postdoctoral Researcher at the University of Gothenburg. He completed his PhD in International Development Studies at Roskilde University, where his doctoral thesis examined the political economy of resource nationalism in the Tanzanian extractive sector. His research focuses broadly on the political economy of development, politics, and extractive sectors hereunder the politics of energy transitions, and the role of state actors in shaping nationalist interventions in the extractive and energy sectors. His research has been published in *African Affairs*, *Oxford Energy Forum*, *Deutsche Welle*, *Le Monde*, among others.

Eileen Dyer Jarnholt, has a PhD in International Development Studies from Roskilde University and Utrecht University. Her research interests include agricultural development, contract farming, natural resource management, political economy and state-business relations. Her dissertation paper was published in 2020 and is titled 'Contact Farming Schemes in Rice and Sugar in Tanzania: Assessing the Implications of Exchange, Power, and Differentiation'.

Opportuna L. Kweka is a Senior Lecturer in Economic Geography in the Department of Geography at the University of Dar es Salaam. She has a PhD from University of Minnesota. Her research is focused on political economy, natural resource governance, water, gender, forced displacement, migration and mobility. Her main publications can be found in the *Journal of Transport Geography, Geoforum, Tanzanian Journal of Population Studies and Development*, among others.

Brenda Kyomuhendo is an Assistant Lecturer in the Department of Marketing and International Business at Makerere University Business School. Her research areas include social media marketing, influencer marketing and entrepreneurship. She has published articles in the *Journal of Developmental Entrepreneurship*.

José Jaime Macuane is an Associate Professor of Political Science and Public Administration at the University Eduardo Mondlane. He has a PhD in Political Science, from the Instituto Universitário de Pesquisas do Rio de Janeiro. His research areas are state and public sector reform, taxation, democratisation, political institutions, and political economy of development and extractives. He has a track record of publications on Africa and Mozambique, in journals such as *African Affairs, Extractive Industries and Society, Cadernos de Estudos Africanos*.

Faustin Maganga is an Associate Professor at the Directorate of Research, Innovation and Consultancy (DRIC) at the St John's University of Tanzania. He has a PhD in Geography and International Development Studies from Roskilde University. He has extensive experience in development research and consultancy, especially related to land rights, land use planning, wildlife forestry management and renewable energy. His key publications can be found in *African Review, European Journal of Development Research*, among others.

Happiness Malle has a Master's in Procurement. She works as a procurement officer at Swala Solutions Ltd which partners with Barrick Gold Mine Tanzania. Happiness is interested in community development and has worked as a research assistant for various projects and researchers on different studies in Tanzania since 2016.

Onesmo Minani is an Advocate, Public Notary and Commissioner for Oaths. He is a practising Advocate of the High Court and Subordinate Courts thereto. He has also served as the CEO of One Answer Microfinance Ltd since 2014. He holds a Bachelor of Laws (LLB) and a Postgraduate of Laws Degree from Mzumbe University, Tanzania. His research interests include smallholder farming, land reform and natural resource governance.

Malin J. Nystrand is an Assistant Professor in Global Political Economy at Roskilde University. She has a PhD in Peace and Development Research from University of Gothenburg. Her research areas include the political economy of investments and social cash transfers, social responsibility and social embeddedness of local business actors, and corruption and post-conflict reconstruction. She has a track record of publications on East Africa and in particular Uganda, in journals such as *Journal of Modern African Studies*, *Third World Quarterly* and *Extractive Industries and Society*.

Rasmus H. Pedersen is a Senior Researcher at the Danish Institute for International Studies. Currently his research is focused on the political economy of energy transitions, comprising issues like resource endowments, resource nationalism, policy coalitions, planning and state capacity, development assistance, electrification and access to energy. Rasmus holds a PhD in International Development Studies from Roskilde University. His key publications can be found in *Extractive Industries and Society*, *Journal of Eastern African Studies*, *Journal of Hazardous Materials*, among others.

Rose Qamara is an Assistant Lecturer at Tengeru Institute of Community Development in Tanzania. She holds an MSc in Forest and Nature Conservation specialising in Policy and Society from Wageningen University and research in the Netherlands. Her research focuses on social-political analysis, especially on environment and natural resources governance, human-wildlife conflicts and food systems.

Padil Salimo has a PhD from the Doctoral School of Social Sciences and Business, Roskilde University, and the Institute of Resource Assessment (IRA), University of Dar es Salaam. Padil is a lecturer at Eduardo Mondlane University and a senior consultant with experience of more than 20 years. His research focus is on oil and natural gas politics, and the political economy of natural resource governance in Africa. His key publications have been included in the book *Extractive Industries and Changing State Dynamics in Africa: Beyond the Resource Curse* (J. Schubert, U. Engel and E. Macamo, eds, Routledge 2018).

George Schoneveld has a PhD and is a Senior Scientist within the Center for International Forestry Research (CIFOR) Value Chains, Finance and

Investment team, based in Nairobi, Kenya. Trained as a business economist, he is managing large research-for-development projects across the global south on inclusive business development, certification and sustainable intensification. George recently led a large-scale evaluation of inclusive business innovations in the cocoa, oil palm, coffee and tea sectors and currently manages inclusive business technical support programmes in Myanmar, Laos, Ghana, Mozambique and Ethiopia.

Arthur Sserwanga is a Professor at Makerere University Business School, Kampala, Uganda. He has a PhD in Entrepreneurship from Makerere University. His research interests include entrepreneurship, taxation, financial crime and accounting. He has authored several articles in journals such as the *European Journal of Business and Management, Journal of Developmental Entrepreneurship*, among others, and has also published books, case studies and working papers.

Emmanuel Sulle is a research advisor at the Aga Khan University, Arusha Campus, Tanzania, and a contributor to the Network of Excellence on Land Governance in Africa. He holds a PhD in Land and Agrarian Studies from the Institute for Poverty, Land and Agrarian Studies (PLAAS). His current research interests include large-scale land deals, land tenure, green economy, convivial and just conservation and agrarian transformation in Africa. His work is published in journals such as *Development and Environment, Journal of East African Studies*, among others, and he has authored several book chapters on agricultural commercialisation, biofuels and tourism.

Acknowledgements

This edited book is the product of six years of research and working together, including five years of fieldwork from 2016 to 2021. It comes out of the work we have carried out under the Hierarchies of Rights research programme funded by the Royal Danish Foreign Ministry through the Danish Consultative Research Committee and the Danida Fellowship Centre. Over the course of six years many people, and in many cases the organizations in which they are embedded, have contributed in greater or lesser ways to make this edited volume a reality. We would briefly like to acknowledge their help, support and generosity here.

First, the research programme was based at the Department of Social Sciences and Business (ISE) at Roskilde University and was coordinated by Lars Buur. We are grateful to the Danish Consultative Research Committee and the Danida Fellowship Centre for a four-year grant that made the research possible, and a two-year extension that allowed us more time to develop our ideas and findings, as well as making sure the programme could be finalized. Besides the generous funding from the Foreign Ministry, the research programme received valuable support from the Swedish Research Council for Malin J. Nystrand's work, as well as various important smaller grants from the Effective States and Inclusive Development Research Centre, University of Manchester, UK.

We are also grateful to ISE, which hosted the programme and became the intellectual home of this book, the research and its development, as well as training the researchers who were funded through the programme, namely Celso Monjane, Thabit Jacob and Padil Salimo. Directly and indirectly the ISE also facilitated the two projects attached to the programme by Eileen D. Jarnholt and Christina Saulich. We thank the ISE administrative staff, particularly the financial and research support staff, who provided invaluable technical support. A special word of thanks is due to the Dean, Peter Kragelund, who provided invaluable assistance and moral support the whole way through, from conception to the very end of the programme. During the later part of the programme the Centre for African Economies (CAE), which in 2021 became the Socio-Economic Research Centre (SECO), became the home for the final outreach activities and later publishing activities. We also want to thank the useful and encouraging advice from members of the research programme's advisory board, namely Ole Therkildsen, Randi Kaarhus, Sam Hickey and Tom Lavers.

The Hierarchies of Rights programme was a collaborative endeavour between ISE at Roskilde University, the Danish Institute for International Studies (DIIS, Copenhagen), Eduardo Mondlane University (UEM, Mozambique) and the University of Dar es Salaam (UDeS, Tanzania) particularly the Institute for Resource Assessment, which generously hosted the programme. At UEM, the project benefitted from the support of the Vice Chancellor, Prof. Orlando Quilambo, and the Dean and Staff of the Faculty of Arts and Social Sciences and of the Department of Political Science and Public Administration, where it was hosted. Special thanks go to DIIS for providing dedicated and strong support for the outreach and working paper series, and to UDeS for facilitating the joint programme with the Doctoral School of Social Sciences and Business, Roskilde University, and UEM for hosting the 2019 comparative outreach activities in Maputo.

The participation of local researchers in Uganda, Tanzania and Mozambique varied across the three countries, but we could not have processed the vast amount of material on which this book and each chapter is based without their assistance and stamina. While numerous researchers could be mentioned, special thanks are due to Carlota Mondlane Tembe, who, besides assisting with the Mozambican research, provided valuable comments and assistance throughout the programme before focusing on her own doctoral work on women and empowerment at UEM. From Mozambique we also thank Rúben Ucucho, for his assistance in the editing process.

The ideas presented in this edited book have profited not only from close intellectual exchange and sparring among the editors and each group of chapter writers, who all came out of the Hierarchies of Rights programme or were associated with it. We also benefitted from a broad network of colleagues in research organizations and projects working on similar or associated ideas and fields of research. In particular, we thank Ole Therkildsen, Sam Hickey, Tom Lavers, Randi Kaarhus, Ellen Hillbom, George Frynas, Richard Saunders, Derek Hall, Tobias Hagmann, Christian Lund, Jesse Ovadia, Aslak Orre, Sérgio Chichava, Bernhard Weimer, Ricardo Soares de Oliveira, Emily Jones, Peter Wilson Leys, Line J. Jacobsen, Ilse Renkens, Christina Saulich, Lindsay Whitfield, Laurids Lauridsen, Salvador Forquilha, Celso Monjane, Nikkie Wiegink and Jason Sumich.

We offer special thanks to Finn Halligan from Edward Elgar Publishing for his understanding and support, which has helped us significantly.

We also wish to acknowledge *Extractive Industries and Society* for permission to use material previously published in several articles during 2019 and 2020, as well as the Taylor & Francis Group for allowing Padil Salimo to revise his chapter.

Finally, we want to acknowledge the invaluable support and assistance of Robert Parkin for editing the chapters for language with such precision and stamina, as well as to Alexandra Porojan for her incredible attention to detail while setting up and reading through the chapters.

Abbreviations

ACT	Agricultural Council of Tanzania
ADC	The biggest privately held trading company in Mozambique
AFDB	African Development Bank
AMA1	Anadarko Mozambique Area 1
ARPONE	Association of the larger farmers in Xai-Xai
ASDP	Agricultural Sector Development Programme
ATOGS	Association of Tanzanian Oil and Gas Service Providers
BMGF	Bill & Melinda Gates Foundation
BRN	Big Results Now
BSGA	Busoga Sugarcane Growers Association
CAADP	Comprehensive Africa Agriculture Development Programme
CAIC	Agro Industrial Park in Chókwè
CARD	Coalition for African Rice Development programme
CCM	Chama Cha Mapinduzi
CDB	Chinese Development Bank
CEAGRE	Centre of Agriculture and Natural Resource Studies
CEO	Chief executive officer
cf	Cubic feet
CHADEMA	Chama cha Demokrasia na Maendeleo
COP26	Climate change conference
Covid	Coronavirus disease
CPI	Investment Promotion Centre
CSA	Cane Supply Agreement
CSOs	Civil society organizations
CSR	Corporate Social Responsibility
CTV	Centro Terra Viva

CUF	Civic United Front
Delta	Big trading group
DUAT	Land use and exploitation rights
ECAS	European Conferences of African Studies
ED&F	British commodity trader
EIAs	Environmental Impact Assessments
ENH	National Oil Company
EPCC	Exploration and Production Concession Contract
ESG	Environment, Social and Governance
ETG	Export Trading Group
EU	European Union
EWURA	Energy and Water Utilities
FAO	Food and Agriculture Organization
FDA	Agricultural Development Fund
FDI	Foreign Direct Investment
FID	Final Investment Decision
FPIC	Free Prior and Informed Consent
Frelimo	Liberation Front of Mozambique
GCA	Consultative Group on Rice
GIZ	Gesellschaft für Internationale Zusammenarbeit
GPS	Global Positioning System
GTZ	German Technical Cooperation
HICEP	Hidráulica de Chokwe – Empresa Pública
HRW	Human Rights Watch
IDPs	Internally Displaced People
IEC	Intra Energy Corporation
IFC	International Finance Corporation
INGOs	International non-governmental organization
INP	Instituto Nacional de Petroléo
JICA	Japanese International Cooperation Agency
Kakira	Kakira Sugar Works
Kaliro	Sugar and Allied Industries Ltd
Kamuli	Kamuli Sugar Ltd

Kapunga	Kapunga Rice Plantation Ltd
KORD	Kakira Outgrowers Rural Development Fund
KSC	Kilombero Sugar Company
KSCL	Kilombero Sugar Company Limited
LC1	Local Council 1
LNG	Liquefied natural gas
LRA	Lord's Resistance Army
MALF	The Ministry of Agriculture, Livestock and Fisheries
MASA	Ministry of Agriculture and Food Security
Mayuge	Mayuge Sugar Industries
MKRS	Mtenda Kyela Rice Supply Company Ltd.
MNCs	Multinational Corporations
MOF	Materials Offloading Facility
MPs	Members of Parliament
mtpa	Annual capacities of flow rates of facilities in million tonnes per annum
MWG	Mbalawala Women's Group
NAFCO	National Agriculture and Food Corporation
NAIVS	National Agricultural Input Voucher Scheme
NARCO	National Ranching Company
NDC	National Development Corporation
NGOs	Non-governmental organizations
NRDP	National Rice Development Programme
NRM	National Resistance Movement
PARPA	Action Plan for the Reduction of Absolute Poverty
PEDSA	Strategic Plan for Agricultural Development
PNISA	National Agriculture Investment Plan
PROIRRI	Sustainable Irrigation Development Project
PS5	Performance Standard 5
RBL-EP	Regadio de Baixo Limpopo – Empresa Pública
RBLL	Rovuma Basin LNG Land
SAGCOT	Southern Agricultural Growth Corridor of Tanzania
SBT	Sugar Board of Tanzania

SCOUL	Sugar Cooperation of Uganda Ltd
SLO	Social License to Operate
SOE	State-owned enterprise
SUDECO	Sugar Development Corporation
TANCOAL	Joint Venture between the National Development Corporation of Tanzania (NDC) and Intra Energy from Australia
TANESCO	Tanzania supply electric company
TANU	Tanganyika African Union
TBL	Tanzania Breweries
TCC	Tanzania Cigarette Company
TIC	Tanzania Investment Centre
TNBC	Tanzania National Business Council
TPC	Tanganyika Planting Company
TPDC	Tanzania Petroleum Development Corporation
TZS	Currency: Tanzanian shillings
UGX	Currency: Ugandan shillings
UK	United Kingdom
UN	United Nations
UPC	Provincial Peasant Union
URT	United Republic of Tanzania
US	United States
USA	United States of America
USAID	US Agency for International Development
USMA	Uganda Sugar Manufacturers Association
UTT PID	Unity Trust of Tanzania, Projects and Infrastructure Development
WanBao	Chinese investment group

Introduction to *Land, Rights and the Politics of Investments in Africa*

Lars Buur, José J. Macuane, Faustin Maganga and Rasmus H. Pedersen

1. INTRODUCTION

Natural resource investments inevitably produce winners and losers and are rarely if ever 'sustainable', even though to a large extent it is sustainability and the green transition that are presently driving extractive investments. However, experience from previous resource booms tells us that this does not necessarily mean that extractive investments are a zero-sum game. After the turn of the millennium, Africa witnessed a surge in investments in natural resources, starting with the petroleum sector, and soon followed by mining and agribusiness (Bryceson and MacKinnon, 2014; Le Billon and Sommerville, 2016; Pedersen and Buur, 2016; Buur et al., 2019), following price spikes in 2008 and again in the early 2010s. This book presents evidence for how these previous booms have affected actors in different African contexts. In the wake of the present recovery of the COVID-19 pandemic, extractive investments have picked up and even accelerated, with new demands for energy and minerals being spurred by the green transition.

Theory suggests that investments in natural resource extraction can help transform African economies by accelerating economic growth, creating jobs and strengthening the links between local economies and the global economy (Auty, 1993; Collier and Venables, 2011). However, theory is one thing, how potentials are managed within the limits of specific national and international political economies quite another. The fact is that extractive investments often wreck the environment and cause all kinds of social, political and economic problems, sometimes referred to as 'illnesses'. At times, these make resource endowments look more like 'curses' than 'blessings' (Ross, 2012; Venables, 2016; Bebbington et al., 2018) when complex processes of extraction and the world market's tentacles are set in motion.

Extractive investments are also often depicted as violating the rights of local populations and leaving them with few benefits. This may in turn lead to social protests and political instability (Frynas, 2000; Watts, 2001), potentially causing investments to be delayed or abandoned, and thereby adding to political uncertainty by further undermining the legitimacy of already weak regimes.

In this edited book, we specifically explore the potential for implementing large-scale extractive investments in natural resources while accommodating the rights of local populations. Based on extensive fieldwork as part of the Hierarchies of Rights: Land and Investments in Africa research programme,[1] we explore the relationships between three specific groups of actors – investors, ruling elites and local populations – with respect to actual large-scale investments in natural resources in the sectors of gas, minerals (coal) and agriculture (sugar and rice) in Mozambique, Tanzania and Uganda. In the analytical framework we propose in this work, we argue that all three groups of actors should be included in the analysis if we are to understand whether and how investments are implemented and whether or not the rights of local populations are accommodated.

We combine our focus on the relationships between investors, ruling elites and local populations with a broad understanding of extractive investments that includes both agricultural investments and extractive investments in, for example, gas and minerals. This draws on an older, Marxist-inspired literature on extractive investments in, for instance, Mozambique from colonialism to the present day (see, e.g., Castel-Branco, 2010) which makes no sharp distinction between agricultural and extractive investments. This literature argues that the colonial economy and the organization of the postcolonial economies that have succeeded them are extractive in their essence, whether of labour for South Africa's industrial complexes (see First, 1983), primary agricultural produce for export (Saulich, 2020) or coal (Monjane, 2019) and other mining and carbonate products for export (Salimo et al., 2020). We argue that much the same goes for Tanzania and Uganda. The broad understanding of extractive investments provides an important backdrop for bringing into the conversation different bodies of literature that are usually kept apart.

This book therefore engages with and takes further three important bodies of literature, namely those on the land-grabbing debate, the resource curse controversy and Corporate Social Responsibility (CSR). The literature exploring natural resource investments and land-grabbing tends to focus on the unequal relationship between investors and the local populations, whose land is being expropriated or otherwise acquired (Cotula, 2012; Hall et al., 2015; Edelman et al., 2013; Wolford et al., 2013). The literature on the resource curse emphasizes the cosy relationship between investors and ruling elites, from which local populations are typically excluded (Beblawi and Giacomo, 1987; Collier, 2010; Ross, 2015; Brooks and Kurtz, 2016). CSR and related interventions have often been promoted as ways for investors to compensate for dysfunctional state authorities, but they tend to be dismissed as mere window dressing (Frynas, 2005; Prno and Scott Slocombe, 2012). This book therefore makes three analytical and theoretical contributions. Firstly, in contrast to most of the existing literature, instead of focusing on just one or two types of relationship, it develops an analytical approach that brings together all three of the main groups of actors involved in the implementation of large-scale natural resource investments: investors, ruling elites and local populations. The analytical framework (see Buur et al., 2017; 2019; 2020) we develop to analyse extractive investments focuses on the *triangular relationship*, not merely the respective dyads, between investors, local populations and ruling elites, inspired by the so-called 'political settlement' approach (Khan, 2010; Whitfield et al., 2015; Behuria et al., 2017).

Secondly, this introduction and the chapters that follow it develop an analytical perspective that moves from a focus on rights as absolute to one that see rights as the outcomes of relationships between the main groups of actors involved in the implementation of large-scale natural resource investments. To work with rights to land, resources and livelihoods in relational terms is far from simple: as works on both land-grabbing and the resource curse argue, investments distribute assets unequally. However, the focus on relations redirects the analytical lens from absolute rights or substantial rights that are non-negotiable to the struggle over, negotiation and accommodation of procedural rights[2] to information, participation and compensation during the implementation of investments. Underpinning any discussion of substantive versus procedural rights is the question of whom extractive investments actually benefit (Pichler et al., 2017).

There are some tough trade-offs to be made here. There is no doubt that extractive investments in natural resources often lead to local populations having their substantive rights 'displaced' by, or maybe more correctly transformed or translated into, procedural rights. This can take the form of, for example, one-off compensation payments, CSR provisions or access to job opportunities. Whereas this can be viewed as illegitimate by certain population groups, as well as by civil-society and political organizations, these transformations may nonetheless be fully legal and may fall within the legal ambit of the state when the latter promotes investments in the name of the national interest or in pursuit of 'the greater good' of economic growth. We would argue that economic transformations that benefit large parts of the population over others, including those with limited power and few resources, are preferable to situations in which socio-economic inequalities persist (and even expand), rights are entirely undermined, and the level of conflict becomes untenable. As Carlos Oya (2013, p. 516) has asked: 'Does the "destruction of existing livelihoods" necessarily imply retrogression? Is there no room for progressive capitalist accumulation, including the creation of new spaces for new and perhaps more manageable struggles (around labour)?' Often opportunities are limited, and expectations are easily derailed (see Frynas and Buur, 2020). Nonetheless, local populations often crave for investments in order to lift up their communities, acquire better and more secure livelihoods, and create better futures for their children.

Thirdly, based on earlier work by Buur et al. (2020), this introduction and the chapters in this book seek to develop further the 'relational approach' to the inclusion of all three key actors identified above – local populations, investors and ruling elites – and the tensions between them. It uses a theoretical approach aimed at understanding why and how investments are implemented and why and how procedural rights are or are not respected as an aspect of extractive natural resource investments. The authors argue further that the chances of large-scale investments in natural resources being implemented while respecting the rights of local populations are at their greatest when they are characterized by 'reciprocal exchange deals' between investors and local populations, 'compatible interests' between ruling elites and investors, and 'mutual recognition' between local populations and ruling elites.

Analytically, one may focus on how little interventions over the last two decades have managed to improve the lot of local populations, making it clear that the underlying relations of structural power in resource extraction (Szablowski and Campbell, 2019) have not changed substantially. In this edited book, we argue that analyses of investments should look at how they are implemented and the extent to which they accommodate the rights of local populations. As this double focus is not common, in the next section we will map the key conceptual discussions we engage with in this volume. In other words, in the remainder of this introduction we discuss how we make use of these bodies of literature, further introduce the questions this collection addresses, describe the methodology underpinning the research of the Hierarchies of Rights research programme, and briefly introduce the remaining chapters.

2.   KEY DISCUSSIONS: MAPPING THE CONCEPTUAL TERRAIN

2.1   The Conceptual Terrain

Who are the most important actors in implementing extractive investments? A diverse and very large body of literature has developed, engaging in debates over large-scale investments in both land and extractives. With considerable sophistication, these studies point out the unequal circumstances in which extractive investments are implemented and rights accommodated or, more often, violated due to inherent structural inequalities (see, e.g., the excellent special issue on 'Contesting Extractive Governance: Power, Continuity and

Change' in *Extractive Industries and Society* edited by Szablowski and Campbell, 2019). Much of the discussion regarding extractive investments focuses primarily on one type of relationship, usually either that between local populations and investors or that between ruling elites and investors. Relationships between ruling elites and local populations are generally overlooked in these discussions. We argue that all three types of relationship between investors, ruling elites and local populations should be taken into account. But how do we understand and conceptually demarcate the three key actors dealt with in this edited volume?

Firstly, we use the term 'local population' for lack of a better one: in other words, we use it cautiously and also with a good deal of pragmatism. Empirically the term 'local populations' may refer to 'smallholders', 'family-based production units', 'kin-based organizations', 'villages' or 'communities' – different countries and contexts have, for good or bad, relied on one or other of these conceptualizations. As we have argued previously (Buur et al., 2019, p. 1197), one of the basic problems with all these terms is that they come with the heavy baggage of intervention by governments, who use them for specific purposes and problems, such as the management of relations. For instance, the common term 'community', with its focus on 'bottom-up' processes, 'self-help', 'empowerment' and so on, has entered the discourse of neoliberal forms of governance (Rose, 1991; Delanty, 2003). We use the broader and more general term 'local population' heuristically, but when it makes *emic* sense we may use some other context-specific term, such as 'community', 'household', 'family unit' or ward.

It is important here to acknowledge cautiously that international, national and local NGOs, for example, often see themselves as representing local populations. We have argued that this assumption may well be appropriate in many cases, but it cannot be taken for granted: investors increasingly outsource community liaison to recognized international NGOs (INGOs) and national organizations (Hilson, 2012). Similarly, states also use NGOs as service providers, for example, as extension officers, for capacity-building and so on. Furthermore, international donors may simultaneously assist states, actively promoting and supporting specific extractive investors, while (I)NGOs assist local populations to promote and facilitate specific investments (Arond et al., 2019). The role of non-governmental organisations (NGOs) is therefore often 'fuzzy', as they act as representatives of multiple and sometimes contradictory interests. In other words, civil-society actors, including international and domestic NGOs, are not simple, homogeneous and unified actors that are easy to define in practice. Civil-society organizations taking the form of NGOs are therefore not given separate, independent positions in our analytical approach because we see them more as intermediaries that may work with any of our three groups, namely local populations, investors or states. We accept the potential criticism of this approach, but would also ask critics to pause for a moment, bracket their criticisms in the Bourdieuesque (Bourdieu and Wacquant, 1992) sense, and ask themselves if all the categories we initially think of are really the most important, or at least consider when they matter in practice, instead of taking their importance for granted a priori.

Secondly, in this book the term 'ruling elites' refers to 'the group of people who wield power as a result of their position in the government, where they occupy offices in which authoritative decisions are made' (Whitfield et al., 2015, p. 24). Importantly, ruling elites operate at different social or scalar levels: national, regional or local, but they often link up in various ways, while at other times pursuing their own specific interests. Furthermore, a basic analytical distinction can be made between state bureaucracies and ruling political elites. Often the relationship is intimate and not easy to disentangle, but important ruling elites frequently rely on bureaucrats to implement policy decisions they favour. In practice the two groups may be hard to distinguish, particularly in countries dominated by a single party, such as Uganda, Tanzania and Mozambique. This is despite the notable differences in how socialist and Marxist-Leninist ideas concerning the supremacy of the 'Party' controlling the 'state' and 'society' are put into effect. For example, in Mozambique there are particular ideas linking 'national unity' to Frelimo, the ruling party, implying that national unity is secured in and through the party's control of the state and society. Here party, state and society are not separated in practice, as they generally are in liberal democratic ontologies (see Buur and Salimo, 2018; Macuane et al., 2018). However, as Therkildsen (2011) has shown for Tanzania, even in party-controlled countries, in certain times and spaces the relevant bureaucracies can also pursue agendas of their own that can undermine government decisions, separating the two spheres of power. Therefore, for us, when and why ruling elites and bureaucracies overlap or are distinguishable is thus an empirical question that needs to be decided contextually in each case study.

Thirdly, in thinking about extractive investments, it is often taken for granted that the category of 'investor' is foreign. In this edited volume, however, the term refers to different combinations of foreign, national and domestic investors in extractive natural resource projects, whether state-owned or private enterprises. In the Hierarchies of Rights research programme, we focused on relatively large-scale investments in gas, coal and agriculture (sugar and rice), often but not always based on some kind of public–private partnership. This often overlooked fact is important: researchers who implicitly fetishize 'the state' as overrun by neoliberal forms of governance and external impositions usually overlook how, through private and public investors, the African state and ruling elites actually pursue their interests. Ideologically they may do so in ways that are at odds with fetishized positions on how states pursue their interests in practice. One example is the assumption that the state will always protect local populations against abusive foreign investors. As several chapters in this book argue (by Jacob, Salimo, Nystrand and Buur), ruling elites and state bureaucracies are not homogeneous and unified. In some cases, different levels of the state are in conflict with other levels or are undermined by the interests of national or provincial ruling elites.

2.2 A Relational Understanding of Rights

Our approach to rights is strongly influenced by the clashes we can observe between local populations' perceptions of their land and livelihood rights, based more on customary or evolving land-tenure systems, and formal rights and tenure regimes backed by the state, which are brought to the fore with large-scale extractive investments. These conflicts often emerge late in the investment process when projects are implemented, and not earlier, when investment decisions are made and projects are approved. Suddenly, the right to information and consultation and to compensation for lost land and livelihoods become burning issues that key investment stakeholders are ill-prepared to handle. As we show, often the state or ruling elites are hesitant and not particularly interested in meeting local populations' demands or accepting their involvement and potential role in making investments work. In some cases, legislation on resettlement and compensation only emerge when investors demand it. In other cases, CSR and the present-day focus on Environment, Social and Governance (ESG) safeguards, involving compliance with various standards – such as International Finance Corporation's (IFC's) demands with regard to resettlement, environmental impact and so on – compel shareholders to force foreign companies to become involved and consult with local populations in order to minimize conflicts.

This raises the question of whether our relational approach leans more towards a traditional legal positivist understanding of rights as social facts, where rights exist even if they are not realized, or more towards a sociological approach to rights (Madsen and Verschraegen, 2013; see also Hilhorst and Jansen, 2012 for the negotiation of rights in specific contexts), where the realization of rights depends on the social context within which they emerge and come to exist. The conundrum is that in some cases rights to land and water, for example, exist in the form of local ideas of access and rights that can sometimes but not always be captured by the term 'customary rights', or ideas of rights in a form that is not necessarily backed by the state formally. Such local or customary ideas clash with both investors' and international organizations' ideas of 'rights' (e.g. rights to consultation, resettlement and compensation) that are often strongly backed by the host state. That is, ideas about substantial rights (often) in the abstract exist for some actors, alongside more emic or local or customary ideas of rights, that clash with notions of rights which arise with investments. Phrased in a slightly different way, and simply for heuristic reasons, by focusing on formal rights in the making, we expand the focus on substantial rights and what the state or ruling elite get out of investments to concentrate on diverse configurations of rights, including procedural rights, that investors have to deal with in their further engagement with local populations.

By accommodation of rights, we thus refer to the extent to which the substantive rights of peoples or populations to land and other resources are transformed into procedural rights, such as rights to information, participation and consultation, resettlement and various kinds of compensation when land is acquired for investment purposes (see, e.g., Veit et al., 2013; Hoops et al., 2015; Lindsay et al., 2017). Substantive rights may also be transformed into jobs or economic opportunities, though in this case the overlap between those who lose substantive rights and those who benefit from this loss is less clear. The differences between and movement from substantive to procedural rights also involve a move from 'thicker' to 'thinner' rights. We acknowledge that substantive rights can often be claimed more effectively from below and that they provide better protection against misuse than procedural rights. However, in many cases conflicts over land and other resources do not reach the courts for a range of governance-related reasons, and even when they do, where the so-called 'ruled by law'[3] principle obtains, the courts are often manipulated. In this regard, much will depend on the contexts in which investments take place, where governance is increasingly shaped by the interweaving of laws, norms, investment codexes, politics and governments nationally or internationally (Szablowski and Campbell, 2019, after Huizenga, 2019; see also Lund, 2021).

We therefore not only focus on rights as 'boundaries of autonomy', but on the power relations that help shape rights and which in turn are themselves partly shaped by rights where rights emerge and become prevalent processes of 'claiming, redefining and "vernacularising" rights' (Mnisi and Claassens, 2009, p. 491). Though economic and social change tends to be inherently conflictual and to lead to unequal outcomes, benefits and rights may be distributed or maintained while investments are being implemented and economies transformed. Essentially, we argue that more inclusive types of economic transformation are needed, while a delicate balance must be struck between implementing investments and accommodating the rights of local populations (Berry, 2009; Pedersen and Buur, 2016). What we see is that, in our African cases, investment projects are used to establish or strengthen authority structures and formal rights, where customary or evolving structures and perceptions of rights existed before.

Time and timing are often very important. Ruling elites at different social levels usually have their own agendas to cater for in the sense of creating economic opportunities, that is, rent-seeking, and ensuring their political survival. They therefore often have less interest in the concerns of the populations they serve and/or represent. The same can be said of investors and development donors, who often enter the field with a limited understanding of the local and national contexts. The short time horizons that extractive companies, governments and development donor organizations work with have turned out to be a weakness, since these are multi-decadal, not short-term processes (McHenry et al., 2017).

To understand how investments are implemented and how rights become intelligible and are socially negotiated, we therefore focus in particular on whether and how local populations are involved and whether they react to investments with protests and resistance. Here it is not always easy to demarcate clearly where substantial rights start or end. For example, compensation that emerges through an investment codex but is not clearly rooted in national law may resemble a procedural right but only later become a formal, state-backed procedural right by becoming part of national legislation. In this volume, Salimo illustrates this process with respect to the right to compensation and resettlement in the Mozambican gas sector, where formal compensation legislation first emerged late in the process after severe violence in the coal sector made gas and oil companies demand formal legislation on resettlement and compensation to be clarified and implemented. Equally, due process and consultation with local populations that originate in an investment codex may become substantive rights over time.

2.3   The Relational Way of Thinking about Investments

The concept of a 'relation' is both simple and complicated. In Euro-American language a relation is intimately linked to both concrete and abstract ideas embodying connectivity, kinship and alliance, including ideas concerning 'structural resemblance or causal connections' (Strathern, 1995, p. 9). We bracket this double feature of the concept, where it is at once an 'abstract construct' (the relation) and a 'concrete' relation (particular or personal) (Strathern, 1995, p. 10). This is because we want to focus on the concrete relations and exchanges between the different positions of investors, ruling elites and local populations (our triangular model of relations, already identified). We acknowledge the 'relational turn' within the social sciences (Latour, 2005; Candea et al., 2015; Strathern, 2017) and find many of these elaborations extremely important and inspiring.[4] Although some of these aspects have clearly influenced our understanding of rights as relations and rights as becoming, our usage in this book is profoundly heuristic. An exchange relation should be understood in its most descriptive sense.

This entails understanding cases of investment from the perspective of relational exchange. This is in part inspired by Marcel Mauss's classic anthropological work (1990) on the exchange of gifts and expectations of a return as a constitutive feature of social relations (see also Graeber, 2001), and in part by the political settlement approach to how the relationships between political and economic elite interests shape policy outcomes (Buur et al., 2012; Whitfield and Buur, 2014; Whitfield et al., 2015; see Buur, 2015 for a summary and explanation of the development of this approach). As we will demonstrate in the following, although different bodies of literature touch upon these exchange relations, they rarely apply a systematic analytical and theoretical approach that includes all three types of relationship.

The relationship between investors and local populations has received significant attention in the literature on large-scale extractive investments. Firstly, there has been a strong focus on dispossession by investors and the conflicts that may arise between investors and local populations in the wake of high global commodity prices in both the early and later literature on land- and resource-grabbing (McMichael, 2009; Tokar and Magdoff, 2009; Matondi et al., 2011), as well as in later land surveys by the mining and petroleum sectors (Ejobowah, 2000; Bourgouin, 2014; Szablowski, 2007; Kirsch, 2014). The interest in CSR, by contrast, has turned to the question of alleviating grievances in order to create the conditions for a Social License to Operate (SLO) (Frynas, 2005; Prno and Slocombe, 2012) to the more recent principle of Free Prior and Informed Consent (FPIC) (Cotula, 2016a, 2016b; Banks et al., 2016). Critics of these approaches (e.g. Harvey, 2014; Le Billon and Middeldorp, 2021; Shapiro and McNeish, 2021) have argued that social development through CSR interventions will not deliver SLOs in the extractive sector, nor fairness in general (Pichler et al., 2017).

Critical writings have indeed often dismissed CSR as 'window dressing' and are more concerned with showing how CSR principles differ from actual practices (Frynas, 2005; Bartley and Egels-Zandén, 2016; Kirsch, 2014). The recent perspectives of Huizenga (2019) and Szablowski (2019) importantly point to the interwoven nature of territorial, regional, national and transnational forms of law, politics and government, bringing scale into the perspective by suggesting that outcomes at one scale can be different from those at another scale. Wiegink (2018), in her work on Mozambique's extractive turn, includes an important analysis of the different temporalities implied by scale. Local populations and foreign and national investors often operate at different scales and temporalities. Investors often see exchanges related to compensation for loss of land and livelihoods as short-term, one-off legal and financial transactions enforced nationally and internationally. Local populations, on the other hand, see them as long-term relations with continuous exchanges and transactions locally.

Secondly, historically the relationship between investors and ruling elites has been extensively discussed in the literature on the resource curse related to extractive investments in which this relationship is often seen as necessarily involving collusion (Karl, 1999; Beblawi and Giacomo, 1987; Beblawi, 1987, 1990; Ross, 2015). However, the literature rarely unpacks the relationship in much detail, which is also the case for more recent studies drawing on the political settlement approach, which emphasizes that policy choices related to investments are 'shaped by incentives arising from the imperatives of ruling elites to remain in power and thus build and maintain political support' (Whitfield and Buur, 2014, p. 127; see also, e.g., the highly important and interesting work by Bebbington et al., 2018 and Usman, 2019).

Larger-scale investors in their turn often seek to shield themselves from the pressure of the ruling elites in order to mobilize resources for the economic survival of their companies through contract-stability clauses permitting international arbitration (Radon, 2007; Cotula, 2015, 2016b) or by alignment with international financial institutions like the World Bank and the International Finance Corporation, the Bank's private investment arm. This seems to suggest that investors in cahoots with ruling elites have the upper hand due to their orchestration or more directly their manipulation of the law and their control over the rules of the investment game. However, as several chapters in this volume suggest, this cannot be taken for granted. Relations are much more unsettled than the literature on extractive natural resources tends to assume, particularly for agricultural investments, but surprisingly also for mining and gas, if to a lesser degree.

Thirdly, as this book suggests, it is rare for ruling elites and local populations to be in agreement with each other. The relationship between local populations and ruling elites is generally the least developed in the literature. The land-grabbing literature started to develop more nuanced approaches after 2012, when it became clear that global land-grabbing was not taking place solely through foreign investments. Domestic investments in production, like palm oil, and sprawling urbanization saw tectonic shifts in land possession taking place rapidly and by and large under the radar, as it happened in Southeast Asia, for example (Hall, 2013). The literature then started emphasizing the role of state actors in facilitating the acquisition of land, as well as the resistance of local populations to investment projects (Wolford et al., 2013; Hall et al., 2015; Edelman et al., 2018). This new focus helped to explain why some projects were never implemented: as became clear from the revisionist turn in works on land-grabbing, a proposal to invest is one thing, actual implementation quite another.

However, the land-grabbing literature still tended to assume a uniform type of relationship between ruling elites and investors. Maybe this is due in part to the fact that, apart from a few, usually urban-based professional groups, in sub-Saharan Africa organized political action from below has rarely influenced national politics either directly or systematically (Rakner, 2011; Waal and Ibreck, 2013). To some extent the political settlement (Khan, 2010) and political survival literature (Whitfield et al., 2015) increasingly emphasizes the role of elections in allowing governments to stay in power and especially how elections may affect relations between ruling elites and local populations (Behuria et al., 2017; Jacob and Pedersen, 2018). These relations may be changing under the influence of repeated elections (Kjær and Therkildsen, 2013), which are gradually forcing ruling politicians to vie for smallholders' support, regional constituencies and votes more generally. This process caters to country and context-specific dynamics. An increasing number of Asian and African countries manage electoral pressures through the use of force, control over who can vote and stand for election, and plain state-organized fraud, as recently experienced in Uganda, Tanzania and Mozambique.

3. THE KEY CHARACTERISTICS UNDERPINNING INVESTMENTS AND RIGHTS

The relational approach allows us to draw on these bodies of literature, touching on various aspects of the relationships between investors, ruling elites and local populations, and also to develop a better understanding of how large-scale extractive investments can be implemented while accommodating the rights of local populations. This implies a move from rather descriptive analyses of exchange relations to a normative but still research-based and theoretically informed agenda. We argue that investments are more likely to be implemented and the procedural rights of local populations respected when relationships are characterized by 'reciprocal exchange deals' between investors and local populations, 'compatible interests' between ruling elites and investors, and 'mutual recognition' between local populations and ruling elites. In short, all three relationships are key to understanding why and how different rights – procedural and substantial rights – are accommodated, change and take their respective forms. The three characteristics of the relations between investors, ruling elites and local populations are shown in Figure I.1 below. This model has been developed by means of an iterative process in which we have moved back and forth between theoretical ideas concerning the three relationships and the empirical findings of our own case studies of concrete investments as part of the Hierarchies of Rights research programme from 2015 to 2022.[5] Our definitions of the three types of actor are discussed in detail in Buur et al. (2017; 2019; 2020), but in summary each of these model characteristics will briefly be discussed here one by one and clarified further.

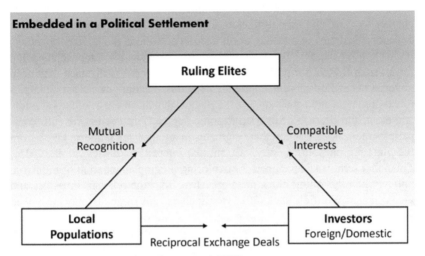

Source: The authors; also available in Buur et al. (2020).

Figure I.1   Model of the key relationships and characteristics

3.1   Compatible Interests

Compatible interests affect the relationship between ruling elites and investors. Generally, the implementation of natural resource investments requires that these two groups, whatever their composition, engage in a series of formal and informal exchange relations, which, at their most abstract level, are concerned with rents and support. Underpinning such exchange relations is the requirement that some sections of the ruling elite have incentives that match those of the investors in order to address the issues of access to key natural resources such as land and water, which are often 'owned' by a diverse set of actors in different types of property regime: the state, local government, chiefs, custom and so on (see Edelman et al., 2018; Peluso and Lund, 2011). They also need to find common ground with regard to the importation and construction of key infrastructure, as well as stabilize property relations sufficiently in exchange for financial and other types of resources that the ruling elite can use to survive electoral competition or exercise patronage politically (Whitfield et al., 2015).

In many ways, the relationship between ruling elites and investors is the most important and often trumps the other relationships. This is the case because this sort of relationship involves the most important socio-economic interests for those who are in charge of the state and its government, as well as of economically powerful investors in the private sector. Even though this is the most important relationship for the implementation of investments, elite and government interests can be undermined by other actors' interests, as the chapter by Buur and Beykirch show for Mozambique, or put under pressure, as Jacob illustrates in his chapter on Tanzania. Still, as the different chapters in this volume clearly suggest, the reason it is the most important relationship for investors is that for projects to be approved in the first instance they need government and ruling-elite approval. What this also implies, for actual implementation, is an open question, but the point is that the interests of the investors and the ruling elites must overlap to some degree. This is what we call 'compatible interests', a coining that originates in another, related term taken from the literature on political survival: 'mutual interest' (Whitfield et al., 2015). This latter term was developed for exploring the implementation of industrial policy when the ruling elites need approval from the relevant investors and vice versa: as Whitfield et al. (2015, p. 18; also p. 289) argued, 'they must need each other'. We will nonetheless suggest that, while interests must be aligned, more often than not they are merely compatible, as they might not be the same.

In simple terms, an investor putting money into complicated (frontier) markets can earn huge rents from being a first mover, but this can also be risky. It is therefore vital for investors to feel that their concerns and their ability to profit from their future investment decisions are addressed. This is true regardless of whether the objective is to promote investments in a particular natural resource sector or of who the investors are: domestic private firms, foreign private firms, state-owned firms, party-owned firms or public–private joint ventures. We therefore argue that investors' relations with the ruling elite are not only crucial but the most important, because without them there would be no investment in the first place. Furthermore, because political support can reduce uncertainty and release different forms of state support that can make investments feasible in the short and long terms, compatible interests are imperative. This also promotes predictability and possibly the most favoured 'credible commitment' by political leaders (Schneider and Maxfield, 1997) in difficult policy environments. However, as the more critical studies of industrial policy suggest, the relationship between ruling elites and investors is neither one-dimensional nor simple. Ruling elites often come to depend on investors, both foreign and domestic, as they often become important taxpayers with the ability to leverage political concessions. Therefore, they may wish to maximize and maintain the benefits of investors' operations, as they increasingly become dependent on them (Kircher, 2014; see in particular Salimo for gas in Mozambique, Jacob for coal in Tanzania, and Sulle et al. and Nystrand et al. for sugar in Tanzania and Uganda).

The importance of domestic and foreign investors for the ruling elites is intimately related to the two-decade-long process of liberalization and democratization under the Washington Consensus, as African politicians could no longer rely solely on state coffers, but had to depend on tax revenues as well as state-organized rent-seeking to fund re-election (Kjær and Therkildsen, 2013). But with increased dependence also comes the fear of investors transferring their loyalties to politicians and parties, including internal factions within the ruling elites who are pursuing particular investments in cahoots with investors (see, e.g., Salimo et al. 2020). Overcoming resistance from ruling coalition factions or other social groups, in the form of local populations and communities or potential foreign or private-sector competitors, is therefore not something that can be taken for granted, as several chapters in this book demonstrate with great clarity. Even though investors, whether domestic or, probably more often, foreign, are often thought of as having considerable 'holding power' (Khan, 2010, pp. 1, 6) in the form of financial muscle and the organizational ability to mobilize regional and international organizations for their own protection, this is not necessarily the case. Nonetheless, they remain vulnerable to local resistance to investments being taken up by international campaigns that can affect their 'reputations' with financial investors (and sometimes with consumers, depending on the type of industry), as well as when renegotiating contracts once the investment has been made and the sunk costs have been racked up (Vernon, 1973). Once investments have begun incurring capital costs, they cannot easily be recovered or transferred, which changes the terrain of power considerably.

It is exactly at this point in time that local populations' initial loss of access to key resources such as land and water will often see investors trying to find a new common ground with them, as delays and interruptions are costly. Relations between investors and ruling elites are therefore prone to change over time as investments mature, ruling elites become dependent on them for regime survival, competition over revenues and rents emerges between top elites and regional and lower-level factions, and local populations respond more broadly to the advent of investments, as they also want to benefit from them.

3.2   Reciprocal Exchange Deals

Reciprocal exchange deals are exchanges between investors and local populations, which are usually uneven and unequal, but can still be considered 'acceptable' to both parties. We know that, despite legislation to stimulate compensation and the sharing of rents from natural resource investments (see EITI, 2019), in countries with governance and democratic deficits – so-called 'ruled by law' countries, which is a key characteristic of many developing countries – the state often lacks an interest in redistributing resource rents to any groups outside its core base. One of the paradoxes, nonetheless, is that many people, including activists, civil-society actors, international donors and global institutions, implicitly assume that states in the Global South and their governments actually want to distribute resources to their populations. The evidence is mixed, as some countries indeed have the idea of redistribution and of sharing national assets or are basing their policies on such ideas (Tanzania is one such country, as Jacob and Pedersen (2018) have illustrated for social protection), while other regimes see redistributions of public goods in narrower terms (see, e.g., Buur and Salimo 2018 for Mozambique), where the ruling elites in charge of the state usually want to survive politically and therefore see and approach resources more like club goods (Salimo et al., 2020).

In such contexts, as long as elections can be rigged and manipulated, electorates in general matter little. But the point is also that local populations see natural resources (be it minerals, water, gas and so on) as 'their resource', whereas ruling elites see them as 'national resources' they are entitled to decide on. As civil society and political activists tend to side with the local perspective for many good reasons, while rarely looking at the national picture, investors are often considerably more insecure than one might expect. For this reason, investors and local populations often try to establish some kind of exchange deal in order to make sure that the latter gain something from the investments and that investors are guaranteed some stability in relation to them (Prno, 2013; Buur et al., 2020, pp. 921–2). This may take the form of direct procedural rights involving due compensation for resettlement or environmental pollution and/or the creation of economic opportunities or the provision of key social services (see Jacob, 2018 for coal in Tanzania; Nystrand et al. for sugar in Uganda, Salimo for gas, and Buur and Beykirch for sugar in Mozambique in this volume). In exchange, local populations usually have to give up land and livelihoods, as well as provide a degree of acceptance for investments over time, which may have contractual underpinnings (see Salimo, 2018 for gas in northern Mozambique). But often they are not well formalized, which in itself can create the basis for continual conflict. Often too, as several cases in our cross-section of examples of investment presented in this book show, investors expect the state to have dealt with local populations and their 'formal rights' to compensation, consultation, arbitration and so forth, not to mention managing the expectations that are associated with major investments. However, as this is rarely done in advance of the investments being made, the question of procedural rights usually becomes a key issue during implementation of the actual investment and will usually cause delays, extra costs and even the breakdown of the investments.

However, what we find is that, in these forms of exchange, investors are principally concerned with access to land and natural resources, relative peace and tranquillity in making their investments, the existence of infrastructure to minimize costs, the availability of a skilled workforce, and a policy environment that is conducive to and protective of their interest in stability and profit. One aspect of this is clearly that investors are interested in keeping often expensive sunk-cost investments safe from sabotage, fire and conflict (see also Buur and Sumich, 2019).

From an investor's point of view, at best the local population is valuable as a source of labour, land and water (depending on the type of industry) – or, in the language of business economics, it is just another business-external factor that needs to be factored in (Reinhardt et al., 2008). More often it is an annoying obstacle to the smooth implementation of a project that has already been agreed with ruling-elite factions and backed by external actors, such as investment banks, multilateral institutions and bilateral donors. However, experience clearly shows that dissatisfied local populations may derail investment projects if they are not properly involved in them and/or compensated for their consequences (Jacob, 2018; Nystrand et al., this volume; Frynas and Buur, 2020).

However, investments differ considerably. If, for example, an investment project involves the 'resettlement' of whole local populations (Salimo, 2018; Wiegink, 2018; Buur and Beykirch, this volume), its implications for livelihood practices and cultural relations are much more severe than, for instance, large-scale agricultural investments with outgrower schemes (Jarnholt, 2020; Buur and Beykirch, Sulle et al. and Nystrand et al. in this volume, for respectively Mozambique, Tanzania and Uganda and the sugar and rice industries). This allows people to stay on their land and become involved in the productive side of the investment.

Nonetheless, there is plenty of room for misunderstandings to arise in exchange deals between investors and local populations (Harvey, 2014), not at least because, as already noted, there is usually a temporal dimension to this relationship that is often misunderstood (see in particular Wiegink, 2018 on coal in Mozambique). Investors will usually expect something in return for what they consider the 'free gifts' they provide to local populations. This could include vague expectations such as 'acceptance', even though it may not always be clear what is expected at all.

At its simplest, investor-driven expropriations and compensation deals often take the form of one-off legal transactions or are thought of as legal one-off deals that may be perceived by receivers or givers as one-off 'gift-giving' activities (though in reality 'there is no such thing as a free gift', as famously suggested by Mary Douglas in the foreword to the 1990 edition of Marcel Mauss's masterpiece *The Gift*). What we often see is a clash between a market-based contractual form of compensation or other payment, which, seen from the perspective of local populations, is nothing other than the expectation of further exchanges being loudly voiced. Community members will often expect much more than the investor is willing to give (Frynas, 2009) in the form of continuous exchanges combined with the ongoing making of claims, based on expectations of a continuing or reciprocal relationship.

It is therefore important to understand that, in our approach, the procedural rights involved and how they develop into a 'reciprocal exchange deal' do not just imply a one-off legal and financial transaction when seen from a relational perspective. A reciprocal exchange deal is influenced by the terms under which it has been negotiated and includes other benefits that each party might derive from it over time. But investors are not all equal. The origin of the investor seems to be the key to understanding the types of exchange relationship that investors tend to develop with local populations. Much critical attention has been paid to corporate investments originating in the Global North (Frynas, 2000; Buur et al., 2017), where investors often worry about reputational risks or wish to adhere to international soft-law standards regulating investments, making them more open to pressure from populations below them than other actors (Frynas, 2005; Szablowski, 2007; McAdam et al., 2010). Investors in emerging markets have traditionally been less focused on voluntary social and environmental standards, though this may change as they become more exposed through their international operations (Patey, 2014; Pegg, 2012). Finally, domestic investors are often closely embedded in both the political and social environments of the investment (Nystrand, 2015). In some cases, this may facilitate exchange relations with local populations, but in other cases it may complicate them (Pedersen and Buur, 2016) because financial and other types of demand for exchanges become excessive.

3.3   Mutual Recognition

Mutual recognition refers in simple terms to relations and exchanges between local populations and ruling elites at the different levels of the state at which such exchanges take place (national, regional or local). This is the relationship that different bodies of literature link to CSR, land-grabbing and the resource curse, which they generally take for granted and never really explore in any detail. There can be many reasons for this oversight, one clearly being the strong focus on powerful foreign investors and their relationships with local populations and ruling-elite actors at the heart of the approval and implementation of a given investment. Here the relationship between ruling elites and local populations may at first sight seem less important for understanding how and why procedural rights concerning compensation, consultation and resettlement are or are not accommodated by natural resource investments. Obviously, the other links are important for understanding the relationship between ruling elites and local populations, but the influence is neither simple nor one-way. We argue that the relationship between ruling elites and local populations is underpinned by a series of exchange relations that often have a long history, this possibly being the reason why it is often overlooked. The exchanges between ruling elites and local populations are more often than not long-term in nature, related to services provided by the postcolonial state that can be exchanged for electoral support, but it can also be based on neglect and/ or ignorance (see Nugent, 2010).

Large-scale investments are embedded in temporal layers that usually each have a long-term contested political history. Ruling elites will evaluate proposed projects as trade-offs between on the one hand their potential to generate rents and increase the state's capacity to control the territory, and on the other hand the risks they may pose to social stability and control. Local populations will judge a natural resource investment in their area based on their previous experiences with investment projects and their previous relationship with ruling elites and the central state. Nugent (2010) suggested that the types of social contract that evolve between African states and their populations can be placed on a continuum between 'coercive' and 'productive' relations.

Nugent (2010, p. 44) also suggests that a 'coercive social contract is one in which the right to govern is predicated on the capacity of the rulers to render intolerable the lives of their subjects'. In contrast, a 'productive contract is one in which the sovereign authority and the subjects/citizens enter into some form of negotiation over how the rule by the former can contribute to the well-being of the latter'. Here we would suggest, with Beetham (2013, p. 266), that productive relations are not only 'acts of consent' in the Weberian sense. Instead, 'what matters for its existence and operation to be made explicit is that there should be a relationship of reciprocity resting upon a mutual recognition of rights and duties, both on the part of the governors and on the part of the governed'.

We highlight, in particular, the nature of exchange relations between local populations and ruling elites, underpinned by what we call 'mutual recognition'. These are relations that come close to what Nugent (2010, p. 45) refers to as a 'productive social contract' based on some form of mediation and recognition between an authority and subjects over 'how the rule by the former can contribute to the well-being of the latter'. In Nugent's analysis, what is exchanged can be tax payments and access to scarce resources, including land, but it can also be extended to other rights, such as the local population's procedural rights to resettlement compensation, participation and consultation.

In our perspective, if mutual recognition is achieved, it can make changes in the property institutions that govern the distribution of economic benefits and rules (see, e.g., Khan, 2010), if not legitimate, then at least sufficiently acceptable in return for desired services and/or protection from abuse by investors or other actors (see Buur et al., 2017, 2019, 2020 for a full discussion). What ruling elites expect from local populations is often recognition of their right to rule, including their right to decide over issues of land and resources. In societies with competitive elections of some sort, this is usually combined with exchanging votes for services, as well as economic opportunities or compensation. In return, local populations expect to be acknowledged as having a special relationship with the land or other resources. They also expect to be protected from transgressions by investors, to receive generous compensation for lost land and livelihoods, and to be provided with 'development' in a more general sense, for example, access to social services, infrastructure, jobs and economic opportunities such as outgrower schemes.

In large-scale investment contexts, where land and resource rights are less standardized and well-defined than in Europe or North America (where resources are 'ruled by law' instead of 'by rule of law'; see Khan and Roy, 2019), these rights and duties are the focus of intense struggles during the implementation of investment projects. Often, the exchange relations that touch upon natural resources and land in postcolonial African countries date back to colonialism and/or the struggle for independence, where independence movements often used resource conflicts to mobilize resistance to the colonial power. This obviously makes extractive investments, especially foreign ones, a potentially contentious issue feeding into local and national political dynamics to various degrees (see Maconachie, 2016 on how this feeds into post-conflict natural resource management scenarios). This is further complicated by the fact that post-independence ruling elites sometimes imposed modernizing projects – and new social contracts – on populations in a violent manner. Core cases here are the socialist Ujamaa and New Society reforms in Tanzania and Mozambique respectively, which sought to transform not only economic development models but also property relations through state-led resettlement schemes (see Buur and Sumich, 2019). In northern Uganda, it was not a modernization project but the Lord's Resistance Army's (LRA) insurgency and the forced resettlement of the population to internally displaced people (IDP) camps that have made land and resources a highly contentious issue in the post-conflict period (see Buur et al. 2019).

As this volume suggests, the level of conflict related to extractive investments hinges on the extent to which local populations are consulted, become involved in the decision and its implementation, and are compensated from and by the specific investment. While the relationship is influenced by that with the investor, relations with the state and ruling elites and the concrete exchanges they are involved in are more important than is often acknowledged. It is clear here that agreed compensation can vanish, and promises may not be fulfilled, as ruling elites need to mobilize rents in order to stay in power and therefore do not want to compensate local populations. Ruling elites may also take the side of the investor during conflicts because they want to implement the political projects they have promised, but in order to do so they have to sacrifice the expectations, rights and livelihoods of local populations.

However, it is important to make it clear that ruling elites contain diverse elite factions and groups at different levels of the state and political system, and therefore also distinct interests that often rub up against each other. We know from the survival of ruling elites' perspectives (Whitfield et al., 2015) that they rely on bureaucrats (usually themselves one of the factions in the ruling elite) to manage natural resource investments and revenues and to run state institutions that are important for their own survival (for Mozambique, see Macuane et al., 2018; for Ghana, see Whitfield, 2018).

4. POLITICAL ECONOMY

The relationship between the three key actors and what characterizes them is intimately related to the wider political settlement in which these relations are embedded, and investments approved and implemented. As we have argued before (see Buur et al., 2020), political settlements are not an external context in which the exchange relations between the three key actors take place, but are deeply entangled in the relationships themselves. How the three relationships evolve is therefore part of reproducing political settlements at different social levels and scales. The political settlement approach (Khan, 2010; Whitfield et al., 2015) focuses on the vertical relations between ruling elites and lower-level factions of the ruling coalition, as well as the horizontal relations between ruling elites and excluded factions, including how a settlement is financed (Behuria et al., 2017) and the role of ideas or ideology (Bebbington et al., 2018). In the political settlement approach, ordinary citizens do not really exist except as voters, electoral constituencies and lower-level factions within the ruling elite, but they do have an important role to play in investment processes (Buur et al., 2019). The three countries from which we present cases in this volume are characterized by different political settlement dynamics, which in each case reveal different degrees of dominance and legitimacy by and of the ruling elites and therefore provide an important backdrop to understanding the investments.

Furthermore, Mozambique, Uganda and Tanzania provide important examples of the diversity of political organizations and settlements we associate with the political settlement approach. Tanzania is generally considered to be governed by a dominant party-state settlement (Gray, 2013), and much the same goes for Mozambique, even though it is much more vulnerable and less ideologically coherent (Macuane et al., 2018; Buur and Salimo, 2018). In contrast, Uganda, notwithstanding its very 'dominant' president, is run under a more competitive clientelist form of settlement (Kjær, 2015; Golooba-Mutebi and Hickey, 2013). Here we will briefly consider the most important aspects of the political settlement of importance for our examples of investment.

4.1   Mozambique: Increased Conflict

Mozambique, even though its political settlement is based on the dominant Frelimo party-state, has fewer universalist underpinnings than in Tanzania (see underneath), as the foundational ideas are related to an understanding of 'national unity' (Hodges and Tibana, 2005) being produced in and through the Frelimo party (Salimo et al., 2020). Foundational ideas like national unity take on particular features in former one-party states like Mozambique that have managed to reproduce power, as they inform the organization of patronage and clientelism along partisan lines (Buur and Salimo, 2018, p. 5; Buur and Monjane, 2017). In Mozambique land is state property, but land-use rights are guaranteed to communities, individuals and organizations (including companies) by constitutional and legal provisions. This is the embodiment of the liberation struggle's ideals about freeing men and land from colonial domination and capitalist exploitation, and it is also closely linked to the idea of national unity in the sense that this model of securing land rights is formally consistent with Frelimo's socialist ideology both before and since independence. But as Buur and Salimo (2018, p. 8) have argued, even though Frelimo formally incorporates various groups and their claims, all policies are 'measured against whether they support or undermine national unity in and through the party'. The same goes for how investments in natural resources are implemented, and how and why, for example, substantial and procedural rights are promoted and honoured.

4.2   Tanzania Stranglehold and New Openings

In Tanzania, the political settlement is also based on a ruling party, Chama Cha Mapinduzi (CCM), and its stranglehold on the state, together with rather intrinsic and long-term powerful ideas related to the state's universal outreach. Though individual rights have been strengthened over the last couple of decades, land and extractive resources in Tanzania remain *de jure* vested in the state, which has retained strong provisions to acquire land compulsorily (Pedersen and Kweka, 2017). More recently, under the late President Magufuli, ideas related to economic nationalism became more pronounced as 'resource nationalism' (Jacob and Pedersen, 2018b; Jacob, 2019). Central to this is a renewed commitment to the CCM's earlier statist ideology and the belief that the state should be the key driving force in economic development (Jacob et al., 2016). This return to the founding ideology of the party was already underway in the early 2010s, but it gained pace with the ascent to power of President Magufuli in 2016 until his death in 2021, a period with a strong emphasis on state-owned enterprises and a declaration of 'economic war' on foreign investors (Jacob and Pedersen, 2018). Under Magufuli the ruling elite coalition became more authoritarian, relying increasingly on repression and clientelist co-option, a move that went hand in hand with centralizing rents and Magufuli's personal involvement in concrete deal-making. How the political settlement for extractive investments will change under the new President Samia Suluhu Hassan is not yet clear, despite a new emphasis on opening the country up once again to foreign investors and attempts to do so.

4.3   Uganda: Control, Violence and Fragility

In Uganda, unlike in Mozambique or Tanzania, the political settlement is more liberal with respect to individualized property rights, at least in formal legal terms. This creates different and more restricted opportunities for its ruling elites, including the President and the state more broadly, to take land except when the President decides to use all the powers of the state to force through particular deals, as we saw more recently regarding his intervention in the oil sector (Bukenya and Nakaiza, 2018). However, the ways in which clientelist political settlements are configured generally means that deals involving land and investors often end up bringing in the Parliament, for example, through local protests targeting area-specific Members of the Parliament (see Nystrand et al., this volume), which have confronted the President for several reasons. The recent elections were nonetheless more violent than usual, as Museveni's ruling coalition clearly felt challenged by new urban youth voters. How this will impact on extractive investments is still unclear.

We argue that these differences in the organization of political settlements are important because what characterizes the relationships between the three key actors in their respective political settlements influences the degree to which the substantial and procedural rights of local populations are respected, as well as how investments can create new types of rights.

5.   A NOTE ON METHODOLOGY

Methodologically, this book is based on an iterative process as part of the Hierarchies of Rights programme and ten case studies that have applied the framework, more or less coherently, as a way to analyse large-scale investments in gas, minerals and agriculture. We have invited a few selected experts, who have worked on the countries, and case studies to complement the edited volume. These are researchers who, from the outset, have participated in the Hierarchies of Rights project and the development of concepts. Most of the chapters have benefitted from discussions with academics who are not directly involved in the research, government officials, development partners and civil-society organizations at various international events. These discussions were important in providing a critical perspective on the research findings that were considered in the elaboration of the chapters.

In contrast to most edited volumes on land-grabbing (Matondi et al., 2011; Edelman et al., 2018) and the resource curse (Bebbington et al., 2018), which have a country-level perspective, our case studies are sectoral and are treated systematically in the sense that they were selected early in the process of the analytical framework being developed. This book therefore does not represent a broader perspective from across the continent, but highly dynamic and cutting-edge analyses of rent-seeking, investment failures, rare successes, and struggles over rights and opportunities related to large-scale investments. Therefore, we do not provide a set of broad research questions but a single focused and clear research question: how and why large-scale investments are implemented, and how the rights of local populations are or are not accommodated. This gives the volume more consistency, as well as enabling comparative research and analysis. We have also carefully considered representativeness, as a book on a series of outliers will not capture the key dynamics related to investments in the three important sectors of gas, minerals and agriculture. The East African countries of Mozambique, Tanzania and Uganda are presently seeing the biggest gas investments in Africa, the most intense coal investments, and a very high number of investments in agriculture and other minerals.

Even though we are focusing on relatively recent experiences, in particular in the decade or so from 2008 to 2021, we recognize that all our cases have longer investment histories spanning the colonial, postcolonial and present neoliberal eras. We see this as a strength rather than a limitation, as we explore cases that have a policy history where novel research can acquire a proper sounding board.

6.   STRUCTURE OF THE BOOK

The wide-ranging and often overlapping themes that this book seeks to explore, related to the implementation of extractive investments in sub-Saharan Africa and how different rights are brought into play, makes it difficult to break down the thematic analysis by placing the discussions neatly in discrete chapters. By organizing the book as a series of sectoral case studies, the most pertinent traces of the themes covered by it are nonetheless given proper space. This has allowed us to explore at great depth what characterized the implementation of extractive investments and how this intersected with different types of rights, as ruling elites, local populations and investors struggled over control in the face of multiple challenges. The sectoral studies follow each other, with Chapters 1 and 2 on Tanzania and Mozambique exploring gas developments and showing how this created spaces for citizenship and intersected with state formation. Closely related to this, Chapter 3 on the coal sector in Tanzania takes the theme of the role of the state further by pointing to its double role here as both investor and the final arbiter of conflicts between local populations and investors. Chapters 4 and 5 shift the focus to extractive investments in the sugar sectors in Uganda and Tanzania respectively, focusing on outgrower schemes and the exchange relations that evolve over time. The last pair of chapters, 6 and 7, focusing on Mozambique and Tanzania respectively, zoom in on rice investments and explore questions related to land and conflict.

Following this structure, Chapter 1 by Opportuna L. Kweka and Rasmus H. Pedersen unpacks how local populations seek to influence petroleum-related investment projects in mainland Tanzania. It argues that local populations exercise greater agency than they are often accorded in the literature. Whereas they are rarely allowed to influence deal-making between the government and companies directly, the evidence suggests that they do influence the implementation of projects, as well as the legal and administrative frameworks governing the sector. The chapter identifies a repertoire of actions that local populations may deploy, namely: riots and resistance related to control over resources; legalism from below, which targets the terms under which land acquisition is carried out; and voting, which aims to reward or punish political leaders who strike deals. In Tanzania's centralized political system, these actions typically target ruling elites and state authorities at various levels more than the international oil companies. The agency of local populations, however, depends on the political economy of petroleum in a country, which may vary over time.

In Chapter 2 by Padil Salimo, conflicts over land related to investments in liquefied natural gas (LNG) in Mozambique are analysed by focusing on the compensation deals and how they have influenced local state-making. The chapter zooms in on sub-Saharan Africa's biggest investments in LNG in the hotly contested Afungi Peninsula, in Palma district, Cabo Delgado province. The investments have caused a rush for land acquisition by international oil companies, private companies, and national and local domestic elite groups. In this process, expectations of economic growth and other anticipated opportunities reconfigured the relationship between local communities and local authorities. Contested land management and insecure land tenure among local communities became critical due to the inability of local government authorities to negotiate and defend fair compensation and resettlement for local communities. The chapter analyses relations between international oil companies and local communities, and the bargaining power of local governments and the ruling elite when large-scale land acquisitions are at stake. The chapter argues that investments in onshore LNG and ruling-elite politics undermined the bargaining power of local government in securing the rights of local communities.

In Chapter 3 by Thabit Jacob, the double role of the state as investor and mediator in the Tanzanian coal sector is explored. Jacob argues that recent research on large-scale investments in natural resources has mainly focused on the role of the state as an investment facilitator and protector of local rights. The ever-increasing role of the state as an investor has received much less attention. At a time of growing resource nationalism and the revival of state-owned enterprises (SOEs), especially in the extractive sector, a gap thus exists in understanding the increasing role of the state as an investor. This chapter uses the case of the Ngaka coal mine, in Mbinga District, south-west Tanzania, to examine how re-emerging resource nationalism and the double role of the state as investor through a revived SOE and its foreign joint-venture partner is shaping relations between the state, the investors and the local population. In particular, the chapter examines the contentious land-acquisition process that paved the way for coal extraction in Ngaka. The chapter argues that the SOE in the form of the National Development Corporation (NDC) and its foreign joint-venture partner relied strategically on Tanzania's resource-nationalist ideology to fast-track coal mining. This also limited local voices and dissent arising from the state-sponsored investments in coal, creating ambivalence and insecurity in the process.

In Chapter 4 by Malin J. Nystrand, Arthur Sserwanga and Brenda Kyomuhendo, we change the sector by analysing shifting relations in the Ugandan sugar sector. The sugar industry in Uganda is of longstanding, the first sugar mills being set up in the 1920s. The industry has for a long time been dominated by a few large domestic business conglomerates with close links to the ruling elite, of which Kakira Sugar Works (Kakira), in the Busoga region, is the largest. Over time Kakira has developed a comprehensive relationship with different parts of the local population, which clearly resembles what Buur et al. (2020) call reciprocal exchange relations between investors and local populations. However, during the last decade, several new sugar mills have emerged, challenging the established relations within and around the sugar industry. This chapter explains how the emergence of new actors in the sugar industry challenged the well-established relationship between Kakira and the local community, as well as the long-established political protection of the older group of large sugar investors, and it also demonstrates the increased importance of local populations and sugarcane farmers in local-level politics in Uganda.

Chapter 5 by Emmanuel Sulle, Faustin Maganga, Rose Qamara, Evans Boadu, Happiness Malle and Onesmo Minani analyses the political economy of the smallholder–investor relationship in the Tanzanian sugar sector. The chapter argues that government and development partners present the part-nership between smallholders and investors in agriculture as an inclusive model. It also shows that, while this might have been the intention, there are also a number of limitations attached to the particular nucleus state–outgrower model used. While the Tanzanian government is implementing nucleated estate–outgrower schemes to boost private-sector participation in agriculture, the chapter argues that, by employing the three pillars of political economy and the natural resources governance approach discussed in the introduction, there are limits to the reciprocal exchange deals that evolve between investors and local populations. The analysis uses the case of sugarcane production between Tanzania's Kilombero Sugar Company Limited and outgrowers to illustrate this finding. The chapter demonstrates how the relationships between ruling elites, investors and local populations shape sugarcane production, imports and the distribution of sugar in the country. The chapter argues that the investor–smallholder relationship is affected by the relationships between investors and ruling elites, as well as by external factors related to the politics of global movements of capital and its ownership.

In Chapter 6 by Lars Buur and Kathrin Beykirch, the focus shifts to extractive rice investments and how and why local exchange deals between Chinese investors and local populations fail. This chapter analyses implementation of the investment in Mozambique by WanBao, a Chinese investor, by focusing on the relationship between it and small-scale rice producers as it evolved over time. It also explores what types of exchange deals farmers involved in rice production established with WanBao. The chapter also analyses the relationships between WanBao, the ruling elite and local populations, as these had an important bearing on how the rice investment was implemented. The authors argue that, if one looks at the farmers who were trained by means of the rice investment, the WanBao initiative can to a considerable extent be considered a success, as it developed something approaching a reciprocal exchange deal, giving farmers access to training, new technologies and inputs. However, seen from a broader perspective in which farmers were excluded from the investment by the local state, while local ruling-elite farmers obtained access to inputs and loans without using them productively, the picture becomes murkier. The fact that the investment failed economically is due less to relations between the investor and local farmers than to the dynamics of the relationships between the investor and the national and provincial ruling elites, which undermined the economic feasibility of this initially promising investment in rice.

In Chapter 7 by Eileen Dyer Jarnholt, Faustin Maganga and George Schoneveld, exchange relations in rice contract-farming schemes in Tanzania are explored. The chapter argues that rice is indeed a vital food crop in Tanzania, both for household consumption and commercial selling. Contract farming is an important agricultural tool through which farmers and larger investors come together to increase the production and quality of the rice crop, thus benefiting both the farmers and investors. This chapter uses the relational model to look at these relationships in two rice contract-farming schemes in Tanzania: Kapunga Rice Plantation Limited and Mtenda Kyela Rice Supply. The empirical data for this chapter come from household surveys and interviews conducted in the Mbeya region in 2015. Agricultural inputs, extension services and land are all types of exchanges that occur in these two cases, though land was only exchanged in the Kapunga case. For the majority of farmers in both cases, their relationship with the investors has been characterized by positive outcomes and reciprocal exchanges, which drives the participants to continue with rice contract farming.

In the Conclusion, we briefly draw the various elements of the analysis from the different sectors and the different relationships between investors, ruling elites and local populations together to reiterate and formulate the key arguments of the book. In exploring the potential for implementing large-scale extractive investments in natural resources while accommodating the rights of local populations, this book advocates the importance of exploring the relationships between investors, ruling elites and local populations with respect to actual large-scale natural resource investments in the sectors of gas, minerals (coal) and agriculture (sugar and rice) in Mozambique, Tanzania and Uganda. We argue that the three groups of actors should be included in the analysis if we are to understand whether and how investments are implemented (as it is not inevitable that they will be) and whether the rights of local populations are or are not accommodated. Furthermore, we have argued that what characterizes the relationships is not without importance. To the extent that these relationships are characterized by 'reciprocal exchange deals' between investors and local populations, 'compatible interests' between ruling elites and investors and 'mutual recognition' between local populations and ruling elites, there is indeed a greater chance for implementation and some kind of accommodation of rights, with benefits for larger sectors of the population. But as we also clearly show in this book, it is indeed rare for economic transformations to benefit large parts of the population over others. Extractive investments, be they in gas, minerals or agriculture, seem to offer limited opportunities for local populations, whose expectations are easily derailed, as Frynas and Buur argue (2020). This is compounded by the fact that local populations often crave investments in order to lift up their communities, acquire better and more secure livelihoods, and create a better future for their children. Those who seem to benefit, however, are rather the ruling elites at different social levels, even though the exact distribution of benefits is highly country-specific.

NOTES

1.   This book is based on extensive fieldwork on large-scale natural resource investments in Mozambique, Tanzania and Uganda in the gas/oil, mining and

agricultural sectors. This fieldwork has been conducted as part of the Hierarchies of Rights research programme at Roskilde University, Denmark.

2. Procedural rights have been defined by Veit and Larsen (2013), Hoops (2015a, 2015b) and Lindsay et al. (2017).

3. Khan and Roy (2019, p. 5) distinguish between countries that operate by pure 'rule of law' principles and those that are 'ruled by law' (Khan and Roy, 2019, p. 5). Their dichotomy between 'rule of law', where those in power bend and use the law to their advantage (the majority of societies), and societies 'ruled by law', where those in power are subject to the law (a relatively few countries mainly situated in northern Europe), is often in practice messier. As we have argued before (Buur et al., 2020, p. 919), it is often the case that the law is enforced somewhere along the continuum between these two contexts. Rights therefore operate on two levels. On the one hand, there are rights related to specific investment projects that we call procedural rights. On the other hand, there is the much longer-term structural evolution of rights regimes that have been promoted by the international donor community in recent decades in many African contexts. The two domains are for obvious reasons interrelated: on the one hand, the long-term rights regime sets boundaries to what land or other resources can be taken and how; on the other hand, the contestations of specific investments may help shape rights regimes in the longer term. But what we often see with natural resource investments is that these long-term evolutions in property regimes are set aside or suspended, so that what local populations are left with are procedural rights at best.

4. In other words, we locate our key theorization in this book elsewhere, not on or in the 'relational turn'.

5. Our approach to model building, as described in Buur et al. (2020), is agnostic, as we regard the three characteristics of the model as convenient devices for organizing our analysis of how and why natural resource investments may accommodate the rights of local populations. Our approach to model building is inspired by Frances et al. (1991, pp. 2–3).

REFERENCES

Around, E., Bebbington, A. and Dammertad, L. (2019) 'NGOs as innovators in extractive industry governance: insights from the EITI process in Colombia and Peru', *Extractive Industries and Society*, 6 (3), 665–74.

Auty, R.M. (1993) *Sustaining Development in Mineral Economies: The Resource Curse Thesis*, London and New York: Routledge.

Banks, G., Scheyvens, R., McLennan, S. and Bebbington, A. (2016) 'Conceptualising corporate community development', *Third World Quarterly*, 37 (2), 245–63.

Bartley, T. and Egels-Zandén, N. (2016) 'Beyond decoupling: unions and the leveraging of corporate social responsibility in Indonesia', *Socio-Economic Review*, 14 (2), 231–55.

Bebbington, A., Abdulai, A.G., Bebbington, D.H., Hinfelaar, M. and Sanborn, C.S. (2018) *Governing Extractive Industries: Politics, Histories and Ideas*, Oxford: Oxford University Press.

Beblawi, H.A. (1987) 'The Rentier State in the Arab World' in H. Beblawi and G. Luciani (eds) *The Rentier State: Nation, State and the Integration of the Arab World*, London: Croom Helm and Istituto Affari Internazionali, pp. 63–82.

Beblawi, H.A. (1990) 'The Rentier State in the Arab World', in G. Luciani (ed) *The Arab State*, London: Routledge, pp. 85–98.

Beblawi, H.A. and Giacomo, L. (1987) *The Rentier State: Nation, State and the Integration of the Arab World*, London: Croom Helm and Istituto Affari Internazionali.

Beetham, D. (2013) *The Legitimation of Power*, London: Palgrave MacMillan.

Behuria, P., Buur, L. and Gray, H. (2017) 'Research note: studying political settlements in Africa', *African Affairs*, 116 (464), 508–25.

Berry, S. (2009) 'Property, authority and citizenship: land claims, politics and the dynamics of social division in West Africa', *Development Change*, 40 (1), 23–45.

Bourdieu, P. and Wacquant, L. (1992) *An Invitation to Reflexive Sociology*, London and Chicago: The University of Chicago Press.

Bourgouin, F. (2014) 'The politics of mining: foreign direct investment, the state and artisanal mining in Tanzania' in D.F. Bryceson, E. Fisher, J.B. Jønsson and R. Mwaipopo (eds) *Mining and Social Transformation in Africa: Mineralizing and Democratizing Trends in Artisinal Production*, Oxon, UK: Routledge, pp. 148–60.

Brooks, S.M. and Kurtz, M.J. (2016) 'Oil and democracy: endogenous natural resources and the political resource curse', *International Organizations*, 70 (2), 1–33.

Bryceson, D.F. and MacKinnon, D. (2014) *Mining and African Urbanisation: Population, Settlement and Welfare Trajectories*, Abingdon, UK: Routledge.

Bukenya, B. and Nakaiza, J. (2018) 'Closed but Ordered: How the Political Settlement Shapes Uganda's Deals with International Oil Companies', CRPD Working Paper, no. 61, Centre for Research on Peace and Development.

Buur, L. (2015) '"Muddling through" by way of modelling: representing complex relationships' in A.M. Kjær, L. Pedersen and L. Buur (eds) *Perspectives on Politics, Production and Public Administration in Africa: Essays in Honour of Ole Therkildsen*, Copenhagen: Danish Institute for International Studies (DIIS), pp. 209–27.

Buur, L. and Monjane, C.C. (2017) 'Elite capture and the development of natural resource linkages in Mozambique' in M. Pichler, C. Staritz, K. Küblböck, C. Plank, W. Raza and F.R. Peyré (eds) *Fairness and Justice in Natural Resource Politics*, London and New York: Routledge, pp. 200–17.

Buur, L. and Salimo, P. (2018) 'The political economy of social protection in Mozambique', ESID Working Paper, no. 103, Manchester University, pp. 1–34.

Buur, L. and Sumich, J. (2019) '"No smoke without fire": citizenship and securing economic enclaves in Mozambique', *Development Change*, 50 (6), 1579–601 https://doi.org/10.1111/dech.12511.

Buur, L., Mondlane, C. and Baloi, O. (2012) 'The white gold: the role of government and state in rehabilitating the sugar industry in Mozambique', *Journal of Development Studies*, 48 (3), 349–62.

Buur, L., Nystrand, M.J. and Pedersen, R.H. (2017) 'The political economy of land and natural resource investments in Africa: an analytical framework', DIIS Working Paper, 2, pp. 1–48.

Buur, L., Pedersen, R.H., Nystrand, M.J. and Macuane, J.J. (2019) 'Understanding the three, key relationships in natural resource investments in Africa: an analytical framework', *Extractive Industries and Society*, 6 (4), 1195–204.

Buur, L., Pedersen, R., Nystrand, M., Macuane, J.J. and Thabit J. (2020) 'The politics of natural resource investments and rights in Africa: a theoretical approach', *Extractive Industries and Society*, 7 (3), 918–30.

Candea, M., Cook, J., Trundle, C. and Yarrow, T. (2015) *Detachment: Essays on the Limits of Relational Thinking*, Manchester: University Press.

Castel-Branco, C. (2010) 'Economia Extractiva e Desafios de Industrializacao em Mozambique' in L. de Brito, C. Castel-Branco, S. Chichava and A. Francisco *Economia Extractiva e Desafios de Industrialização em Mozambique*, Maputo: IESE.

Collier, P. (2010) 'The political economy of natural resources', *Social Research*, 77 (4) , 1105–32.

Collier, P. and Venables A.J. (2011) *Plundered Nations? Successes and Failures in Natural Resource Extraction*, London: Palgrave Macmillan.

Cotula, L. (2012) 'The international political economy of the global land rush: a critical appraisal of trends, scale, geography and drivers', *Journal of Peasant Studies*, 39 (3/4), 649–80.

Cotula, L. (2015) *Land Rights and Investments Treaties: Exploring the Interface*, Land, Investment and Rights series. London, UK: IIED.

Cotula, L. (2016a) *Foreign Investment, Law and Sustainable Development: A Handbook on Agriculture and Extractive Industries, IIED Natural Resource Issues*, London: J. Mayers, IIED.

Cotula, L. (2016b) '"Land Grabbing" and International Investment Law: Toward a Global Reconfiguration of Property?' in A.K. Bjorklund (ed.) *Yearbook of International Investment Law and Policy 2014–15*, New York: Oxford University Press, pp. 177–214.

Delanty, G. (2003) *Community*, London: Routledge.

Edelman, M., Hall, R., Borras Jr., S.M., Scoones, I. and Wolford, W. (2018) *Global Land Grabbing and Political Reactions "From Below"*, London and New York: Routledge.

Edelman, M., Oya, C. and Borras Jr., S.M. (2013) 'Global land grabs: historical processes, theoretical and methodological implications and current trajectories', *Third World Quarterly*, 34 (9), 1517–31.

EITI (2019) *Progress Report 2019: Extractive Industries Transparency Initiative*, accessed 19 November 2022 at https://eiti.org/sites/default/files/attachments/eiti_progress_report_2019_en.pdf.

Ejobowah, J.B. (2000) 'Who owns the oil? The politics of ethnicity in the Niger Delta of Nigeria', *Africa Today*, 47 (1), 28–47.

First, R. (1983) *Black Gold: The Mozambican Miner, Proletarian and Peasant*, London: Harvester Press.

Frances, J., Levacic, R., Mitchell, J. and Thompson, G. (1991) 'Introduction' in G. Thompson, J. Frances, R. Levacic and J. Mitchell *Markets, Hierarchies & Networks: The Coordination of Social Life*, London, Thousand Oaks and New Delhi: SAGE Publications, pp. 1–19.

Frynas, G. and Buur, L. (2020) 'The presource curse in Africa: economic and political effects of anticipating natural resource revenues', *Extractive Industries and Society*, 7 (4), 1257–70.

Frynas, J.G. (2000) *Oil in Nigeria: Conflict and Litigation between Oil Companies and Village Communities*, Munster, Germany: Lit Verlag.

Frynas, J.G. (2005) 'The false developmental promise of corporate social responsibility: evidence from multinational oil companies', *International Affairs*, 81 (3), 581–98.

Frynas, J.G. (2009) 'Corporate social responsibility in the oil and gas sector', *Journal of World Energy Law Business*, 2 (3), 178–95.

Golooba-Mutebi, F. and Hickey, S. (2013) 'Investigating the links between political settlements and inclusive development in Uganda: towards a research agenda', ESID Working Paper, no. 20, pp. 1–49.

Graeber, D. (2001) *Towards an Anthropological Theory of Value: The False Coin of Our Own Dreams*, New York (US) and Houndmills (UK): Palgrave.

Gray, H. (2013) 'Industrial policy and the political settlement in Tanzania: aspects of continuity and change since independence', *Review of African Political Economies*, 40 (136), 185–201.

Hall, D. (2013) 'Primitive accumulation, accumulation by dispossession and the global land grab', *Third World Quarterly*, 34 (9), 1582–604.

Hall, R., Edelman, M., Borras, Jr., S.M., Scoones, I., White, B. and Wolford, W. (2015) 'Resistance, acquiescence or incorporation? An introduction to land grabbing and political reactions "from below"', *Journal of Peasant Studies*, 42 (3/4), 467–88.

Harvey, B. (2014) 'Social development will not deliver social licence to operate for the extractive sector', *Extractive Industries and Society*, 1 (1), 7–11.

Hilhorst, D. and Jansen, B. (2012) 'Constructing rights and wrongs in humanitarian action: contributions from a sociology of praxis', *Sociology*, 46 (5), 891–905.

Hilson, G. (2012) 'Corporate social responsibility in the extractive industries: experiences from developing countries', *Research Policy*, 37 (2), 131–7.

Hodges, T. and Tibana, R. (2005) 'A Economia Política Do Orçamento em Moçambique', *Publicações Universitárias e Científicas*, Principia.

Hoops, B., Marais, E.J., Mostert, H., Sluysmans, J.A.M.A. and Verstappen, L.C.A. (2015) *Rethinking Expropriation Law I: Public Interest in Expropriation (Property, Environment & Law)*, Hague, The Netherlands: Eleven International Publishing and JUTA.

Huizenga, D. (2019) 'Governing territory in conditions of legal pluralism: living law and free, prior, and informed consent (FPIC) in Xolobeni, South Africa', *Extractive Industries and Society*, 6 (3), 711–21.

Jacob, T. (2018) 'State Caught in the Middle: Coal Extraction and Community Struggles in Tanzania 8', Danish Institute for International Studies, Copenhagen, Denmark, pp.1–24.

Jacob, T. (2019) 'When good intentions turn bad: the unintended consequences of the 2016 Tanzanian coal import ban', *Extractive Industries and Society* , 7 (2), 337–40 https://doi.org/10.1016/j.exis.2019.02.009.

Jacob, T. and Pedersen, R.H. (2018) 'Social protection in an electorally competitive environment (1): The politics of Productive Social Safety Nets (PSSN) in Tanzania', ESID Working Paper, no. 109, pp.1–31.

Jacob, T. and Pedersen, R.H. (2018b) 'New resource nationalism? Continuity and change in Tanzania's extractive industries', *Extractive Industries and Society*, 5 (2), 287–92.

Jacob, T., Pedersen, R.H., Maganga, F. and Kweka, O. (2016) 'Rights to land and extractive resources in Tanzania (2/2): the return of the state', DIIS Working Paper (12), pp. 1–38.

Jarnholt, E.D. (2020) 'Contract farming schemes in rice and sugar in Tanzania: assessing the implications of exchange, power and differentiation', PhD dissertation, Roskilde University and University of Utrecht.

Karl, T. (1999) 'The perils of petroleum: reflections on the paradox of plenty, in fueling the 21st century – The new political economy of energy', *Special edition of The Journal of International Affairs*, 53 (1), 31–48).

Khan, M. (2010) 'Political settlements and the governance of growth-enhancing institutions', Research Paper Series on Governance for Growth, School of Oriental and
African Studies, University of London, accessed 1 January 2015 at http://mercury
.soas.ac.uk/users/mk17.

Khan, M. and Roy, P. (2019) 'Digital identities: a political settlements analysis of
asymmetric power and information', Working Paper 015, School of Oriental and
African Studies, University of London, pp. 1–32.

Kirsch, S. (2014) *Mining Capitalism: The Relationship between Corporations and
Their Critics*, Oakland: University of California Press.

Kjær, A.M. (2015) 'Political settlements and productive sector policies: understanding
sector differences in Uganda', *World Development*, 68, 230–41.

Kjær, A.M. and Therkildsen, O. (2013) 'Competitive elections and agricultural sector
initiatives in sub-Saharan Africa' in M. Böss, J. Møller and S.-E. Skaaning (eds),
Developing Democracies: Democracy, Democratization, and Development, Aarhus
University Press, pp. 116–37.

Latour, B. (2005) *Reassembling the Social: An Introduction to Actor-Network-Theory*,
Oxford: Oxford University Press.

Le Billon, P. and Middeldorp, N. (2021) 'Empowerment or imposition? Extractive vio-
lence, indigenous peoples, and the paradox of prior consultation' in J. Shapiro and
J.A. Mcneish (eds), *Our Extractive Age: Expressions of Violence and Resistance*,
New York: Earthscan from Routledge, pp. 71–93.

Le Billon, P. and Sommerville, M. (2016) 'Landing capital and assembling "investable
land" in the extractive and agricultural sectors', *Geoforum*, 82, 212–24.

Lindsay, J., Deininger, K. and Hilhorst, T. (2017) 'Compulsory land acquisition in
developing countries: shifting paradigm or entrenched legacy?' in I. Kim, H. Lee
and I. Somin (eds) *Eminent Domain: A Comparative Perspective*, Cambridge:
Cambridge University Press, pp. 118–55.

Lund, C. (2021) *Nine-Tenths of the Law: Enduring Dispossession in Indonesia*, New
Haven and London: Yale University Press.

Maconachie, R. (2016) 'The extractive industries, mineral sector reform and
post-conflict reconstruction in developing countries', *Extractive Industries and
Society*, 3 (2), 313–15.

Macuane, J.J., Buur, L. and Monjane, C.M. (2018) 'Power, conflict and natural
resources: the Mozambican crisis revisited', *African Affairs*, 117 (468), 415–38.

Madsen, M.R. and Verschraegen, G. (2013) 'Making human rights intelligible: an
introduction to a sociology of human rights' in M.R. Madsen and G. Verschraegen
Making Human Rights Intelligible: Towards a Sociology of Human Rights, Onati
International Series in Law and Society, Oxford: Hart Publishing, pp. 1–22.

Matondi, B.P., Havnevik, K. and Beyene, A. (2011) *Biofuels, Land Grabbing and Food
Security in Africa*, London and New York: Zed Books.

Mauss, M. (1990) *The Gift: The Form and Reason for Exchange in Archaic Societies*,
New York: Norton.

McAdam, D., Boudet, H.S., Davis, J., Orr, R.J., Scott, W. and Levitt, R.E. (2010).
'"Site Fights": Explaining Opposition to Pipeline Projects in the Developing World',
Sociological Forum, 25 (3), 401–27.

McHenry, M.P., Doepel, D.G. and Urama, K.C. (2017) 'Making extractive industries-led
growth inclusive: an introduction', *Extractive Industries and Society*, 4 (2), 235–9.

McMichael, P. (2009) 'Food sovereignty, social reproduction and the agrarian question' in H. Akram-Lodhi and C. Kay *Peasants and Globalization: Political*

Economy, Rural Transformation and the Agrarian Question, New York: Routledge, pp. 288–312.

Mnisi, S. and Claassens, A. (2009) 'Rural women redefining land rights in the context of living customary law', *South African Journal of Human Rights*, 25 (3), 491–516.

Monjane, C.M. (2019) 'Rethinking the political economy of commodity-based linkages: insights from the coal sector in Mozambique', Roskilde University Doctoral Thesis, Doctoral School of Social Sciences and Business, Roskilde University and The Institute of Resource Assessment, University of Dar es Salaam, accessed 9 November 2022 at https://rucforsk.ruc.dk/ws/files/67091435/PHD_DISSERTATION_CELSO_MONJANE.pdf.

Nugent, P. (2010) 'States and social contracts in Africa', *New Left Review*, 63, 35–68.

Nystrand, M. (2015) 'The rationale of taking social responsibility: social embeddedness of business owners in Uganda', Doctoral thesis, Gothenburg University, accessed 9 November 2022 at https://gupea.ub.gu.se/handle/2077/38753.

Oya, C. (2013) 'Methodological reflections on "land grab" databases and the "land grab" literature "rush"', *The Journal of Peasant Studies*, 40 (3), 503–20.

Patey, L. (2014) *The New Kings of Crude: China, India, and the Global Struggle for Oil in Sudan and South Sudan*, London, UK: Hurst and Company.

Pedersen, R. and Buur, L. (2016) 'Beyond land grabbing: old morals and new perspectives on contemporary investments', *Geoforum*, 72, 77–81.

Pedersen, R.H. and Kweka, O. (2017) 'The political economy of petroleum investments and land acquisition standards in Africa: the case of Tanzania', *Research Policy*, 52, 217–25.

Pegg, S. (2012) 'Social responsibility and resource extraction: are Chinese oil companies different?', *Resources Policy*, 37 (2), 160–67.

Peluso, N.L. and C. Lund (2011) 'New frontiers of land control: introduction', *The Journal of Peasant Studies*, 38 (4), 667–81.

Pichler, M., Staritz, C., Küblböck, K., Plank, C., Raza, W. and Peyré, F.R. (2017) *Fairness and Justice in Natural Resource Politics*, London and New York: Routledge.

Prno, J. (2013) 'An analysis of factors leading to the establishment of a social licence to operate in the mining industry', *Resources Policy*, 38 (4), 577–90.

Prno, J., and Scott Slocombe, D. (2012) 'Exploring the origins of "social license to operate" in the mining sector: perspectives from governance and sustainability theories', *Research Policy*, 37 (3), 346–57.

Radon, J. (2007) 'How to negotiate an oil agreement' in M. Humphreys, J.D. Sachs and J.E. Stiglitz, *Escaping the Resource Curse*, New York, USA: Columbia University Press, pp. 89–113.

Rakner, L. (2011) 'Institutionalizing the pro-democracy movements: the case of Zambia's Movement for Multiparty Democracy', *Democratization*, 18 (5), 1106–24.

Reinhardt, F.L., Stavins, R.N. and Vietor, R. (2008) 'Corporate social responsibility through an economic lens', *Review of Environmental Economics and Policy*, 2 (2), 219–39.

Rose, N. (1991) *Powers of Freedom: Reframing Political Thought*, Cambridge: Cambridge University Press.

Ross, M. (2015) 'What have we learned about the resource curse?', *Annual Review of Political Science*, 18, 239–59.

Ross, M.L. (2012) *The Oil Curse: How Petroleum Wealth Shapes the Development of Nations*, Princeton: Princeton University Press.

Salimo, P. (2018) 'The politics of LNG: local state power and contested demands for land acquisitions in Palma, Mozambique' in J. Schubert, U. Engel and E. Macamo (eds), *Extractive Industries and Changing State Dynamics in Africa: Beyond the Resource Curse*, London and New York: Routledge.

Salimo, P., Buur, L. and Macuane, J.J. (2020) 'The politics of domestic gas: the Sasol natural gas deals in Mozambique', *Extractive Industries and Society*, 7 (4), 1219–29.

Saulich, C. (2020) 'Accessing global value chains: the politics of promoting export-driven industrialisation and upgrading in the Mozambican cashew processing industry', CAE Working Paper 2020, p. 5, accessed 9 November 2022 at https:// typo3.ruc.dk/fileadmin/assets/isg/02_Forskning/CAE/CAE_working_paper-2020-5 .pdf.

Schneider, B.R. and Maxfield, S. (1997) 'Business, the state, and economic performance in developing countries' in S. Maxfield and B.R. Schneider *Business and the State in Developing Countries*, Ithaca, NY: Cornell University Press, pp. 3–35.

Shapiro J. and J.A. Mcneish (2021) *Our Extractive Age: Expressions of Violence and Resistance*, Earthscan from Routledge, accessed 19 November 2022 at https://library .oapen.org/bitstream/handle/20.500.12657/48472/9781000391589.pdf.

Strathern, M. (1995) *The Relation*, Cambridge, UK: Prickly Pear Press.

Strathern, M. (2017) 'Persons and partible persons' in M. Candea, *Schools and Styles of Anthropological Theory*, London: Routledge, pp. 236–46.

Szablowski, D. (2007) *Transnational Law and Local Struggles: Mining, Communities and the World Bank*, Portland, USA: Hart Publishing.

Szablowski, D. (2019) '"Legal enclosure" and resource extraction: territorial transformation through the enclosure of local and indigenous law', *Extractive Industries and Society*, 6 (3), 722–32.

Szablowski, D. and Campbell, B. (2019) 'Struggles over extractive governance: power, discourse, violence, and legality', *Extractive Industries and Society*, 6 (3), 635–41.

Therkildsen, O. (2011) 'Policy making and implementation in agriculture: Tanzania's push for irrigated rice', DIIS Working Paper 26, pp. 1–48.

Tokar, B. and Magdoff, F. (2009) 'An overview of the food and agriculture crisis', *Monthly Review*, 61 (3), accessed 1 January 2017 at http://monthlyreview.org/2009/ 07/01/an-overview-of-the-food-andagriculture-crisis/.

Usman, Z. (2019) 'The successes and failures of economic reform in Nigeria's post-military political settlement', *African Affairs*, 119(474), 1–38.

Veit, P.G., Larsen, G. and Easton, C. (2013) 'Overlapping property rights: when rights to natural resources conflict with rights to land', Africa Biodiversity Collaborative Group (ABCG) and World Resources Institute, accessed 19 November 2022 at https://pdf.usaid.gov/pdf_docs/PA00JWGV.pdf.

Venables, A.J. (2016) 'Using natural resources for development: why has it proven so difficult?', *Journal of Economic Perspectives*, 30 (1), 161–83.

Vernon, R. (1973) *Sovereignty at Bay: The Multinational Spread of US Enterprises*, Harmondsworth, England: Penguin Books.

Waal, A.D. and Ibreck, R. (2013) 'Hybrid social movements in Africa', *Journal of Contemporary African Studies*, 31 (2), 303–24.

Watts, M.J. (2001) 'Petro-violence: community, extraction, and political ecology of a mythic commodity' in N.I. Peluso and J.M. Watts *Violent Environments*, Ithaca, NY: Cornell University Press, pp. 189–212.

Whitfield, L. (2018) *Economies after Colonialism: Ghana and the Struggle for Power*, Cambridge: Cambridge University Press.

Whitfield, L. and Buur, L. (2014) 'The politics of industrial policy: ruling elites and their alliances', *Third World Quarterly*, 35 (1), 126–44.

Whitfield, L., Therkildsen, O., Buur, L. and Kjær, A.M. (2015) *The Politics of African Industrial Policy: A Comparative Perspective*, New York: Cambridge University Press.

Wiegink, N. (2018) 'Imagining booms and busts: conflicting temporalities and the extraction-"development" nexus in Mozambique', *Extractive Industries and Society*, 5 (2), 245–52.

Wolford, W., Borras, S.M., Hall, R., Scoones, I. and White, B. (2013) 'Governing global land deals: the role of the state in the rush for land', *Development and Change*, 44 (2), 189–210.

1. Community participation in Tanzania's petroleum sector

Opportuna L. Kweka and Rasmus H. Pedersen

1. INTRODUCTION

Until a couple of decades ago, negotiating petroleum contracts was largely an issue between ruling political and bureaucratic elites and investors; local populations did not play any significant role in the process (Radon, 2007). They were also largely ignored in the broader literature on the petroleum industry in developing countries. However, following in the wake of the violent conflict in the Niger Delta in Nigeria in the late 1990s, academic research was undertaken focusing specifically on their plight (Ejobowah, 2000; Pegg, 2015). They have since emerged as increasingly relevant stakeholders in oil and gas projects, and a host of social and environmental standards have been developed, primarily targeting the behaviour of private international oil companies (Watts, 2005; Cotula, 2016). This may be relevant to ensure the stability of operations, but it does not shed much light on the role that local populations may play in the implementation of investments. Similarly, the resource curse literature has identified a correlation between large-scale petroleum extraction, conflict and ultimately civil war (Ross, 2015), potentially pointing to rebellion as a local population strategy to gain more control over and increase benefits from extractive resources, while remaining almost silent on other types of agency.

Based on a review of recent scholarship on the role of local populations in petroleum investments, empirical research into a number of petroleum investments and petroleum-related projects in mainland Tanzania, and the political processes structuring such projects, this chapter unpacks local strategies of exerting an influence on the development of the petroleum industry. The chapter makes two arguments. First, it argues that local populations exercise greater agency than is often depicted. Whereas local populations are rarely, if at all, allowed to influence the striking of deals between governments and companies directly, the evidence suggests that they can influence their implementation, as well as the legal and administrative frameworks that govern the sector. In Tanzania, we can observe a repertoire of actions that have been employed to influence deals and increase the benefits from projects: riots and resistance related to control over resources; legalism from below, which targets the particular terms under which land is acquired; and voting behaviour that aims to reward or punish the ruling politicians who influence the legal and institutional frameworks that structure investments.

Secondly, and consequently, we argue that the agency of local populations depends on the political economy of petroleum in a given country. Tanzania is interesting in this regard because ownership and control over land and natural resources is vested in the nation and is managed by the government on behalf of the people. This means that the government is strongly involved in the implementation of projects (Pedersen and Jacob, 2017). As a 'new oil' country, Tanzania allows us to better study the impact of the advent of international social standards in a different context than the more loaded processes in 'old' producer countries like Nigeria and Angola. Our findings suggest that local populations' attempts to influence deals tend to target the ruling politicians more than the international oil companies making the investments. This was all the more pronounced due to the intense electoral competition that prevailed before authoritarian tendencies were gradually introduced in Tanzania in the second half of the 2010s and which made the political system more sensitive to the interests of rural populations (Paget, 2017; Jacob and Pedersen, 2018).[1] Our findings therefore point more to the existence of politicised processes involving local and national politics than is often acknowledged in the literature. These findings feed into emerging bodies of literature that point to the crucial role of the state authorities in structuring the implementation of social standards, for instance, Corporate Social Responsibility (CSR) and land acquisition (Frynas, 2009; Pedersen and Kweka, 2017).

This chapter is based on intensive fieldwork from 2015 to 2017 along the Indian Ocean coast in the southern half of Tanzania, where most gas reserves have been found. Around 150 in-depth qualitative interviews were conducted with a wide range of stakeholders, including local people directly affected by investments, local authorities, NGOs, government officials and company representatives. Generally, the research focused on four elements; (1) project designs and project implementation; (2) to what extent local populations' procedural rights to information, participation and compensation for land were adhered to; (3) local engagement with investors; and (4) the political processes that aimed to reform the legal and administrative framework governing the sector over the same period.

The next section provides a brief literature review on the role of local populations in petroleum investments, showing that they have gained some prominence, but still tend to be depicted as passive objects for interventions by investors and ruling elites. The understanding of the more politicised relations between local populations, investors and ruling elites in the petroleum sector is still little developed. The following three sections unpack some of the actions local populations have carried out to influence investment processes in Tanzania, first through riots and resistance related to a pipeline project, secondly through legal action by bringing cases to court and appealing to leaders at various levels, and thirdly through strategic voting. The sixth section discusses the implications of these actions, arguing that local populations only have limited impact on investment decisions and implementation, but seem to have traction in terms of influencing the policymakers into designing or approving the overall policies. Lastly, this section is followed by a conclusion.

2. COMMUNITIES AS SUBJECTS TO BE PROTECTED: A LITERATURE REVIEW

Local populations have gained more prominence in the literature on petroleum in Africa over the last decade and a half, but rarely in a way that depicts them as actors with much agency. In the general literature on petroleum, they only appeared for real around 2000, mostly due to conflicts in the Niger Delta in Nigeria in the previous decade (Ejobowah, 2000; Pegg, 2015). It is also only quite recently that the plight of local populations has become an issue with respect to the negotiation of petroleum contracts (Radon, 2007). Calls for 'meaningful' engagement with communities have become more vocal (Wilson et al., 2016; OECD, 2016; OECD, 2017). Even so, they still tend to be seen as objects to be protected by investing extractive companies more than as relevant stakeholders to be involved in actual negotiations. Relatedly, the more business-focused literature has recently started emphasising the extra operating costs that companies may incur from conflicts with local populations (Davis and Franks, 2014). Consequently, a host of standards have been promoted, typically emphasising the responsibility of the extractive companies to prevent grievances and address the livelihood concerns of local populations.

Indeed, the extractive sectors have become pioneers in developing the sorts of social policies that have become increasingly important for transnational businesses investing in developing countries. Most importantly, CSR interventions have been implemented in numerous ways, mostly voluntarily, in order to accommodate the concerns of host communities at various levels (Frynas, 2005; Frynas, 2008). The advent of the CSR agenda overlapped with the launch of the UN's Global Compact initiative in 2000, which encouraged businesses to implement sustainability goals wherever they operated (Watts, 2005). The more academic CSR literature has increasingly pointed to the key role of the host state in shaping the outcomes of companies' CSR interventions (Frynas, 2009; Scherer and Palazzo, 2011). The responsibility of international financial institutions to ensure compliance with environmental and social standards was also institutionalised during this period (Szablowski, 2002; 2007).

The role of these more or less voluntary standards has only increased in recent years. The concept of the Social License to Operate (SLO) has become a powerful framework for firms' interactions with local communities, whose acceptance they should seek not merely as a one-off but through ongoing consultations (Prno and Scott Slocombe, 2012; Prno, 2013). The notion of Free, Prior and Informed Consent (FPIC) is stronger in legal terms, as it has been incorporated into the United Nations Declaration on the Rights of Indigenous Peoples of 2007 and outlines the responsibility of state governments to obtain indigenous communities' consent prior to making any major land-based investments (Cotula, 2016). Though this idea originated in Latin America, NGOs and researcher activists have subsequently sought to promote this standard on extractive companies around the world (Greenspan, 2014; Oxfam, 2015). However, it has met resistance from governments in Sub-Saharan Africa, and it is less clear whether it actually affects relations between local populations, investing companies and ruling elites in the region and, if so, how.

The larger body of literature on the resource curse is similarly vague on the agency that local communities may exercise in order to influence operations. It has tended to focus more on the lower than expected economic growth, dysfunctional institutions and clientelist politics that are often following in the wake of large natural resource investments and resource-driven windfalls (Collier, 2010; Ross, 2012; Hilson, 2014). However, it does point to a correlation between the discovery of natural resources – in particular oil – and civil war, especially if the resource is found in peripheral areas with marginalised ethnic populations (Hunziker, 2014; Ross, 2015). In less war-prone areas, research shows that, whereas local populations in mineral-producing localities do benefit from resources in the form of rising living standards and improved livelihoods, extraction also leads to increasing levels of inequality, environmental degradation and dispossession, something that the present authors suggest may help explain the recurrent social discontent that often accompanies resource extraction (Loayza et al., 2013).

Finally, recent research in the field between the literature on democratisation and that on extractive resources has identified a correlation between the size of economic transfers from resources and the likelihood of local leaders being re-elected (Maldonado, 2014). These two bodies of literature thus suggest that local populations may play a role in influencing political processes in resource-rich areas. However, existing research does not really unpack how and why this plays out. The need to unpack investment-related processes that involve local populations is also the theme of an emerging body of research on petroleum investments and land in Africa, which has pointed to the importance of statutory legal and institutional frameworks guiding the acquisition of land for investment purposes (Akujuru and Ruddock, 2014; Ekhator, 2015; Emuedo and Abam, 2015; Pedersen and Kweka, 2017; Pedersen and Jacob, 2017). In short, the literature on the more politicised relations between local populations, investors and ruling elites in the petroleum sector is still limited: local populations still tend to be depicted either as passive objects when faced with interventions from investors and ruling elites in the petroleum sector, or as participants in or victims of organised crime, violence and civil wars in resource-rich, but peripheral areas. Whereas this may be part of the picture in some cases, in the following sections we identify a larger repertoire of actions that local populations have employed to influence deals and increase the benefits to them of projects, namely riots and resistance, legalism from below and voting behaviour.

3. RIOTS AND RESISTANCE

In scholarly research on Tanzania, there has been a strong tradition of emphasising the successful post-colonial nation-building of the country's first President, Julius Nyerere. While there have been cases of political intervention and unrest targeting the Asian minority linked to the latter's dominance in the business sector in the early years after independence, ethnicity is generally seen as much less important in politics than it is in most neighbouring countries (Barkan, 1994; Aminzade, 2013; Boone, 2014; Cheeseman et al., 2018). It therefore came as a surprise to many when, in 2012 and 2013, the population in the country's southeastern regions rioted and aired separatist sentiments prompted by the government's decision to construct a pipeline to transport natural gas from the gas field of Mnazi Bay south of Mtwara town to the commercial centre of the country, Dar es Salaam. Over several days, people went into the streets to express their anger, as they felt that the gas extracted in the region should have been used locally to generate economic activity and jobs.

The pipeline project had been several years in the making, but with limited involvement by the local population. Gas had already been found in Mnazi Bay in 1982, but the domestic market was then deemed too small to justify the costs of extraction and associated infrastructural development. However, Artumas, a Canadian company, began production in 2007 based on a production-sharing agreement from 2004, and supported by Dutch development assistance (Bofin and Pedersen, 2017). The initial gas-to-electricity project was rather modest, being restricted to providing a more stable power supply with an 18MW power plant to the then poorly supplied southeast of the country. Given the decision in 2012 to construct a pipeline to Dar es Salaam, production was increased from 2–3 million cf/day (cubic feet per day) in the early years of production for TANESCO's power plant in Mtwara to up to 80 million cf/day and an option for a further increase to 130 million cf/day later (Wentworth, 2010;

Maurel & Prom, 2014). This was a USD 1.2 billion project, 95 per cent of which was financed through a loan from the China Export Import Bank held by the Tanzania Petroleum Development Corporation (TPDC). The loan was conditional: prior to finalising the loan agreement, contracts were signed with Chinese companies for construction (Bofin and Pedersen, 2017). Combined with new power-plant facilities in Dar es Salaam, the pipeline was envisaged as helping address the glaring gap in power supply between the need for electricity and the limited production capacity that the rest of the country was experiencing.

What is noteworthy about the riots that ensued was the fact that their main targets were not the international oil companies involved in the Mnazi Bay project, but government and ruling-party offices, which were ransacked and, in some instances, burnt to the ground. This contrasts with the conflicts over large-scale mining from the 1990s onwards, when the mining companies were more conspicuously implementing projects in the context of limited central and local government capacity and therefore became targets for local resistance (Lange, 2008). However, with the increasing emphasis on the party-state's involvement in Tanzania's extractive projects, conflict dynamics have changed (Pedersen and Jacob, 2017; Jacob, 2018). Indeed, the decision to construct the pipeline was clearly a government decision, as the then Minister of Energy and Minerals, Sospeter Muhongo, was very vocal on the issue, arguing that the company that would be implementing the project would be a state entity, TPDC (Confidential, 2013a).

At the heart of the protests were decade-old feelings that the southeast had been marginalised in the country's development (Seppälä and Koda, 1998; Must, 2018). An often-cited element in this was the fact that a tar road connecting these regions to the rest of country, though having been promised for decades, was only finalised after 2010, when major new gas resources along the Indian Ocean rim were found. Unheard of in Tanzania, there were even open displays of threats to secede from the country, and although rioters rarely targeted individual outsiders directly, they did tell people from other regions to go home. Since then these sentiments have subsided, due in part to repression, and whereas the threat of secession has been aired again since, the general conclusion is that this was more a rhetorical device in order to show the genuineness of the grievances, rather than expressing a deep-felt wish to secede (Ahearne and Childs, 2018).

One of the main reasons for the rioting was the lack of information from the government and the lack of consultation with the local population. Access to information in general, and more specifically information related to the project, is still very limited even among some NGOs, who are working to raise awareness to the local communities. In the absence of such information, local communities have used all possible materials they possess, from the limited media presence to gossip and rumours. According to Abu-Lughod (1985) and Scott (2008), rumours and gossip are forms of resistance often used by the weak when confronting more powerful authorities. Whereas the then President Kikwete in 2010 had announced that Mtwara would be a 'new Dubai' (Stølan et al., 2017), the decision in 2012 to construct a pipeline came as a surprise. Kikwete's aim in making such a statement was to win the election in 2010 in Mtwara where the opposition party, the Civic United Front (CUF), had had a stronghold for a while. Having done so, in 2012 he changed to a policy of transporting gas to Dar es Salaam. As a result, local people found that the industries they had imagined being built in Mtwara and the associated employment opportunities were becoming less tangible. The local politicians from the ruling party were merely informed about the pipeline decision, a top-down procedure that was perceived as rather impolite by Tanzanian standards, where consultations are often conducted even when decisions have already been taken (interview with district councillor, 28 September 2017). This fuelled decades-old feelings of marginalisation.

By comparison, the local population's relations with the international oil companies tend to be more peaceful, partly because of these companies' transfers of resources to local populations in exchange for land and resources. The first gas project in Mtwara, which began producing gas and power for the local area in 2006–07, had been implemented by a private oil company, Artumas, which followed the international standards of the private-sector arm of the World Bank, International Finance Corporation (IFC), in respect of rates of compensation. These were more generous than the standards that were applied to the new pipeline under the auspices of TPDC, which followed more restricted Tanzanian compensation schedules and rates of compensation. Artumas and the succession of companies that came to acquire the right to operate in Mnazi Bay after Artumas (currently the French company Maurel and Prom) invested further in CSR. Every year there is a dialogue about priorities between the company and the local population involving planned social investments in the affected areas, for instance, the construction of school classrooms, road repairs and boreholes (interview with local leader, 28 September 2017).

The national authorities' response to the riots came in several phases, at first being quite heavy-handed, involving the introduction of the police, with people being beaten up, imprisoned and several being killed. To this day, tensions are strong, and the representatives of national authorities are on the alert for anything that might stir new riots. The local population is thus perceived to be more troublesome than those in other regions of the country. The authorities therefore closely monitor and regulate the people and organisations that engage with the local populations, or, as put by one government official, they 'coordinate':

> We have our own way to handle communities. You should coordinate what should reach local people and what should not reach the communities. We have to train the communities to come back on track. (Interview with government official in Mtwara, 23 October 2017)

A part of this is the perception, among some central government officials, that the riots were stirred by external actors, who were supposedly unhappy with the pipeline. Some point to oil importers, who had hitherto profited from the importation of fuel for power production by trying to undercut the gas-to-electricity project. Others point to the international oil companies, who were believed to be against the state-led project (interview with current government representative, 27 September 2017; interview with former government representative, 8 June 2018).

However, the resistance also had more constructive outcomes in terms of exchanges that aimed to improve relations between the ruling elites, the national oil company (TPDC) and local populations. Whereas the riots came as a surprise to national decision-makers, the debate soon came to focus on two things. First was the need to address and 'manage' people's expectations. Led by Paul Collier, donors had already been pushing for the development of a communications strategy to manage expectations, but the agenda was now being taken up by the government too (see URT and Collier, 2013). In addition, TPDC began expanding its CSR activities by paying villages to take care of the areas around the pipeline, for example, by cutting the grass and also 'protecting' the pipeline. Secondly, according to some officials the riots led to an intensified focus on local content provisions and other ways of increasing local benefits from production (interview with government official, 27 April 2017). Indeed, the 2015 Petroleum Act provides for quite detailed and binding requirements on local content, CSR and training (Jacob et al., 2016). The local content agenda, however, was also partly driven by the interests of the national political and economic elites, which did not necessarily overlap with those of the local populations and therefore did not necessarily benefit these populations to any significant degree (for more on this, see the discussion below). Apart from riots and resistance, local populations sought to influence the terms of the investments in other ways, as described in the next section.

4.   LEGALISM FROM BELOW

Whereas the resistance analysed above originated in dissatisfaction with the overall decisions of the political elite and was linked to a longer history of certain populations feeling marginalised, many smaller actions are deployed by local populations to influence the implementation of specific investment projects, typically without challenging the right of the political and administrative elites to take the decisions about them. These cases predominantly originate in feelings that procedural rights – that is, the rights to information, participation and compensation – have been violated. A host of cases have been brought to court as acts of what Julia Eckert (2006) has termed 'legalism from below', that is, 'protest that uses legal terms against the transgressions of law by state agents and other bodies of governmental authority'. In the Tanzanian case, however, we should add that local populations not only protest against transgressions of the law as it is, but also transgressions against how they believe the law *should* be, which is bound up in feelings of injustice. Typically, however, they lose these cases, as the laws provide the state authorities with quite far-reaching powers in comparison with ordinary people and local communities. Possibly, therefore, many people first seek to influence decisions and their implementation through appeals to local leaders before going to court.

The starting point of some of these cases is the fact that individuals and groups of people come forward, claiming that they had not received compensation, despite having the right to it. This provides for a sensitive dynamic at the local level, because projects are typically implemented with the involvement of local authorities and leaders. Therefore, by complaining about the lack of compensation, individuals are also pointing their fingers at their own leaders. One instance of this was the acquisition of land for the gas-related Dangote project around 2010,[2] when people complained about the lack of compensation. Indeed, implementation of the project had been fast-tracked to such an extent that procedural mistakes very likely happened. Valuations of land and livelihoods were conducted at a very short notice, and people received limited information about the procedures and their rights (interview with village leader, 20 February 2016; see also Pedersen and Kweka, 2017). Village leaders denied these claims and did not support the complainants when they went to court against Dangote and the district authorities, which had also been involved in the acquisition process, as had the Tanzania Investment Centre (TIC). Whether the village leaders were acting on behalf of the district authorities and the investor, or whether the complainants were merely trying to get compensation without genuine rights, could not be established by our research, but the reduction in the number of complainants during the process suggests that the latter might have been applicable in some cases. The complainants eventually lost the case, but at least one of the village chairmen resigned, or was forced to do so, and was replaced by one of the complainants.

Related to the gas investments that poured into the gas-rich regions after major discoveries of deep-sea gas offshore in the Indian Ocean in 2010, a virtual land rush and investment rush could be observed in the first half of the 2010s. The development of a liquified natural gas (LNG) plant to process and compress the gas for export was expected to cost USD 20–40 billion and generate thousands of jobs (Baunsgaard, 2014). Most of the bigger projects involved various types of state actors, from those engaged in the expansion of infrastructure to ever more speculative enterprises such as fertiliser factories, industrial parks and urbanisation schemes. Of the latter, major urbanisation schemes in all the potential host cities of an LNG plant – Kilwa, Lindi and Mtwara – were initiated in the last two. The district authorities teamed up with the Unity Trust of Tanzania, Projects and Infrastructure Development (UTT PID), a unit under the Ministry of Finance set up to 'unlock idle capital' from previously privatised government enterprises. The main and only shares UTT PID still owns are in Tanzania Breweries (TBL) and the Tanzania Cigarette Company (TCC), which were both doing well even at the time of privatisation. The UTT PID has been investing in real estate through partnership with municipal councils, where it provides the funds for surveying urban and town land through the process of formalisation. The UTT PID is entirely a profit-making organisation with a CEO and some autonomy in decision-making. It therefore sells the surveyed plots at a higher price, splitting the profits from the sales with the local municipal councils (interview with UTT representative, 1 September 2015; see also Pedersen and Kweka, 2017).

In these cases, the urbanisation schemes provoked major conflicts with local landholders. However, they ended up quite differently for the inhabitants, differences that are illustrative of the political dynamics related to such investments. In Mtwara, people had previous experience of similar urbanisation projects and knew that they would be given low monetary compensation compared to the prices the land would be sold for afterwards. Remaining with only a little land of bad quality after the scheme, they would also find it hard to acquire new land to live on and farm in the area. In the new project, they were scheduled to 300 Tanzanian Shillings per square metre in compensation, knowing that the land would be resold for between 4000 and 8000 Tanzanian Shillings. They therefore initially rejected the project and the compensation deal when they were asked for permission prior to the project start in 2012–13. Although the state authorities have far-reaching powers to compulsorily acquire land, they generally also seek consent at the local level to make the projects go smoothly. Only under pressure from the district commission, and after obtaining promises on the size and quality of land they would receive as part of the compensation package, so they could stay in the area and have the land surveyed, did they accept the deal, but only unhappily:

> We would not have been able to stop the project. Because it was a plan of the government to expand the city, so we had to accept [it]. Under normal circumstances

people would have rejected the project. But we could not say no. (Interview, local leader in Mtwara, 17 February 2016)

However, the project stalled due to the involvement of the Prime Minister's Office and the Ministry of Lands, after protests over similar projects involving the UTT and other developers elsewhere in the country (see, for instance, *The Guardian*, 2016). Supposedly, it was the above-normal profit margins for the implementing entities, reportedly at up to 300 per cent of the capital invested, that provoked the backlash. In Mtwara, the profit margin would be lower, supposedly around 100 per cent (interview with district official, 17 February 2016). Possibly because they had managed to increase their take, however, the local people now wanted to get the process finished because they had stopped investing in perennial crops and buildings, and just wanted to have the compensation and move on with their lives. They therefore formed a committee to push for the deal to be finalised, and they also contacted their leaders, first the elected district leaders and the regional commissioner, though in the end they also wrote to the Prime Minister's Office. They also opened a court case in the High Court in Mtwara to push for the project to be completed. A later interview with a local observer suggests that the areas have now been surveyed in collaboration with Ardhi University in Dar es Salaam, and that land has been given back to the initial landholders as part of the compensation (interview, 24 April 2021). The latter, however, were supposed to pay for having the land surveyed themselves, which some of them are struggling to do.

In Lindi, the local landholders who were trying to influence the UTT project were less fortunate, as the municipality and UTT implemented their urbanisation scheme and earned their profits, each of around 5 billion Tanzanian Shillings. Whereas those in the affected area did accept the project when it was introduced to them, some were unhappy about the level of compensation. Of the 700 who were compensated, 199 subsequently complained in court that they felt cheated, though some later withdrew their complaints. Unlike those affected by a similar project in Mtwara, they acted without the support of their local leaders at the sub-district level. Most of the complainants were dissatisfied with the level of compensation, which was at least 25 times and possibly up to 45 times below the price the land would later be sold for (Pedersen and Kweka, 2017). To many, another issue was that they only received information concerning the level of compensation very late in the process, basically on the same day the compensation was paid. While this is common practice in Tanzania to avoid speculation (interview with a ministry official, 26 February 2016), it also reduces transparency for those affected considerably. Nonetheless, acting without the support of their own elected leaders at the sub-district level, the local people lost the case against the district authority.

The mere discovery of large-scale offshore gas deposits in the Indian Ocean therefore created a virtual land rush to those areas that could potentially benefit from the development of the gas. This brought with it projects of a speculative nature that were initiated on the expectation of a future inflow of associated industries and the creation of thousands of jobs. In Tanzania's rather statist land-tenure regime, this meant significant levels of involvement by district authorities which, in partnership with other developers, sought to profit from these new opportunities. The locally affected populations could not challenge the decisions of political and administrative elites to initiate projects, but they could seek to influence the terms they were offered through 'legalism from below'. Being weakly protected by the law, they typically lose the cases over land acquisition that they do bring to court. However, they could and did seek to influence projects through letters and petitions to district and national political leaders, as demonstrated in Mtwara. To be successful, they needed the involvement and support of their leaders at the sub-district level. There were thus exchanges between local populations and the national ruling elite to undercut the alliance between district elites and investors. The link between the local and national political economies of gas becomes more apparent when we look at electoral politics.

5.   INFLUENCE THROUGH VOTING

Decision-making on extractive investments is quite centralised in Tanzania, something which limits the room for protest and dissent. Until 2015, the ever more competitive electoral cycle presented an opportunity to express dissatis-faction and influence investment dynamics through the ballot box. The pattern in this respect is not quite the same in Mtwara, where the gas is currently being produced, or in Lindi, where an LNG plant is planned to be constructed using gas from offshore deep sea. In Mtwara, there is a widespread sentiment that the gas should be kept in the area, and the opposition parties successfully campaigned on this topic. In Lindi, on the other hand, people are generally happy that gas – and gas projects – will be brought to the area, and voting there was therefore less influenced by the issue of control over gas and associated investments. This section will go through these electoral dynamics in each of the areas involved and assess whether the procedures for investing in natural gas and making related investments had any influence.

The protests over the gas pipeline in 2013 began in Mtwara town, but they soon spread to the gas-producing areas to the south of the town, in Msimbati and Madimba, two relatively remote rural areas. There, the expression of dis-content took its own distinct form. Firstly, the general discontent over the gas was demonstrated by logs being placed across the roads to prevent the passage of government traffic. Secondly, bombs were thrown at the buildings of a local marine park that had been established just prior to extraction. The construction of the buildings was unpopular because it was from them that the authorities controlled much of the land and water resources and also sought to control dynamite fishing in the area (interview with former village leader, 27 July 2016). Whereas people in Mtwara town wanted the gas to stay in the region, those in the gas-producing areas wanted it to stay in their areas and be used to generate job opportunities there. An additional source of discontent in the gas-producing areas was that the Mtwara Rural District authority chose to distribute the revenues from the local minerals tax, the 0.3 per cent service levy on annual gross revenues, evenly across the district, thus giving the gas-producing areas no advantages in this regard.

However, the Tanzanian authorities regained control over the area using the full force of the state apparatus, and young men in particular were beaten severely. This heavy-handed response and the gas issue in general affected people's voting behaviour. Those traditionally supporting the Chama Cha Mapinduzi (CCM) and even CCM councillors found it hard to defend the ruling party in this situation. Many people, aware that further protests would not bring anything positive to the area, waited for election day to come. A journalist put it this way:

> The 2015 elections were a result of the people being quiet. They thought: 'let us be quiet but show during the elections.' Most people said they were frustrated and were waiting to express their anger in the ballots. (Interview, 23 October 2017)

Whereas the CCM controlled 34 out of the 37 seats (92 per cent) in the rural district councils in these areas after the 2010 elections, it only controlled 17 out 29 seats (59 per cent) after the 2015 elections. The district council in the gas-producing area itself, Msimbati, switched from the CCM to one of Tanzania's main opposition parties, the CUF.

In Mtwara town, which has its own local government authority, the pattern was even more dramatic for the ruling party. Generally, the 2015 elections were also mired in national politics. Early on, the CUF chairman, whose strongholds are Zanzibar and the coastal areas on the Tanzanian mainland, areas with majority Muslim populations, had declared that the major issue in the elections was the ownership of natural resources. The CUF called on Muslims to organise so as to make sure they received something out of the resources (Confidential, 2013b). Indeed, this fuelled the feeling among many in Mtwara that they were not benefiting very much from the gas being produced in their area. There had been large expectations regarding future employment, which, however, only materialised slowly. Furthermore, most jobs were day jobs or short-term contract work as guards, cleaners and cooks. This also explains why, to some extent, the riots and resistance targeted non-local people who had migrated into the area. Some local people used the words 'people from the North' to refer to the in-migrants who are employed in the Dangote cement industry. In addition, there was dissatisfaction with the UTT-funded project mentioned above. After the 2010 elections, the CCM controlled 25 out of 28 seats (89 per cent) in the municipality. After the 2015 elections it lost control completely, winning only 12 out of 29 seats (41 per cent). As a result, the next mayor of Mtwara city council came from the CUF. The opposition also made inroads into the number of MPs from the entire region, though the CCM retained the majority.

In Lindi the story was different, as were the dynamics related to gas. As Lindi was not a gas-producing area, the construction of a pipeline would bring benefits from gas closer to the town, instead of taking it away from the area. Gas was therefore not a major issue during the 2015 elections (interview with journalist, 26 October 2017). Similarly, the outcomes of the urbanisation project involving the UTT funds mentioned above were ambiguous, as the community was divided. On the one hand, those who were in business sup-ported the project because they expected to increase their customer base and their sales. Furthermore, the citizens in Lindi experienced the UTT-funded project as positive because the revenues that flowed from it allowed spending on popular projects, like the paving of roads and the equipping of school labo-ratories (interview with district official, 22 February 2016).

On the other hand, many of those who were farmers did not support the project because they found that their land was being taken from them without proper compensation and that they would become poorer as they lost their source of livelihood. Therefore, even though those affected by the project tried to elect other representatives, they did not manage to do so. The opposition parties did make inroads into the CCM's majority, but this was linked to the general mobilisation by opposition parties in urban areas in Tanzania more than to conflicts over gas. The opposition went from 2 out of 20 seats in the municipality in 2010 to 8 out of 20 in 2015. Whereas the opposition parties did double their quota of MPs in the region from 2 out of 8 in 2010 to 4 out of 8, they lost their seat in Lindi Town.

Decision-making processes related to gas projects in Tanzania are fairly centralised nationally, and the direct influence of local populations on projects in between elections is therefore limited. As the heavy-handed response to the riots in Mtwara demonstrates, repression by state organs controlled by the ruling elites was always a possibility. However, local populations did seek to exercise influence through voting, which in the historically competitive 2015 elections resulted in landslide wins for the opposition parties in Mtwara because of dissatisfaction with the ruling party's handling of gas. In Lindi, which would generally gain from gas projects, election campaigns were less directly influenced by the gas agenda. Overall, many of those who voted for the opposition parties undoubtedly did so to send a protest signal to the ruling politicians that their legitimacy was wearing thin. Whether they believed that anything would actually change much is less clear. As authoritarian tendencies grew stronger in Tanzania after 2015, this avenue of influence closed. The 2020 elections resulted in landslide victories for the ruling party across the country, but, according to most independent observers, they were far from free and fair.

6.　TOWARDS A LOCAL POLITICAL ECONOMY OF PETROLEUM INVESTMENTS IN TANZANIA

Much of the literature on oil and gas investments tends to depict local populations as hapless victims with no or limited influence on petroleum projects or as participants in or victims of organised crime, violence and civil war in resource-rich, but peripheral areas. Policy-wise, this has led to efforts to promote social standards and CSR, typically emphasising the responsibility of international oil companies in this regard. Lately, the FPIC has begun to place a greater emphasis on states' responsibility to gain indigenous communities' consent prior to major land-based investments, but it has met resistance from governments in Sub-Saharan Africa. We have argued that local populations employ a repertoire of actions to influence projects and thereby exercise greater agency than is often depicted. In Tanzania's rather centralised and statist political and land-tenure systems, these actions typically target ruling elites and state authorities at various levels.

An important distinction should be made between direct influence on the implementation of specific projects and less direct influence on the policy frameworks guiding investors. While local populations are rarely allowed to influence investment decisions and only have limited impact on implementation, once projects have been set in motion, their activities seem to gain more traction, which makes an impression on the policymakers who are designing or approving the overall policies. This points to more politicised processes than is often acknowledged in the literature. Most conspicuously in this regard is the Petroleum Act of 2015 and the Draft Land Policy of 2016, both of which explicitly seek to improve the lot of existing holders of land rights, as well as local populations in the gas-producing areas.

It can be hard to establish exactly which event filters into the policymaking process. However, interviews and evidence point to the riots in Mtwara as one of the factors that contributed to the passing of the Petroleum Act. The Act not only caters for strong provisions in respect of CSR and local content, but also provides for state institutions to monitor the enforcement of these provisions (interview with government official, 27 April 2017; see also Jacob et al.,

2016). In the Draft Local Content Policy that came out a year after the riots, addressing rising local expectations is regarded as necessary:

> Delivering local benefits to the communities where oil and gas companies operate is no longer an option. It is a commercial necessity – and one that is increasingly mandated by law in many countries [...] companies in the oil and gas industry face rising expectations to do more than simply mitigate negative impacts, serve as sources of tax/royalty revenue and act as good neighbours. (URT, 2014)

People in Mtwara were consulted during the drafting process (interview with person involved, 4 August 2016). Similarly, the Draft Land Policy of 2016 mentions the land acquisition processes in the country that have led to dissatisfaction and complaints locally and which it promises to address: 'The main areas of concern include inadequate compensation payments, delay in paying compensation and lack of transparency on valuations for compensation and payment of compensation' (URT, 2016). Such provisions were introduced after years of relentless campaigning by civil society and opposition parties, pointing to conflicts and dissatisfaction in mining areas, and stating that Tanzania was not receiving enough out of its resources.

This put pressure on the ruling party – which, combined with increasing electoral competition, at least until authoritarian tendencies gradually became stronger after 2015 – made it change direction (Jacob and Pedersen, 2018). In this respect, the local populations' tactics, which we observed and analysed above, aimed at influencing politics through the ballot box, has probably contributed too. But do such changes have any impact on the ground?

There is certainly a great deal of hype surrounding the local content provisions – a virtual local content rush – at the national level, as state institutions and private-sector actors position themselves to benefit from the opportunities that may arise. The national oil company, TPDC, also pushed for tough local content requirements, which it hoped to use to increase its capacity (interview with government official, 27 April 2017). A Local Content Department was first introduced under the National Economic Empowerment Council, initially as part of the Prime Minister's Office but later moved to Energy and Water Utilities (EWURA); it aims to coordinate the relevant activities in the country as a whole. The Association of Tanzanian Oil and Gas Service Providers (ATOGS), chaired by a former chief secretary and inaugurated by the Vice President, was also established to prepare the private sector and monitor progress. However, such interventions are more focused on national than local actors, and it remains to be seen whether the latter will benefit to any significant extent. We remain sceptical, as the interests of the country's political and economic elites seem to have priority.

By comparison, the enforcement of the CSR provisions, which will almost exclusively benefit local populations, has received less attention. Most companies do engage with local populations in various ways, some more structured than others. The provision that companies must pay a service levy amounting to 0.3 per cent of their annual gross revenues that came into force with the Local Government Finances Act of 1982 (Ngowi and Potts, 2019) is upheld and administered by the local district and municipal authorities. Furthermore, some change is observable in the interface between the legal and regulatory requirements and company engagement, though not always to the advantage of the local populations that are directly affected by gas production. In Kilwa District, due to the new CSR provisions in the 2015 Petroleum Act that require the development of a CSR plan in collaboration with local district authorities, a less direct relationship between the population on the gas-producing Songo-Songo island and the producing company has developed. In Mtwara, these provisions had not led to any significant changes at our last visit in 2017, where some CSR was still largely being decided by the companies themselves in dialogue with local village authorities. There, however, the district authorities also chose not to earmark funds for host villages, which were opposition strongholds, when distributing the revenues from the service levy on activities in the district. Supposedly, however, this practice had been questioned and was being reconsidered (interviews with local leaders, 28 September 2017).

7.   CONCLUSION

Systematic empirical research into the role and influence of local populations on petroleum and related investments has been limited. Most attention has been paid to the obligation of international oil companies to ensure local benefits through CSR and local content requirements. Based on empirical research in mainland Tanzania, this chapter has sought to unpack the broader repertoire of actions that local populations may employ to influence projects in areas where gas and gas-related projects are being implemented. Our findings point to more diverse processes and outcomes than are often depicted. First and foremost, exchange relations between local populations and ruling elites are more important than is often acknowledged in much of the literature. An important element in the Tanzanian case is the growing role of state institutions in facilitating and conducting economic activities as part of the country's growing resource nationalism.

The chapter has focused on specific projects, as well as the politics that structure them. Overall, it has revealed more politicised processes than are often acknowledged in the literature. It identifies three main ways in which local populations seek to influence investment processes and increase the benefits they receive from projects, namely resistance and riots related to the ownership of resources; legalism from below, which particularly targets the terms under which land acquisition is carried out; and voting behaviour, which aims to reward or punish those political leaders who are in a position to influence the overall institutional framework that structures investments. All these interventions target the state authorities more than the international oil companies. Although the attempts to influence specific gas projects have had limited effect, the more politicised interventions seem to have had some impact.

In Mtwara, local people put pressure on the ruling politicians through protests and riots, as well as with their votes, signalling that the legitimacy of their rule was wearing thin. This contributed to the legal changes that aimed at making local content and CSR more ambitious and binding. However, the political and economic elites seem to pay more attention to the enforcement of the local content provisions, which offer opportunities nationally, than to the aspects that would benefit the gas-producing areas. Local populations have received some support in terms of social services and revenue, but there is a need to enforce the service levy and for CSR to be provided systematically in order to build local capacity that can help ensure that local content also focuses on local populations at the village and district levels. Continued pressure by local populations may be required to make the latter happen. However, the space for such pressure diminished when the late President Magufuli came to power in 2015, and it is too early to say if his successor, President Samia Suluhu Hassan, will change anything. She has signalled more openness towards local populations in expressing their grievances, but she has also insisted that she is no different from Magufuli and that she is continuing where Magufuli left off (Citizen, 2021a and 2021b).

NOTES

1. Fieldwork was conducted with a focus on planned and ongoing projects, which were typically underway before authoritarian tendencies gradually grew stronger in Tanzania from around 2015 onwards. This paper therefore analyses events that took place in contexts of increasingly competitive elections and does not really cover the dynamics under the late President Magufuli.
2. Around 2010, the Nigerian Dangote Industries initiated a project to establish a major cement factory just outside Mtwara town in southern Tanzania. The site for the construction of these plants was chosen because of rich limestone deposits in the area and its proximity to local gas finds. Though delayed, gas eventually came to fuel the factory.

REFERENCES

Abu-Lughod, L. (1985) 'A community of secrets: The separate world of Bedouin women', *Journal of Women in Culture and Society*, 10(4), 637–57.

Africa Confidential (2013a) 'Protests fuel political crisis', *Africa Confidential*, 54(12), 6.

Africa Confidential (2013b) 'Rocky road to gas economy', *Africa Confidential*, 54(23), 4–5.

Ahearne, R. and Childs, J. (2018) 'National resources? The fragmented citizenship of gas extraction in Tanzania', *Journal of Eastern African Studies*, 12(4), 1–20.

Akujuru, V.A. and Ruddock, L. (2014) 'The determination of compensation payable in the Niger Delta for compulsory acquisition and the need for a sustainable practice', *Journal of Sustainable Development in Africa*, 16(2), 102–14.

Aminzade, R. (2013) *Race, Nation, and Citizenship in Postcolonial Africa: The Case of Tanzania*, New York, USA: Cambridge University Press.

Barkan, J.D. (1994) *Beyond Capitalism vs. Socialism in Kenya and Tanzania*, Boulder, USA: Lyenne Rienner Publishers.

Baunsgaard, T. (2014) 'United Republic of Tanzania: Selected issues', IMF Country Report No. 14/121, IMF.

Bofin, P. and Pedersen, R.H. (2017) 'Tanzania's oil and gas contract regime, investments and markets', DIIS Working Paper, 1.

Boone, C. (2014) *Property and Political Order in Africa: Land Rights and the Structure of Politics*, New York, USA: Cambridge University Press.

Cheeseman, N., Collord, M. and Reyntjens, F. (2018) 'War and democracy: The legacy of conflict in East Africa', *Journal of Modern African Studies*, 56(1), 31–61.

Citizen (The) (2021a) 'President Samia directs regional governments to allow freedom of expression', *The Citizen*, 6 April 2021.

Citizen (The) (2021b) 'President Samia disappointed with kind of debate in Parliament', *The Citizen*, 18 April 2021.

Collier, P. (2010) 'The political economy of natural resources', *Social Research*, 77(4), 1105–32.

Cotula, L. (2016) *Foreign Investment, Law and Sustainable Development: A Handbook on Agriculture and Extractive Industries*, London, UK: IIED.

Davis, R. and Franks, D. (2014) 'Costs of company-community conflict in the extractive sector', Research report, CSR Initiatives at Harvard Kennedy School, US.

Eckert, J. (2006) 'From subjects to citizens: Legalism from below and the homogenisation of the legal sphere', *Journal of Legal Pluralism*, 38(53/54), 45–75.

Ejobowah, J.B. (2000) 'Who owns the oil? The politics of ethnicity in the Niger Delta of Nigeria', *Africa Today*, 47(1), 28–47.

Ekhator, E.O. (2015) 'The impact of the African Charter on Human and Peoples' Rights on domestic law: A case study of Nigeria', *Commonwealth Law Bulletin*, 41(2), 253–70.

Emuedo, C. and Abam, M. (2015) 'Oil, land alienation and impoverishment in the Niger Delta, Nigeria', *European Journal of Research in Social Sciences*, 3(2), 8–23.

Frynas, J. (2009) *Beyond Corporate Social Responsibility: Oil Multinationals and Social Challenges*, UK: Cambridge University Press.

Frynas, J.G. (2005) 'The false developmental promise of corporate social responsibility: Evidence from multinational oil companies', *International Affairs (Royal Institute of International Affairs 1944–)*, 81(3), 581–98.

Frynas, J.G. (2008) 'Corporate social responsibility and international development: Critical assessment', *Corporate Governance: An International Review*, 16(4), 274–81.

Greenspan, E. (2014) *Free, Prior, and Informed Consent in Africa. An Emerging Standard for Extractive Industry Projects*, US: Oxfam America's Research Backgrounder, Oxfam.

Guardian (The) (2016) 'Government set indicative price for land', *The Guardian*, 25 May 2016.

Hilson, G. (2014) 'The extractive industries and development in sub-Saharan Africa: An introduction' *Resources Policy*, 40(C), 1–3.

Hunziker, P. (2014) 'Civil conflict in petroleum producing regions', DIIS, Eidgenössische Technische Hochschule ETH Zürich, no. 22367.

Jacob, T. (2018) 'State caught in the middle: Coal extraction and community struggles in Tanzania', DIIS Working Paper, 8.

Jacob, T. and Pedersen, R.H. (2018) 'New resource nationalism? Continuity and change in Tanzania's extractive industries', *Extractive Industries and Society*, 5(2), 287–92.

Jacob, T., Pedersen, R.H., Maganga, F. and Kweka, O. (2016) 'Rights to land and natural resources in Tanzania (2/2): The return of the state', DIIS Working Paper, 12.

Lange, S. (2008) *Land Tenure and Mining in Tanzania*, Bergen, Norway: Chr. Michelsen Institute.

Loayza, N., Mier y Teran, A. and Rigolini, J. (2013) 'Poverty, inequality, and the local natural resource curse', Policy Research Working Paper, no. 6366, World Bank.

Maldonado, S. (2014) 'The Political Effects of Resource Booms: Political Outcomes, Clientelism and Public Goods Provision in Peru', Research report, SSRN library, US.

Maurel and Prom Group (2014) 'Signature of a Gas Sales Agreement for Mnazi Bay and Msimbati Gas Fields in Tanzania: A second source of cash flow for the group', accessed 17 November 2022 at https://www.maureletprom.fr.

Must, E. (2018) 'Structural inequality, natural resources and mobilization in southern Tanzania', *African Affairs*, 117(466), 83–108.

Ngowi, P.H. and Potts, D. (2019) 'Extractive industry revenues and their expenditure in local government authorities: The case of the gold service levy in Geita District Council in Tanzania' in D. Potts (ed.) *Tanzanian Development: A Comparative Perspective*, UK: James Currey, Cambidge University Press, ch 14.

OECD (2016) 'OECD due diligence for meaningful stakeholder engagement in the extractive sector', Preliminary version, OECD.

OECD (2017) 'OECD due diligence guidance for meaningful stakeholder engagement in the extractive sector', OECD.

Oxfam (2015) 'Community Consent Index 2015: Oil, gas and mining company public positions on free, prior and informed consent', Oxfam.

Paget, D. (2017) 'Tanzania: Shrinking space and opposition protest', *Journal of Democracy*, 28(3), 153–7.

Pedersen, R.H. and Jacob, T. (2017) 'Reconfigured state-community relations in Africa's extractive sectors: Insights from post-liberalisation Tanzania', *Extractive Industries and Society*, 4(4), 915–22.

Pedersen, R.H. and Kweka, O. (2017) 'The political economy of petroleum investments and land acquisition standards in Africa: The case of Tanzania', *Resources Policy*, 52(C), 217–25.

Pegg, S. (2015) 'Introduction: On the 20th anniversary of the death of Ken Saro', *Extractive Industries and Society*, 2(4), 607–14.

Prno, J. (2013) 'An analysis of factors leading to the establishment of a social licence to operate in the mining industry', *Resources Policy*, 38(4), 577–90.

Prno, J. and Scott Slocombe, D. (2012) 'Exploring the origins of "social license to operate" in the mining sector: Perspectives from governance and sustainability theories', *Resources Policy*, 37(3), 346–57.

Radon, J. (2007) 'How to negotiate an oil agreement' in M. Humphreys, J.D. Sachs, J.E. and Stiglitz (eds) *Escaping the Resource Curse*, New York, USA: Columbia University Press, pp. 87–114.

Ross, M.L. (2012) *The Oil Curse: How Petroleum Wealth Shapes the Development of Nations*, Princeton, USA: Princeton University Press.

Ross, M.L. (2015) 'What have we learned about the resource curse?', *Annual Review of Political Science*, 18, 239–59.

Scherer, A.G. and Palazzo, G. (2011) 'The new political role of business in a globalized world: A review of a new perspective on CSR and its implications for the firm, governance, and democracy', *Journal of Management Studies*, 84(4), 899–931.

Scott, J.C. (2008) *Weapons of the Weak: Everyday Forms of Peasant Resistance*, US: Yale University Press.

Seppälä, P. and Koda, B. (1998) *The Making of a Periphery: Economic Development and Cultural Encounters in Southern Tanzania*, Dar es Salaam, Tanzania: Mkuki na Nyota Publishers and Nordiska Afrikainstitutet.

Stølan, A., Engebretsen, B., Berge, L.I.O., Somville, V., Jahari, C. and Dupuy, K. (2017) 'Prospects for peace in a petro-state: Gas extraction and participation in violence in Tanzania', REPOA, *CMI Brief no 51*, 16(10), 1–4.

Szablowski, D. (2002) 'Mining, displacement and the World Bank: A case analysis of Compania Minera Antamina's operations in Peru', *Journal of Business Ethics*, 39(3), 247–73.

Szablowski, D. (2007) *Transnational Law and Local Struggles: Mining, Communities and the World Bank*, Portland, USA: Hart Publishing.

United Republic of Tanzania (URT) (2014) 'Draft local content policy of Tanzania for oil and gas industry', Press Release, 7 May 2014, Dar es Salaam: Ministry of Energy and Minerals, Government of Tanzania, accessed 17 November 2022 at https://www.tnrf.org/files/draft_local-content-policy-of-tanzania-for-oil-gas-industry.pdf.

United Republic of Tanzania (URT) (2016) 'Draft National Land Policy', email to the author from Womenslandrights, 11 November 2016.

United Republic of Tanzania (URT) and Collier, P. (2013) 'Tanzania gas sector scoping mission', October, pp. 15–19 and December, pp. 10–13, 2012; Final Report, 21 February 2013.

Watts, M.J. (2005) 'Righteous oil? Human rights, the oil complex, and corporate social responsibility', Annu. Rev. Environ. Resour., 30, 373–407.

Wentworth (2010) 'Annual General Meeting presentation', Wentworth Resources Limited, Continental Hotel Oslo, Norway, 17 September 2010.

Wilson, E., Best, S., Blackmore, E. and Ospanova, S. (2016) *Meaningful Community Engagement in the Extractive Industries: Stakeholder Perspectives and Research Priorities*, London: International Institute for Environment and Development.

2. LNG investments in Mozambique: compensation deals and the dynamics of local state-making

Padil Salimo[1]

1. INTRODUCTION

In 2010, Mozambique was confirmed as an emerging player in the global energy sector. Over 180 trillion cubic feet (cf) of natural gas were formally discovered in the Rovuma Basin, located in northern Mozambique, specifically in Cabo Delgado province. Massive investments are taking place to build liquified natural gas (LNG) infrastructure onshore and offshore in the Rovuma Basin. Currently, there are three LNG projects, only one offshore, operated by Eni, which became the first project to exploit natural gas from Coral South commencing in 2022. In November 2022, the country witnessed the first LNG export shipment.[2] The other two projects will be onshore located on the Afungi Peninsula, in Palma district. These projects involve several of the 'giants' of the oil industry, like the American Exxon Mobil and the French Total, as well as the minor Italian industry player Eni, which is operating jointly with Exxon Mobil. Together, the three projects will produce around 32 million tonnes per year (mtpa) of LNG (see Salimo, 2018).

The volume of investments in the Rovuma Basin is massive, nearly $60 billion over ten years. On 18 June 2019, Anadarko reached a Final Investment Decision (FID)[3] for $20 billion, but then the company was bought by Occidental, who later sold all its assets in Africa to Total. ExxonMobil's FID is presently postponed due to low oil and gas prices following the COVID-19 pandemic, and this delay could last even longer due to the worsening insecurity caused by Islamist attacks in Cabo Delgado. The prospects of the investments have generated a massive demand for land acquisition in Palma district, as well as in Mocimboa da Praia district in Cabo Delgado. The LNG project in Afungi was initially projected to occupy an area of 7,000 ha and would have directly affected more than 2,500 people living in the area, who have been included in the resettlement project, as well as other families from the neighbourhoods of

Maganja, Senga, Palma Sede and Monjane, who are also due compensation for economic losses.

Several studies of large-scale investments in the extractive industry that are related to foreign direct investment (FDI) show two distinct effects. On the one hand, FDI creates elevated expectations relating to possible contributions to social and economic development (Melina and Xiong, 2013; Deininger, 2011; Frynas and Buur, 2020). On the other hand, it creates suspicion and fear about security of land tenure and access to resources that are indispensable for the survival of local communities (Cotula et al., 2009; Borras et al., 2011; Wittmeyer, 2012; Schoneveld, 2014; Jayne et al., 2014). Borras et al. (2011) argue that investments resulting in deals involving large-scale land acquisitions are ambiguous and often lead to dispossession of land, loss of livelihoods, environmental degradation and loss of access to the land and natural resources upon which local populations depend. This is highly problematic when the power of the local authorities is weak with respect to the competing interests of the ruling elites in the context of large-scale investments in natural resources. Indeed, large investments in extractive investments that demand large-scale land acquisitions in Africa and the displacements of local populations are repeatedly observed to affect people's ability to access basic livelihoods (Cotula et al., 2009). This being the case, the questions are: what kind of local state emerges with large-scale investments in LNG, and how does this affect the rights of the local populations?

In Mozambique, recent examples of the marginalization of local populations affected by coal-mining projects have been observed in Tete Province, where there have been serious violations of fundamental rights (Mosca and Selemane, 2011; Human Rights Watch (HRW), 2013), including the loss of land and other sources of livelihood. This example serves as a warning to local communities in the Afungi Peninsula, as well as the surrounding areas, where populations are living in uncertainty with regard to both land tenure and their livelihoods as the LNG developments loom. Multinational oil companies, private-sector actors and ruling elite groups have been exerting pressure on the local government officials who formally manage local land acquisitions, while, from the other side, the processes by which investors are acquiring the land are being contested by local communities and civil-society organizations.

Hence, there is a fear that the land to be allocated in compensation may not be appropriate for agriculture and that other opportunities emerging from the large-scale investments will not benefit the local populations. This view has been influenced by a common debate around the implications of large-scale investments in natural resources, which emphasizes the negative impact on the affected communities and therefore neglects the potential of such investments to effect positive transformations of traditional economic and social practices, as well as the way in which communities explore land use.

This chapter analyses the relations between international oil companies and local populations concerning negotiations for compensation for land generated by the investments in LNG infrastructure. Key to the analysis is an examination of the role played by local government, also called local authorities in this chapter. I argue that weakness of the local authorities' bargaining position and their inability to manage the competing pressures of the multinationals and the ruling elites leave them unable to defend the interests of local communities, whether by protecting their tenure or by securing 'good deals' for them in terms of compensation for land.

This research is based on a review of the existing literature on large-scale land acquisitions and investments in natural resources in Africa, combined with extensive fieldwork conducted in different phases during the period from 2015 to 2018, involving interviews in various places and institutions in Maputo and Cabo Delgado province, observation and discussion meetings in Palma with community groups, and participation in community consultations on compensation and resettlement organized jointly by the government and the multinational oil companies. The interviews in Maputo focused on actors in the petroleum sector, government, the private sector, civil-society organizations (CSOs) and academia. In Cabo Delgado, particularly in Pemba, Palma and Mocimboa da Praia, interviews were conducted with government officials, private-sector actors, members of CSOs, local communities and others.[4]

Following this introduction, the chapter will analyse the way in which land management has been implemented in the context of the massive onshore LNG investments, and how the government adopted mechanisms for land acquisition that privileged investors and the powerful ruling elite groups. The third section analyses how deals for compensation were negotiated between investors and local communities, and what has been the role of the ruling elite in the process. The fourth section analyses the local government's power and authority underpinning land management and compensation and how its power and authority fares given the powerful influence of the central ruling elite over local government. This is followed by an analysis of the dynamics of relations between investors, local communities and the ruling elite regarding compensation for land losses and the type of local state that emerges. The final part of the chapter is the conclusion.

2.   LNG INVESTMENTS AND LAND ACQUISITION IN PALMA

On 20 December 2006, the government of Mozambique signed an exploration and production concession contract (EPCC) with Anadarko from the USA and Eni from Italy. This followed an announcement in July 2005 of the results of the second round of bidding for petroleum licences. In 2020, French Total bought Anadarko's concession. The National Oil Company, the ENH, the sole representative of the state in each of the petroleum exploration blocks where the companies had stakes, was also a signatory to each concession contract.[5] The massive volume of proven natural gas reserves discovered by Anadarko/Total and Eni led to an agreement between the concessionaires and the government to develop an onshore LNG facility, to be utilized by both concessionaires of Areas 1 and 4. For this purpose, Anadarko/Total and Eni, the offshore operators of Areas 1 and 4 in the Rovuma Basin, signed an agreement in December 2012 that allows both companies to work jointly in constructing LNG plants and other related infrastructure (Gqada, 2013).

The LNG project's aim is to respond to the challenges of development and the monetization of the gas reserves discovered in these two blocks. The location of the gas fields and their distance from their main markets in Asia and Europe pose significant financial and technological challenges, since the conventional model of supplying natural gas via a pipeline is unfeasible. LNG technology is considered to be the best option, although it is capital intensive and, in comparison with pipelines, relatively new to the industry. There were at least seven sites as options[6] for the onshore LNG infrastructure, but the Afungi Peninsula was eventually selected.[7] The government of Mozambique indicated that it did not want the operators in Areas 1 and 4 to develop their own separate logistical infrastructure to serve the gas-gathering system. Instead, it insisted that the investments in natural gas production were to be done in such a way that they promoted the country's industrial development by investing in the private sector and facilitating job creation.[8]

Before 2010, Palma District was a remote rural region with minimal economic infrastructure. When news regarding the unprecedented investment in LNG in Afungi broke, the local government was completely unprepared for the enormous pressure on land acquisition that would follow. The land administration capacity was inadequate, both before the investment in LNG started and after (Salimo, 2018). The government located in Maputo has shown no sign of making the necessary investment to develop the technical and human resources capacity to deal with the phenomenon of large-scale investments.

In February 2012, the governor of Cabo Delgado province, Eliseu Machava (who later became secretary-general of the ruling party from 2014 to October 2017), issued an official order which instructed the district governments of Palma and neighbouring Mocimboa da Praia not to grant any DUAT (Direito de Uso e Aproveitamento da Terra; i.e. land use and exploitation rights).[9] Some actors, including several within the government, initially viewed this decision to suspend allocations of DUATs as an opportunity for the local government to strengthen its organizational and technical capacity to manage land issues by buying time, although others were concerned that the moratorium might undermine development in the form of investments in infrastructure, commerce and services as consequence of the barriers imposed over access to land.[10] However, it later transpired that members of the ruling elite (members of the important families that participated in the liberation war, for example) were able to exploit the situation because, while allocations of DUATs were restricted for ordinary citizens, the process of allocating land continued for key ruling elite groups and other powerful business actors. Thus, one administrative decision ensured that key members of the ruling elite, from Cabo Delgado and beyond, gained control of the land, particularly in Palma.

The absence of a 'territorial plan' directing future development of the district was part of the narrative used to justify the provincial government's formal freeze on allocations. In a response to the challenges in 2016, the district government of Palma drew up two detailed land-planning documents. The first presented the area where international investors were expected to be located as an industrial zone, while the second plan focused on tourism, something which the local government had some knowledge about. The provincial governor of Cabo Delgado approved both plans. Another three plans were drafted and approved in April 2016, detailing housing expansion plans for the villages of Nkumbi, Nkalanga and Manguna, which comprise a total area of 994 ha.[11] In contrast to what most good governance and rights approaches would have suggested, the formal planning processes, and with them ideas about the land and rights attached to such processes, emerged and took shape with the investments. They were not in place before the LNG gas investments began to take shape and to become a reality. However, even though such instruments of territorial planning are important for an informed and relatively well-organized process of land management and allocation to be created, they are not sufficient to guarantee that the processes related to land acquisition will be played out within the formal mechanisms and desired standards of territorial development and land rights, as many other contextual and informal practices also have a role to play.

Administrative capacity in Mozambique is generally weak and characterized by inefficiencies. This is particularly the case in land management and land governance and is not limited to the local government level. Several studies have shown that the problem is to be found at every level of land administration, and the relevant bodies are seldom able to perform their statutory functions efficiently (Weimer and Carrilho, 2017; Cabral and Norfolk, 2016; USAID, 2007). The political economy of land management in Mozambique is complex. To some extent, poor capacity favours both members of the ruling elite with interests in land and bureaucrats who can exploit the inefficient enforcement of the institutional framework to manipulate the allocation of land to their advantage. The contextual reality says much about the nature of the state that exists in Mozambique.

The pressure on land acquisition in Palma is related to multinational oil companies' need to secure large tracts of land for their onshore natural gas operations. As part of the ruling elite's efforts to maintain control over land access and use amid the onshore LNG investments, in 2012 ENH requested a huge parcel of land with an area of 25,700 ha in Palma.[12] The aim was officially to protect specific state interests that are inherently associated with land and sovereignty, but the intention was also to secure a certain amount of leverage with the international oil companies in negotiations over natural gas operations, as they would be dependent on ENH for access to land.[13] But the government guaranteed only 7,000 ha, and on 12 December 2012 issued the DUAT to Rovuma Basin LNG Land (RBLL), a shell company created the previous month by ENH and one of the major initial investors, Anadarko Mozambique Area 1 (hereafter AMA1). The remaining 18,000 ha were not officially allocated, as no DUAT for them was issued. However, local government officials and key informants within the central government institutions insisted nonetheless that ENH does indeed control the land.[14] In 2016, the district government of Palma made a presentation to a number of stakeholders interested in investing in Palma.[15] The slideshow suggested that the 18,000 ha in Afungi were reserved for ENH to use in 'future' industrial and urban projects.

RBLL was created specifically to acquire the DUAT. Although the 7,000 ha were allocated to RBLL for the development of onshore LNG infrastructure by operators in Areas 1 and 4 of the Rovuma Basin, RBLL is not a concessionaire for natural gas, meaning that it could not satisfy the aims under which the land was acquired. As a result, RBLL had to transfer the DUAT to an operator. This arrangement was adopted to avoid the dispersal of natural gas projects along the coast of Palma, something that would have led to a loss of ENH control and therefore a reduction in the government's leverage over companies investing in gas production. However, because RBLL is not a concessionaire of petroleum exploration and production, it had to ask the government to transfer its DUAT to AMA1. This was done via an 'Assignment of Exploration Agreement', signed a day after the DUAT was issued to RBLL.[16] Under this agreement, RBLL ceded its exploration rights to AMA1 for the implementation of the LNG project. The aim of this was twofold. Firstly, it formalized AMA1's right to implement the project, including the design, construction, operation and maintenance of all equipment related to the LNG infrastructure. Secondly, this cleared the way for AMA1, as the lead company in the LNG project, to conduct an Environmental Impact Assessment, a key instrument for approval of a Resettlement Plan for people living in or using the 7,000 ha area, on which, in its turn, implementation of the entire LNG project would depend.

The idea of ENH controlling the acquisition of and access to land is of considerable importance to the government, even though it has never been addressed openly. Eni, the offshore LNG investor, has requested land in Quionga, a coastal village located close to Afungi, as a complementary site for future natural gas infrastructure, arguing that the massive volume of natural gas in the Rovuma Basin will generate a demand for more land. However, the government has not approved its request.

3.   LAND AND DEALS FOR COMPENSATION

Land acquisition by investors in Mozambique must comply with the formal institutions that oversee land acquisition. The land and petroleum legal frameworks (Law 68/1997 and Law 21/2014, respectively), as well as the legislation relating to resettlement resulting from economic activities that only come into existence after investments had been made (Decree 31/2012), are the key instruments informing national practices related to land acquisition by investors in the oil and gas sector. Additionally, companies are committed to abide by international standards regarding best practice, with significant emphasis on the International Finance Corporation (IFC) Performance Standard 5 (PS5).[17]

The LNG project onshore on the Afungi Peninsula will physically and economically affect close to 6,000 families, whose livelihoods depend on their use of the land and sea, access to both of which will be reduced by the project. On the land, there will be a number of total exclusive zones for the sole use of the companies investing in LNG and of 'noise buffer zones', so the populations that currently reside in and use those areas will not be substantially affected when they are relocated. Meanwhile, fishermen will have no access to the security exclusion zone around the jetties and the materials offloading facility (MOF), while the pipeline corridor will be sealed during the construction phase and possibly permanently. In general, the dominant livelihood activities of the populations of Afungi and the villages of Maganja, Senga, Palma Sede and Monjane revolve around agriculture and fishing.[18] The Resettlement Plan indicates that at least 1,508 households will be directly affected by implementation of the project, with 556 affected both physically and economically, that is, in terms of their livelihoods.[19] A further 952 households will need to be compensated economically. In addition, 3,285 fishermen, most of whom live in Afungi, will no longer have access to the open sea via the area covered by the maritime infrastructure, such as the MOF and the marine terminal services.[20]

The 7,000 ha in Afungi were acquired without any community consultation, which in itself is illegal according to both the land and the investment regulations, which both stipulate the requirement of community consultation. The remaining 18,000 ha requested by ENH are not currently a matter of debate, as this land is not directly integrated into the present LNG project. Yet, it is considered an 'area reserved to the state', represented by ENH, and the people who currently occupy the land will surely be affected by future projects. Therefore, despite the absence of discussion on this particular area, it has the potential to generate considerable conflict over land rights in the future.

Returning to the acquisition of the 7,000 ha, the local communities and CSOs have exerted pressure on the government to review the allocation of the DUAT, given that there was no community consultation, despite it being a legal requirement. For instance, in 2015, Centro Terra Viva (CTV), a CSO working in advocacy and research on land issues in Mozambique, commissioned an independent study to analyse the allocation of land to RBLL. The study, which was conducted by the well-respected João Trindade (see Trindade et al., 2015), reinforced the claims of local communities and CSOs relating to the lack of community consultation and labelled the process 'illegal'.

The government acknowledged that certain procedures had not been adequately followed in Afungi, but that did not lead to a decision to nullify the DUAT that had been awarded to RBLL and then transferred to AMA1. The multinational oil companies with stakes in RBLL continue to deny any responsibility regarding the claims, insisting that due process relating to the acquisition and transfer of the DUAT was followed according to the legislation. This being the case, the main concern moved from the acquisition of the land to standard performance procedures that were directly related to the implementation of the LNG project. The company, AMA1, expressed an interest in conducting a community consultation process, focusing on compensation and resettlement. Over four years from 2013 to 2016, AMA1 held four community consultations as well as various informal meetings with community groups.

In 2015, a third community consultation was organized amid significant criticism from CSOs due to previous allocations of land to investors having been made without any community consultation. The local government manipulated community leaderships to cancel out voices within their communities that were not in favour of the project. The committees created to represent community interests in the consultation process became fragmented, as conflicting perspectives regarding the resettlement process and compensation emerged. A report by the Provincial Peasant Union (UPC) of Cabo Delgado stated that the disagreements among the committee members could be attributed to the salaries that some of them had started to receive from the multinational oil companies.[21] Additionally, there has been criticism of a lack of transparency and a failure to involve keys actors within the local communities and CSOs in the consultation process.

Community members argue that their contributions have not been given due consideration or been subject to due process, and that the companies are dragging their feet over both compensation and resettlement packages. Land restoration and some activities relating to compensation have still not been finalized, which is impacting negatively on local residents' social and economic lives, as they are not allowed to develop certain durable activities within the project site.[22] AMA1 commissioned the Centre of Agriculture and Natural Resource Studies (CEAGRE) at the Eduardo Mondlane University in Maputo[23] to conduct a research project on how the proposed compensation for agricultural crops was in line with the principles established under the PS5. The PS5 advises companies to avoid involuntary resettlement whenever possible and to minimize its impact on the displaced through mitigation measures against the long-term social stress and impoverishment, by providing fair compensation and improving living conditions.[24] The study recommended inclusion of a number of crops that were not mentioned in the proposed scheme, as well as an upward revision of the prices of those crops that were mentioned.

Although the oil companies included the local communities in some of the discussions about compensation, the proposed packages failed to meet community expectations related to the process and the compensation. The villagers feel that they were sidelined in the main negotiations over compensation for their land, crops and other assets, and argue that the compensation framework represents a deal between investors and the government. This was supported by CSOs working with the local populations in the hope of promoting their rights and strengthening their capacity to negotiate better deals with the oil companies and the government.[25] However, CSOs, most of which were based in Maputo, encountered various problems, and their efforts have proved to be largely ineffective (Salimo, 2018).

Despite the key role the community has been assigned by the state through different pieces of legislation, including the land law (Law 19/97), the petroleum law (Law 21/2014) and the Decree 31/2012 on resettlement and compensation, in practice the local communities' capacity and power to negotiate compensation and hold a fair dialogue with powerful groups, such as the investing companies and the state, was indeed poor.[26] This is not only because the local communities lack knowledge of their rights with regard to land governance and possess an insufficient understanding of the petroleum industry, it is also because of the strategies and tactics deployed by gas investors and the state. For example, the divide-and-conquer tactics have resulted in certain community members receiving salaries from the oil companies, while others have been promised rewards by local government officials. Furthermore, the local government itself has generally backed the investors over questions relating to implementation of the project, giving little consideration to the local communities' demands. Lastly, no information was shared prior to the community consultations, so local communities had little reliable information on which the various parties involved could base their expectations.

However, the most significant factor has been the politics behind the relations between the companies and the local communities, in a context where the companies are often connected with the ruling elite centrally, both parties being far less concerned to meet the local communities' demands than to pursue their own overlapping interests. As a consequence of these dynamics, the negotiations for compensation between the companies and the local populations were generally undermined. In practice, the key process and issues relating to the negotiations are controlled and directed mainly by the central ruling elite of the Frelimo party, primarily consisting of the key dominant families that controlled the Guebuza and Nyusi governments, due to the magnitude of the rents expected from these investments. Members of this elite have maintained a certain level of control over the benefits from the current project and have done all they can to ensure that the compensation scheme will neither jeopardize the implementation of future projects nor divert substantial opportunities for rent away from their hands.

4. LOCAL GOVERNMENT: FRAGMENTED POWER AND AUTHORITY

The LNG investments have the potential to affect a reconfiguration of local government power and authority, potentially strengthening local governments' ability to govern local populations, as they become important brokers between national and local concerns, as well as national and international ones. A key question is how influential this power might be, bearing in mind the centralized nature of politics in Mozambique (Weimer and Carrilho, 2017). There are many examples of large-scale investments in natural resources throughout Africa raising serious concerns over inadequate compensation and their negative impacts on the living standards of the affected populations (Jayne et al., 2014; Borras et al., 2011). These experiences have prompted the emergence of CSOs that engage with local populations to oppose poor deals and violations of their rights (Lund and Boone, 2013).

As Lund and Boone (2013, p. 3) argue, the activities of these CSOs in the context of profound struggles over rights to the land may also challenge the existing power and authority of local governments. The main question behind the power and authority of the local government in relation to land use is: who has the political power to impose one interpretation at the expense of others? Lund and Boone suggest that prevailing interpretations of disputes over land will have implications not only for the actors involved, but also for the existing institutional arrangements that guarantee land tenure relations. Then, as these authors observe, the politics that generate any changes in these interpretations could shape authority relations in how control over land is distributed.

As discussed earlier, the process of acquiring land in Palma violated both formal institutional procedures and the basic governance mechanisms outlined in Mozambique's land legislation, and it has been strongly contested as a result. The potential delay in following the formal mechanisms for accessing the land was considered too risky for the central-level ruling elite who wanted the land, and for this to happen, it was crucial to secure state participation. Through their control over the state, it was possible for the elite to control the mechanisms for determining land allocation. The authority to decide on the allocation of such a large area of land that was required for the LNG investments rests legally with the central government in Mozambique, either at the ministerial level or in the Council of Ministers, which is controlled by the President. In contrast, the administrative and management processes rest with local government. However, de facto, decisions made by the powerful Frelimo ruling elite trump any formal mechanisms. For example, RBLL, the shell company to which the 7,000 ha in Afungi were assigned, was designed to be able to integrate future gas concessionaires operating in the Rovuma Basin as shareholders, but the mechanisms involving land allocation were made by bypassing the legal procedures.

Eni joined RBLL in 2014, at which point shares in the company were divided equally between Eni, ENH and AMA1.[27] This arrangement gave the government leverage in its negotiations with the multinationals through ENH's control of access to the land. The debate among the key government institutions in the petroleum sector revolved around concerns that allocating land to multinational oil companies might threaten Mozambique's sovereignty. The argument was, if infrastructure for other projects were constructed along the coast to serve the natural gas operations in Rovuma Basin, ENH would have less control in a context of weak financial and technological capabilities for significant participation in these projects. In 2013, when the government refused Eni's application for a DUAT in Quionga village,[28] on the coast south of Palma, it justified its decision by saying that its preferred policy was for unification of the gas project's infrastructure in Rovuma Basin; in other words, geographical dispersal was to be avoided. In order to secure control of access to the land, the Instituto Nacional de Petróleo (INP) recommended transforming the area requested by Eni into a 'state reserve' (*reserva do estado*) and then giving ENH the role of managing it, as opposed to 'owning' or leasing it.

Against this backdrop, local governments have little power to take decisions that conflict with those of the central-level ruling Frelimo elites, even in the face of clear violations of formal institutional procedures. These violations occurred because institutional mechanisms in a country ruled by law, in contrast to rule of law (Khan and Roy, 2019), will always allow the rulers to bypass it, thus distorting the formal laws, as Buur et al. (2020) suggest. Such practices, when confronted by increasing demands for fair compensation from local populations and CSOs, have seen local state officials align their actions with the ruling elite's interests, even though this undermines their authority locally. This has contributed to the local government being reconfigured in order to address the emerging challenges of securing deals between investors and local communities.

One possible consequence of the CSOs' criticisms of the ways in which the land was allocated and of the dissatisfaction with the mechanisms of community consultation in Palma may have been the appointment of three new district administrators within the space of just three years. It is important to take into consideration the fact that investments in LNG represent an opportunity for the central-level ruling elite to reinvigorate the country's economy after the debt scandal[29] (Macuane et al., 2018), but it also represents an important source of rents for the ruling elite, which could be used to secure its grip on power. As such, there is a danger that members of the elite will hamper the local government's efforts to protect community rights and secure fair compensation for the local population.

5.   RULING ELITE POLITICS AND IMPLICATIONS FOR LOCAL STATE-MAKING

The context in which economic transformation is proceeding in Mozambique – specifically with respect to mineral and hydrocarbon discoveries (Monjane, 2019) – means that it is imperative to promote foreign investments through land allocations (Cabral and Norfolk, 2016; Fairbairn, 2013) and the security of land tenure for local communities. One ambivalent aspect is that the state plays the principal role in both guaranteeing local communities' security of land tenure and granting land-use rights to investors. At its most basic level, it does this by enforcing the implementation of existing formal mechanisms and deciding when to diverge from the formal rules. As part of this, members of the ruling elite may reshape or bypass these mechanisms to serve their own interests (Khan, 2010; Whitfield and Buur, 2014).

As argued above, the ruling elite and other powerful groups are able to exert significant influence over land governance and land management. In this regard, Lund and Boone (2013) argue that the balance of power among those who hold various forms of institutional authority over land issues governs who is most likely to succeed in achieving their aims. This view agrees with that of Pedersen and Kweka (2017), who conclude that any research into petroleum investments and land acquisition in Africa would benefit from widening the focus to encompass the broader political economy of land and petroleum investments, rather than concentrating solely on the behaviour of the oil companies. This is because they are unlikely to be the only or most important actors in deciding how land is acquired. Such research is driven by the issue of the type of local state that is constituted as a consequence of large-scale investments in LNG and its related ability to protect local community rights within the context of those investments.

The key to understanding what drives changes at the heart of state power is recognizing the potential influence of a variety of societal forces. This being the case, the dynamics involving the multiple actors that interact with and outside the state may have a significant impact on the nature of the state that emerges in the event of large-scale natural resource investments. These multiple actors – members of the ruling elite, multinational oil companies, CSOs, donors and other international agencies, and local populations – all have their own interests to defend. Therefore, due to the high economic value of large-scale investments, their relations are usually conflictual, as they may need to engage in tense negotiations in relation to specific issues, such as compensation deals, future business opportunities and protecting the interests of particular groups. Decisions made by the ruling elite may serve to exacerbate this tension and generate further contestation, while the competing demands of right-holders and other important actors may constrain the state and therefore influence new paths of state-making.

For example, the oil companies must consider the interests of the central-level ruling elite in order to secure the successful implementation of their projects (see Buur et al., 2019; 2020). Likewise, members of the ruling elite must take the oil companies' interests into account because they need to secure revenue and other benefits from the multinationals' investment in the LNG project (see Buur et al., 2020). By contrast, both sides have largely ignored local government, which has been left ill-equipped to perform its principal local role: protecting the local community's rights and interests during negotiations for compensation. As a result, the local population has been largely sidelined during the negotiations about compensation in Cabo Delgado, weakening its already fragile bargaining position. One consequence of this is the perception within the local community that the government is the 'enemy of the people', while the oil companies are more open to accommodating community interests, but are not allowed to do so by ruling elite interests. In interviews, residents of Quitupo and Maganja in Palma expressed concerns about government corruption and insisted that they would prefer to receive their compensation from the companies directly, rather than the state. In contrast, the Frelimo-controlled state insists that compensation be paid to the state first, after which local communities can receive their share.[30] Similarly, in August 2015, during the third community consultation, representatives of the local population declared that they did not trust the government (or the state) to manage the funds that had been allocated for resettlement and compensation.

Nevertheless, CSOs and the 'mobilized' local communities have managed to effect changes in both local and central government behaviour. In 2015, the new central administration acknowledged that the CSOs had an important role to play in negotiations over compensation and resettlement. In this regard, it distanced itself from the problems of previous years, ranging from a lack of community consultation on land acquisitions to an absence of transparency in the consultation process on resettlement and tensions between the state and CSOs.[31]

Despite CSOs enjoying far from universal acceptance within the local community, the local state has managed to alter the central state's perception of the local community's demands, and indeed the role of civil society itself, but not enough to avoid the youth insurgency that has been hitting Cabo Delgado since 2017 (dos Santos, 2020; Morier-Genoud, 2020). Even though the local state, in an attempt to gain further legitimacy locally, tried to increase the local community's leverage during negotiations with investors by educating the local population on their rights to land and natural resources, actively defending the villagers' interests and fighting for more social and economic benefits from the LNG project, the unholy alliance between the central government and the investors prevailed.

6.   CONCLUSION

This chapter has analysed the relationship between multinational oil companies (the investors) and local communities during negotiations about compensation for land lost due to LNG investments. This issue has been examined by highlighting the role played by the local government in the negotiation process vis-à-vis its ability to protect the interests of the local population. The principal conclusion is that the negotiations over compensation, relating to land and economic losses, are intertwined with the contested nature of local government politics vis-à-vis central government interests. In general, the local government has been sidelined during these negotiations, which have been dominated by the central ruling elite and the investors. This has eroded the local government's authority and its ability to protect the local community's interests. Therefore, the type of state that has emerged in the wake of the investments in LNG has been strongly influenced by ruling elite politics, which has both undermined and delegitimized local government. This in turn has had a detrimental impact on the relationship between investors and local communities, which has been distorted due to a lack of information and poor rights awareness, and because the ruling elite has become too influential in determining the path of negotiations over compensation.

NOTES

1.   Padil Salimo holds a joint PhD in Social Science from Roskilde University in Denmark and the University of Dar es Salaam in Tanzania. This chapter is part of the PhD programme, funded by the Danish Ministry for Foreign Affairs under the Hierarchies of Rights Programme. The chapter is a revised version of a previous chapter published both in a book edited by Jon Schubert, Ulf Engel and Elísio Macamo (2018), *Extractive Industries and Changing State Dynamics in Africa:*

       Beyond the Resource Curse, USA: Routledge; and in his doctoral thesis Padil Salimo (2022), 'Governing petroleum in Mozambique: contentious governance reforms and deal-making', Doctoral thesis, Roskilde Universitet.

2.   Eni (13 November 2022), 'Mozambique's first LNG cargo departs from Coral Sul FLNG, offshore the Rovuma Basin', accessed 19 November 2022 at https://www.eni.com/en-IT/media/press-release/2022/11/eni-coral-first-cargo.html.

3.   Wood Mackenzie (17 June 2019), 'Mozambique LNG under starter's order: Anadarko FID "largest sanction ever" in sub-Saharan Africa oil and gas', accessed 11 November 2022 at https://www.woodmac.com/press-releases/mozambique-lng-fid/.

4.   Fieldwork started in 2015 with several meetings held in Maputo and Cabo Delgado province (in Pemba, Mocimboa da Praia and Palma districts). The gathering of information also involved focus-group meetings with members of the local communities in Palma Sede, Quitupo, Maganja and Senga. Preliminary results of this research have been presented in a seminar and conferences at the Institute for Advanced Studies (STIAS) of the University of Stellenbosch; the Institute for Poverty, Land and Agrarian Studies (PLAAS) of the University of Western Cape; the Institute of Resource Assessment (IRA) of the University of Dar Es Salaam; and at the 5th IESE Conference in Maputo.

5.   See the 'Exploration and Production Concession Contract for Area 1 "Offshore" of the Rovuma Basin', 20 December 2006, agreed between the government, AMA 1 and ENH; and the 'Exploration and Production Concession Contract for Area 4 "Offshore" of the Rovuma Basin', 2006, agreed between the government, Eni East Africa SpA (EEA) and ENH. Both available at www.inp.gov.mz, accessed 11 November 2022.

6.   The sites were identified between Pemba and the Tanzanian border, with the seven then narrowed down to three, namely the Afungi Peninsula in Palma District, the Londo Peninsula in Metuge District and the Cabo Delgado Peninsula.

7.   Personal interview with key officials at INP and ENH, confirmed with narratives in Chapter 5, 'Consideration of Alternatives', in the AMA1 socio-economic, marine and terrestrial ecology study, conducted by Environmental Resources Management (ERM) and Impacto.

8.   This is aligned with the industrialization policy through natural gas investments, as established in the Natural Gas Master Plan, approved by the government in 2014.

9.   Governo da Província de Cabo Delgado, Ofício No 33/GG/CD/2012, 27 February 2012. The same document was sent to the offices of the Head of State, Prime Minister, Minister of Agriculture and Minister of State Administration.

10.   Personal interviews with senior officials of the district government in Palma, April 2017.

11.   A PowerPoint presentation prepared by the district government of Palma, 20 September 2016. Complementary information obtained from personal interviews with technicians from district services for planning and infrastructure.

12.   This figure is confirmed by details on the localization map annexed to the provisional DUAT allocated to Rovuma Basin LNG Land (RBLL), issued in Maputo on 12 December 2012, authorized by the Minister of Agriculture and issued by the National Directorate of Land and Forest. The document also states that the 7,000 ha of land allocated to RBLL is unoccupied, which later became the main

source of conflict between local communities and CSOs on the one hand and the government and multinational oil companies on the other.

13. Personal interviews with officials in key sectors of the government, who argued that this kind of operation was adopted, despite bypassing the law, to ensure that land was not directly allocated and controlled by multinational oil companies, therefore guaranteeing that state sovereignty is not under threat. The government's intentions have been to keep the land for the development of natural gas infrastructure projects under the control of the ENH, and thus put this company at the centre of the negotiations with multinationals on the land needed to host the LNG project and other natural gas-related projects in the Rovuma Basin.

14. In interviews, members of the district government in Palma consistently mentioned that the 18,000 ha of land have been earmarked for ENH's future urban development projects.

15. The presentation took place on 20 September 2016.

16. That is, 13 December 2012.

17. The Environmental Impact Assessment approved by the government in 2014 and the Resettlement Plan approved in 2016 both refer to the specific use of PS-5 and the government of Mozambique's Decree 31/2012.

18. See Anadarko (2015), 'Resettlement Plan'. Not published.

19. See Anadarko (2015), 'Resettlement Plan'. Not published.

20. Decree 87/2013 assigned a concession for maritime terminals and logistics in Pemba and Palma to Portos de Cabo Delgado (PCD), but Decree 4/2016 amended those rights and transferred them to concessionaires in Areas 1 and 4. This regulates how the concessionaires of the Rovuma Basin project meet the requirements of international LNG standards applicable to the Rovuma Basin project infrastructure in both land and maritime areas with regard to ownership rights, operations and management, and safety and maritime traffic control. The concessionaires of the Rovuma Basin project are granted exclusive rights of access and operations over maritime and land areas where the facilities are constructed, and effective control over all Rovuma Basin project infrastructure, including the LNG marine terminal and the materials offloading facility.

21. UPC (2016), *Consultas Públicas, Manipulação e Falta de Respeito aos Direitos das Comunidades*, Cabo Delgado.

22. Focus group with local communities in three villages – Quitupo, Maganja and Palma – April 2017.

23. The centre was commissioned to conduct an independent study evaluating the company's proposed scheme for compensation for crops under the LNG project in order to verify whether the proposal was aligned with the 'total cost of replacement' established in PS5. See Chiulele (2014).

24. The PS5 is focused on 'Land Acquisition and Involuntary Resettlement'. For details of the principles underlying PS5, see IFC (2012), 'Performance Standard on Environmental and Social Sustainability: Performance Standard 5', World Bank Group, 1 January 2012, accessed 11 November 2022 at https://www.ifc .org/wps/wcm/connect/24e6bfc3-5de3-444d-be9b-226188c95454/PS_English _2012_Full-Document.pdf?MOD=AJPERES&CVID=jkV-X6h.

25. Anadarko (2012), 'Community Investment Plan (CIP) 2013–2014'. Not published.

26. Interviews with key actors in Quitupo and Maganja, June 2016 and April 2017.

27. 'Rovuma Basin LNG Land', *Bulletin of the Republic*, series 3, no. 68, 22 August 2014.

28. In a letter of 22 April 2013 to the former Minister of Mineral Resources (Ref. No. 145/ENI/13), Eni expresses an interest in obtaining a DUAT for a site in Quionga and discusses the regulatory and contractual framework.
29. The debt scandal refers to hidden debt organized by the former President Guebuza and present President Nyusi in cohort with many members of the Frelimo party that came to the fore in 2016, when huge loans by three state-owned enterprises (SOEs) forced the International Monetary Fund (IMF) and the international donor community to suspend budgetary support. This has ruined the economy.
30. Interviews in Quitupo and Maganja, April 2016 and April 2017.
31. The new government took the decision to postpone the public community consultation that was scheduled to take place a few months after the government's inauguration. This decision gave the new administration time to understand the project, but more importantly it signalled a positive change in its attitude towards CSOs, which had previously been viewed as enemies of development, as the government invited them to participate as relevant stakeholders. An independent evaluation of land allocations to concessionaires in Palma, Afungi, commissioned by CTV (see Trindade et al., 2015) has since been used by the government as a key document to inform the next stage of interventions in Palma. Relations with CSOs have improved, a network for consultations between government, CSOs, companies and other stakeholders has been created, and a network involving these actors has been established and consolidated to deal with land issues.

REFERENCES

Borras, S.M. Jr., Hall, R., Scoones, I., White, B. and Wolford, W. (2011) 'Towards a better understanding of global land grabbing', Journal of Peasant Studies, 38(2), 209–16.
Buur, L., Pedersen, R.H., Nystrand, M.J. and Macuane, J.J. (2019) 'Understanding the three key relationships in natural resource investments in Africa: an analytical framework', *The Extractive Industries and Society*, 6(4), 1195–204.
Buur, L., Pedersen, R.H., Nystrand, M.J., Macuane, J.J. and Jacob, T. (2020) 'The politics of natural resource investments and rights in Africa: a theoretical approach', *The Extractive Industries and Society*, 7(3), 918–30.
Cabral, L. and Norfolk, S. (2016) 'Inclusive land governance in Mozambique: good law, bad politics?', IDS Working Paper 47, Brighton: Institute of Development Studies and Swiss Agency for Development and Cooperation, accessed 11 November 2022 at https://opendocs.ids.ac.uk/opendocs/bitstream/handle/123456789/12187/Wp478 .pdf;jsessionid=5E756739CC5A3F2FDD8C39AB2A25B998?sequence=1.
Chiulele, R. (2014) 'Avaliação do relatório da compensação das culturas independentes para o Project de Desenvolvimento de Gás em Moçambique (PDGM)', *Maputo: Centro de Estudos de Agricultura e Recursos Naturais*, UEM.
Cotula L., Vermeulen, S., Leonard, R. and Keeley, J. (2009) Land grab or development opportunity? Agricultural investment and international land deals in Africa, London and Rome: IIED/FAO/IFAD
Deininger, K. (2011) 'Challenges posed by the new wave of farmland investment', Journal of Peasant Studies, 38(2), 217–47, accessed 11 November 2022 at www.shus .unimi.it/wp-content/uploads/2012/01/jpeasantst_032011.pdf.
dos Santos, F.A. (2020) 'War in resource-rich northern Mozambique – six scenarios', *CMI Insights*, 2, 1–18, accessed 19 November 2022 at https://open.cmi.no/cmi

-xmlui/bitstream/handle/11250/2655944/War%20in%20resource-rich%20northern %20Mozambique%20%20–%20Six%20scenarios?sequence=1&isAllowed=y.
Fairbairn, M. (2013) 'Indirect dispossession: domestic power imbalances and foreign access to land in Mozambique' in Wolford, W., Borras, S., Hall, R., Scoones I. and White, B. (eds), Governing Global Land Deals: The Rule of the State in the Rush for Land, Malden, MA and Oxford: John Wiley & Sons.
Frynas, J.G. and Buur, L. (2020) 'The presource curse in Africa: economic and political effects of anticipating natural resource revenues', *The Extractive Industries and Society*, 7(4), 1257–70, at https://www.sciencedirect.com/science/article/abs/pii/ S2214790X20301568.
Gqada, I. (2013) 'A boom for whom? Mozambique's natural gas and the new development opportunity', Occasional Paper No. 151, Governance of Africa's Resource Programme, South Africa: SAIIA, accessed 15 May 2022 at http://www.saiia.org.za/ occasional-papers/349-a-boom-for-whom-mozambique-s-natural-gas-and-the-new -development-opportunity/file.
Human Rights Watch (HRW) (2013) What is a House without Food? Mozambique's Coal Mining Boom and Resettlements, New York: HRW.
Jayne, T.S., Chamberlin, J. and Headey, D.D. (2014) 'Land pressures, the evolution of farming system, and development in Africa: a synthesis', Food Policy, 48, 1–17.
Khan, M.H. (2010) 'Political settlements and the governance of growth-enhancing institutions', Unpublished paper SOAS, University of London, accessed 11 November 2022 at https://eprints.soas.ac.uk/9968/1/Political_Settlements_internet.pdf.
Khan, M. and Roy, P. (2019) 'Digital identities: a political settlement analysis of asymmetric power and information', Working Paper 015, School of Oriental and African Studies, University of London, pp. 1–32.
Lund, C. and Boone, C. (2013) 'Introduction: land politics in Africa – constituting authority over territory, property and persons', Africa, 83(1), 1–13.
Macuane, J.J., Buur, L. and Monjane, C. (2018) 'Power, conflict and natural resources: the Mozambican crisis revisited', *African Affairs*, 117(468), 415–38.
Melina, G. and Xiong, Y. (2013) 'Natural gas, public investment and debt sustainability in Mozambique', IMF Working Paper, Washington, DC: IMF.
Monjane, C.M. (2019) 'Rethinking the political economy of commodity-based linkages: insights from the coal sector in Mozambique', Doctoral thesis, Roskilde University.
Morier-Genoud, E. (2020) 'The jihadist insurgence in Mozambique: origins, nature and beginning', *Journal of Eastern African Studies*, 14(3), 396–412.
Mosca, J. and Selemane, T. (2011) El Dorado Tete: os mega projectos de mineração, Maputo: Centro de Integridade Pública.
Pedersen, R.H. and Kweka, O. (2017) 'The political economy of petroleum investments and land acquisition standards in Africa: the case of Tanzania', Resources Policy, 52, 217–25.
Salimo, P. (2018) 'The politics of LNG: local state power and contested demands for land acquisition in Palma, Mozambique' in Schubert, J., Engel, U. and Macamo, E. (eds), *Extractive Industries and Changing State Dynamics in Africa: Beyond the Resource Curse*, USA: Routledge, pp. 89–111.
Schoneveld, G.C. (2014) 'The geographic and sectoral pattern of large-scale farmland investments in sub-Saharan Africa', Food Policy, 48, 34–50, https://doi.org/10.1016/ j.foodpol.2014.03.007.
Trindade, J.C., Cruz, L. and José, A.C. (2015) 'Avaliação jurídica independente aos processos de licenciamento dos projectos minerais e hidrocarbonetos', Maputo:

Centro Terra Viva, accessed 11 November 2022 at www.oam.org.mz/wp-content/uploads/Avaliacao-Juridica-Independente-aos-Processos-de-Licenciamento-dos-Projectos-Mineiros-e-Hidrocarbonetos-.pdf.

USAID (2007) Land Use Rights for Commercial Activities in Mozambique, Washington, DC: United States Agency for International Development.

Weimer, B. and Carrilho, J. (2017) Political Economy of Decentralization in Mozambique: Dynamics, Outcomes, Challenges, Maputo: IESE.

Whitfield, L. and Buur, L. (2014) 'The politics of industrial policy: ruling elites and their alliances', Third World Quarterly, 35(1), 126–44.

Wittmeyer, H. (2012) 'Mozambique's "land grab": exploring approaches to elite policymaking and neoliberal reform', Unpublished paper, College of Saint Benedict and Saint John's University, accessed 11 November 2022 at http://digitalcommons.csbsju.edu/polsci_students/3.

3. The double role of the state: the state as investor and mediator in the Tanzanian coal sector

Thabit Jacob

1.   INTRODUCTION

Recent studies of large-scale investments in land and natural resources have mainly focused on the role of the state and state elites as facilitators of investments made by multinational corporations (MNCs) (Lee, 2006; Carmody, 2013; Ayers, 2013; Kelly and Peluso, 2015; Pearce, 2016). The literature on land-grabbing has also underscored the role of state elites and government agencies in facilitating the flow of foreign capital, which in many cases has led to inadequate consultation and the forced eviction and displacement of local populations in areas where these investments are being implemented (Cotula et al., 2009; Daniel and Mittal, 2009; Wolford et al., 2013). Recent research has further emphasized that deals may be domestically driven and that, while land acquisitions may be morally questionable, they are not necessarily illegal (Hall, 2011; Pedersen and Buur, 2016).

Hence, while the role of the state as a facilitator of natural resource investments has been studied, there is little understanding of its role as an investor or joint-venture investor. This chapter argues that there is a need to widen the discussion to focus on the re-emergence of the state as an investor through state-owned enterprises (hereafter SOEs), as witnessed in recent coal investments in Tanzania. Through an analysis of the Ngaka coal mine, this chapter focuses on the diverse and changing relationships SOEs and joint ventures have with local populations using TANCOAL's Ngaka coal mine in Mbinga District, south-west Tanzania, as a case study, with a particular focus on exploring investor–investor relationships.[1]

The chapter offers an opportunity to explore local conflicts over state-led coal extraction. It argues that, while the SOE in the form of the National Development Corporation (NDC) and its foreign joint-venture partner relied strategically on the Tanzanian government's use of the state to fast-track coal mining, it also limited local voices and dissent arising from the state-sponsored investments in extraction, creating ambivalence and insecurity in the process.

We know that research advocating that the state should acquire a greater stake in resource investments expects state ownership of mining investments through SOEs to increase local acceptance of mining investments and to reduce tensions with local populations after many years of conflicts between small-holders and foreign companies (Collins, 2009).[2] However, recent research in Tanzania suggests that investment-related conflicts are increasingly changing to a situation in which the interests of local populations and smallholders compete with those of the state through revived SOEs (Jacob et al., 2016). The double role of the state as both an investor and the final arbiter of different rights is therefore not straightforward but can potentially cause ambiguity and conflict.

The chapter draws on and contributes to Buur et al.'s (2017; 2019; 2020) analytical framework on land and natural resource investments in Africa, which unpacks the complex triangular relationship between investors, local populations and ruling elites and their respective bureaucracies. This chapter reveals a more complicated situation in this three-way relationship. Whereas Buur et al. tend to see the state, and especially the ruling elites, as mainly playing the role of investment facilitators and protectors of local populations and smallholders' land rights and livelihood security, the chapter argues that the Tanzanian state has a double role as both an investor and the final arbiter of different forms of rights.[3] State-led resource investments therefore have significant implications for the ability of local populations to benefit from such investments, as this chapter will show. But – and this is important – the double role of the state also offers opportunities for some sections of the local population to press for further inclusion and access to benefits from the investment. The chapter argues that the holding power of the different actors – that is, the ruling elites, the state, investors and local populations – is the key to understanding the various actors' ability to influence a given situation (on the concept of holding power, see the recent contribution by Behuria et al. (2017), which builds on early work by Mushaq Khan, 2010). Buur et al. (2019, p. 1202, note 15) define the concept of 'holding power as "the capability of an individual or group to engage and survive in conflicts" (Khan, 2010, p. 6)'. More specifically, they argue 'that it is made up of two sets of factors, namely the ability to impose costs on others and the ability to absorb costs inflicted by others'. Holding power is therefore intimately related to the more general question of the distribution of power in society, which relates to 'the relative holding power of different groups and organizations contesting the distribution of resources. Holding power is partly based on income and wealth but also on historically rooted capacities of different groups to organize and the networks they belong to' (Khan, 2010, p. 1; quoted from Buur et al., 2019, p. 1202, note 15).

The material for this chapter is based on in-depth ethnographic interviews, participant observation and documentary analysis. The empirical materials discussed in this chapter consist of semi-structured, in-depth interviews with local community members in Mbinga District, supplemented by additional data collected between 2015 and 2017 in the commercial capital, Dar es Salaam, and in Songea, Ruvuma's regional headquarters. Participant observation included a guided tour of TANCOAL's Ngaka coal mine. In Dar es Salaam, in-depth, semi-structured interviews were conducted with key informants, including TANCOAL officials, government officials affiliated with the then Ministry of Energy and Minerals, and NDC representatives. These were supplemented by three ethnographic field trips to Mbinga and the two adjacent villages of Ruanda and Ntunduwaro between 2015 and 2017, where formal and informal interviews were conducted with ward, village and sub-village leaders, relocated local land-users, leaders of political parties and TANCOAL officials stationed at the mine. The empirical material also includes a transcription of a two-and-a-half-hour village meeting on land and compensation issues held in Ntunduwaro village in 2016. Triangulation was used to verify and cross-check data collected from various sources.

The chapter is organized as follows. The second section explores the historical relationship between the state and local populations before the start of coal extraction, showing how this has evolved over time. In their theoretical framework, Buur et al. (2020) have emphasized the need to understand the relationship between local populations and the state historically, asking whether it has been based on mistrust, violence or ignorance? This is important to understand in the case presented in this chapter because historical relations between ruling elites, and by extension the state, and local populations will often shape present-day relations and affect the legitimacy of the SOE in respect of these investments. After the historical analysis, the chapter then discusses the prevailing situation in relation to the Ngaka coal mine and explores local conflicts related to the joint-venture investment involving the state-owned NDC and its Australian partner, the Intra Energy Corporation (IEC), an Australian stock exchange-listed company. The chapter examines what characterizes the relationship between the joint-venture investment and the local population. The final section discusses the implications of the empirical findings and concludes the chapter.

2.   HISTORICAL PERSPECTIVE: THE STATE AND LOCAL POPULATIONS IN THE RUVUMA REGION

Rural populations in various parts of the globe have experienced a history of socio-economic, political and cultural control and oppression by ruling elites under the guise of social transformation and modernization (Scott, 1998). Tanzania is no exception to this. Although the protection of the rights of local populations in mining and oil and gas investments has improved over the last couple of decades (Pedersen et al., 2016), they have been the weaker party compared to the state and investors, whether the latter be local or foreign. The historical interaction between the state and local populations has been riddled with tensions.

The Ruvuma region has a long history of resettlement under the colonial administration of the Germans and later the British. The first resettlement programme was carried out by the Germans in 1905 to pave the way for the establishment of a game reserve, which later became the present-day Selous game reserve (Monson, 1998; Neumann, 2001). Local resistance to German colonial rule led to the Maji Maji rebellion of 1905–06, which was brutally suppressed by the Germans, forcing many people to flee to other parts of the region and to neighbouring Mozambique (Edwards, 2003). In 1944, the British, now the colonial power, embarked on a resettlement scheme in order to extend the area designated for the Selous reserve (Neumann, 2001).

The heavy-handed approach towards the local population continued under the post-independence villagization policy of Julius Nyerere, the founding father of modern Tanzania, and his Ujamaa socialist and self-reliant experiment (see next section). However, the experience of Ujamaa for local populations was uneven, particularly in the Ruvuma region, which includes Mbinga District, where the Ngaka coal mine is located. Historically, the relationship with the state is of particular importance here, as it created mistrust and problems related to the legitimacy of the state in the rural Ruvuma region, which still influences the nature of state–community relations today.

2.1   Ujamaa: Producing a New Society

Ujamaa and its villagization policy were adopted in 1967 after the Arusha declaration, when Tanzania officially became a socialist state. Villagization aimed to transform rural Tanzania by moving people from scattered villages into government-planned nucleated settlements and by encouraging communal farming in the new villages. The resettlement exercise started as a voluntary process that was justified by development rhetoric and the greater ease of service delivery in the new villages, but it later became increasingly coercive and top-down in nature, due to its slow initial progress. By 1973 only 15 per cent of the population had been resettled. Nyerere and provincial party officials became increasingly frustrated with the rural population's slow response in forming Ujamaa villages. Government and party officials in charge of implementation came under pressure and resorted to coercion and abusive practices to achieve targets set by the party-state, which made it clear that the careers of local government officials and party cadres depended on the policy's rapid implementation (Boesen et al., 1977; Von Freyhold, 1985; Jennings, 2002; Schneider, 2006; Jennings, 2008).

In 1973 the government passed an enabling legislation, the Rural Lands (Planning and Utilisation) Act, which made resettlement more compulsory. The Act gave the government extensive administrative powers by empowering the President to declare any area a 'development area'. Under the same Act, the Minister for Regional Administration had powers to end existing rights to land in any area where it was planned to establish Ujamaa villages. Also, in 1973, the then ruling Tanganyika African Union (TANU) declared that all farmers in rural areas should be in Ujamaa villages by 1976. In 1975, another influential Act was passed, the Villages and Ujamaa Villages Act, which further reinforced the villagization programme by giving TANU officials more power to establish villages (Fimbo, 2004; Pedersen et al., 2016).

A combination of legislative and coercive measures saw the number of registered Ujamaa villages increase fourfold between 1972 and 1976. By 1976, over 6 million people were living in Ujamaa villages across Tanzania, a very significant portion of the rural population,[4] in what Michael Jennings dubbed 'one of Africa's largest resettlement campaigns' (Jennings, 2008, p. 5).

The resettlement process was heavy-handed, destroying social structures and disrupting existing customary arrangements, while increasing the party-state's control over land (Boesen et al., 1977; Von Freyhold, 1985; Coulson, 1982; Shivji, 1998; Jennings, 2002; Schneider, 2006). Villagization was characterized by excessive use of force on the part of the state, a total disregard for existing customary rights and a lack of any consultation with rural populations. Veteran legal and land-rights scholar Issa Shivji, who assessed the process, criticized it for undermining collective rights in rural areas. He noted the following:

> Post-colonial administrators [in independent Tanzania] did not even go through the motions of consultation, [but rather] directives from the top implemented bureaucratically and often enforced through legal and extra-legal coercion have been the typical modus operandi. (Shivji, 1998, p. 10)

While villagization was heavy-handed, its impacts were not uniform across Tanzania, some regions being more affected than others. There was minimal resettlement in areas of large coffee and tea plantations, such as the Northern and Southern Highlands (Odgaard, 1986; Raikes, 1986). Conversely, resettlement was widespread and more brutal in the southern regions of Lindi, Mtwara and Ruvuma, which had fewer plantations than the rest of Tanzania. Besides the lower level of capitalist market integration, another reason for this was that the southern regions bordered on war-torn Mozambique. Here resettlement was framed as a way of protecting the local population from the war on the other side of the border (Boesen et al., 1977; Von Freyhold, 1985; Jennings, 2002; Schneider, 2006).

The longer history of post-independence nation- and state-formation is important for more recent investments. While investments, when approved, are often seen as the point of departure for the creation of new relations between investors, states and local populations, they are in fact socially embedded (Nystrand, 2015; Buur and Nystrand, 2020) in processes of state-formation that often involve misrecognition and abuse instead of mutual recognition (Buur et al., 2020). Tanzania is no exception here.

2.2   Echoes of the Past

Although it has been over 40 years since villagization was implemented, and memories of its authoritarian modes of resettlement may not be as important today, social memory still influences the attitudes of local populations towards state-driven policies, including state-approved investments. The successive Tanzanian governments of Presidents Ali Hassan Mwinyi (1985–95) and Benjamin Mkapa (1995–2005) paid great attention to foreign investors and promoted neoliberal economic policies and practices that undermined the rights of local populations, leading to evictions of smallholders in various parts of the country.[5]

In the mining sector, relationships between the state and local populations changed dramatically at the peak of the neoliberal reforms under the administration of President Mkapa (1995–2005), when the state was desperate to attract Foreign Direct Investment (FDI). In efforts to improve FDI flows under a World Bank-sponsored and locally supported mining-reform programme, artisanal miners from different parts of the country were forcibly removed from their areas by state security forces to pave the way for foreign mining companies. This was more prevalent in the gold sub-sector, especially in Lake Region areas such as Bulyanhulu, Geita and North Mara (Lange, 2008; Schroeder, 2010; Emel et al., 2011). The state famously labelled artisanal miners 'intruders' (Holterman, 2014, p. 62). The most infamous eviction case was the so-called 'Bulyanhulu tragedy' of August 1996, when over 50 people were allegedly killed while artisanal miners were being forcibly evicted by state security forces to pave the way for the establishment of the Bulyanhulu gold mine by the Kahama Mining Corporation Limited (Nambiza, 2007; Lange, 2011; Makene et al., 2012). This was a wholly owned subsidiary of Canada's Sutton Resources, later acquired by the Barrick Gold Corporation in 1999 (LEAT, 2002).

While it is not claimed that the Nyerere, Mwinyi and Mkapa governments were similar or that they acted in the same ways, it is suggested that there were continuities in terms of the treatment of local populations by different administrations. Under the guise of 'nation-building' under Nyerere, local populations suffered heavily from villagization, as already discussed. On the other hand, the partnership between the state and foreign capital under the Mwinyi and Mkapa administrations promoted foreign investments in wildlife, tourism and large-scale mining, all of which led to mixed outcomes, including violations of smallholders' rights and increased conflicts, especially in areas where local populations resisted such investments. In short, the treatment of local populations and smallholders shows important continuities over the years, but contemporary developments have given way to differences.

The most significant difference in recent years occurred in 2010, when the Kikwete administration paved the way for the revival of SOEs in the mining sector with a new Mining Act. This represented a departure from the policies of previous administrations, which had focused on foreign investments. SOE-led projects were framed as 'unique projects' in which the state had a direct stake, as opposed to former mining projects in the country, which were 100 per cent owned by foreign companies. SOE-led investments reflect several aspects of the related political dynamics, which include a potential, if only rhetorical realignment with Nyerere's policies of self-reliance, as well as a renewed focus on mining as a potential source of rents for the ruling elites. These rents can emerge from local service and procurement contracts, revenues and royalties that are used locally, as well as straightforward bribes (see Jacob, 2017).

More recently, the Magufuli government intensified the SOE-led investment policies started by Kikwete. After assuming office at the end of 2015, the late President Magufuli enacted a series of policy reforms that have dramatically changed the governance of mining investments. These policy changes included three new pieces of legislation enacted in July 2017 (see Jacob and Pedersen, 2018) and mining regulations in 2018, which among other things proclaimed Tanzania's sovereignty over its natural resources, provided for the mandatory (16 per cent) involvement of SOEs in all mining operations and allowed them to acquire up to 50 per cent of the shares in mining companies.

Given the recent enthusiasm for SOE-led investments, a possible unintended consequence of the policy emphasis has been heightened tensions between the state and local populations, as local communities are increasingly being persuaded or coerced to support extraction projects carried out by state-owned enterprises (Pedersen and Jacob, 2017; Jacob and Pedersen, 2018). Even though today's coercive strategies differ from those of the Ujamaa villagization schemes of the 1960s and 1970s, present-day strategies echo past strategies. This is discussed in the next section, where any form of refusal to support SOE-led investments is considered 'unpatriotic' and even 'un-national'.

3.   COAL EXTRACTION AND CONTESTATION

In Mbinga District, located in the Ruvuma region, south-western Tanzania, which has been the scene of mining and FDI-steered state developmentalism, the state-led NDC joined its Australian partners to embark on coal extraction. Historically local populations have been loyal to the ruling Chama Cha Mapinduzi (CCM) but due to conflicts related to the investments recent electoral trends indicate that the situation is changing. The emergence of new political players has led to the erosion of previously dominant CCM coalitions at the sub-national level. One of the main reasons for the breakdown in relations between the CCM and its traditional supporters in Mbinga District is local dissatisfaction over recent compensation arrangements related to land expropriations. As a result of this dissatisfaction, opposition political parties have ended up being seen as the trusted voice in some of the local issues that have not traditionally arisen in the area, which has been dominated politically by the CCM.

As an SOE, the NDC was determined to fast-track the land-acquisition and compensation process and move ahead with coal extraction as fast as possible, as the revenues were seen as a possible source of rents for the CCM's ruling elites at different national and local levels (see Jacob, 2020 for a broader analysis). However, villagers resisted what they perceived to be a 'low level of compensation' (field notes, Mbinga, July 2017). This brought them into conflict with the local state in Mbinga, which was backed by both the regional government in Ruvuma and national government institutions. A number of unfulfilled promises, made by the state-backed investor in the Ngaka coal mine, aggravated the conflict.

3.1   Supporting a 'State-Led Project': Fast-Tracking Land Acquisition and Conflict

The influence of the SOE and regional and local state officials in shaping consultation processes was immense. The SOE-led mining project was framed by NDC officials and national and local politicians as a 'unique project' that would benefit Tanzania and should be supported by all Tanzanians. Villagers were also constantly reminded that this was a project in which the state has a direct stake, as opposed to other mining projects in the country, which are 100 per cent owned by foreign companies. There was a need, they were told, to support a state-owned company that represents 'all Tanzanians'. This framing was very strategic in controlling dissent in efforts to legitimize coal extraction. As one villager put it:

> When the NDC and land people came for consultation, we were told the project is led by the NDC, and the Australian company is just a partner. […] our Member of Parliament and Regional Commissioner said we must support the government of President Kikwete. (Interview, Ntunduwaro village, September 2015)[6]

The quote above is a reference to the soft efforts deployed by state actors to limit opposition and dissent in local communities, which has characterized the recent wave of state-led extractive and energy investments. The ruling elites frame the latter as the key to promoting economic growth, modernizing energy provision and securing the nation's energy supply. This framing is associated with claims that issues of national importance and urgency should supersede local rights (Jacob, 2017; Pedersen and Jacob, 2017). In other words, SOE officials and ruling elites at the regional and national level tried to shape consultation processes locally in ways that increased tensions and mistrust, particularly when promises were not followed up and when trust was broken between the ruling elites and the local populations.

After reluctantly giving what many locals consider their 'coerced consent', coal mining was allowed to start in 2011. However, the consultation process and overall compensation plan were dominated by local dissent and opposition, which was ignored after the government forced villagers to vacate their lands to pave the way for coal extraction. Villagers claimed to have been compensated for only their buildings and crops, not the full market value of their homes (interviews, Ntunduwaro, Mbinga, 2016). Those resisting the low compensation rates were labelled 'enemies of development' (interviews, Ntunduwaro, Mbinga, 2016–17). Low levels of compensation were initially accepted due to threats that the government would take the land anyway and that villagers therefore had to accept whatever was offered. They were told by the area's MP and NDC representative that the government 'was doing them a favour' (interviews in Ntunduwaro and Rwanda, 2016–17).

Nonetheless, communities in Ntunduwaro and Ruanda increasingly showed their frustration with the state-backed coal investments, dominated by the convergence of interests between the ruling elite (the CCM and the SOE) and the foreign investor. It should be noted that, before coal extraction began in August 2011, a meeting between TANCOAL and village members was held in January 2011 at which the NDC and its Australian joint-venture partner outlined their plans for improving community relations. The initial promises made at the meeting included, among other things, the provision of electricity, a clean water supply, prioritizing employment opportunities for the local population, improving local schools (with the construction of housing for staff and new classrooms) and dispensaries, establishing a vocational training centre, and minimizing the environmental impacts (dust and effluent control) from mining the coal. Many of these promises remain unfulfilled to this day.[7] In addition, poor compensation and the lack of farmland have hit some community members hard. Without plots to cultivate food and cash crops, many are now surviving as casual labourers working on farms belonging to other villagers.

3.2 Contesting Land Acquisition: the State's Power Fully Displayed

In mid-2012, villagers started small-scale local protests targeting TANCOAL officials and Gaudence Kayombo, the local CCM MP of what was then the Mbinga East constituency, over delays in holding talks to resolve legitimate compensation demands in accordance with Tanzanian legislation. On the morning of 9 October 2012 local protests culminated in dozens of well-organized villagers gathering to block trucks transporting coal from the mine and to demand payment of what they called 'deserved compensation' (interview with Ntunduwaro village chairman, July 2016).

In a major show of force, the district and regional governments responded to the protests by sending in heavily armed specialist anti-riot police units, regular police and the army to join the private security guards who were already stationed at the mine. Eleven people, including the village chairman, were arrested and detained after clashes with the police. The mine had to suspend operations for several days following orders from the Regional Commissioner, Said Mwambungu. Villagers expressed their dismay at the allegedly unnecessary use of force by the special anti-riot police squad and the presence of the army during the crackdown on the peaceful blocking of the road. As one of those who took part in the clashes stated:

> We are not used to dealing with the field force (special anti-riot police). It was very scary. At least the normal police are close to people. (Ngaka villager, 2016)

On the other hand, an official from the Mbinga District supported the brutal response by the security forces and emphasized that it was the only option left to the government:

> We realized that villagers were angry and well organized, and it was too much for TANCOAL's private security guards to handle. We had to bring the special anti-riot police from the district and regional headquarters, and they did a great job. It was

a serious decision, but it had to be done to protect our investment. (Mbinga District official, 2016)

In May 2013, the conflict erupted again when the villagers organized protests over delayed compensation payments, but they finally accepted what was generally perceived by many to be a low level of compensation, which had been pushed down by the Tanzanian state out of a fear of losing out on revenues and rents from the investment if compensation deals were increased. The Australian investor was ready to pay higher levels of compensation, but this was rejected by the national SOE.

Grievances against the NDC and its partners remain high today. In the aftermath of the 2012 and 2013 conflicts, security at the mine was increased. By 2014, the total security budget had doubled, according to TANCOAL, and the number of private security guards stationed at the mine had almost tripled (interview with TANCOAL's operations officer in Ngaka, August 2015). This was in addition to the occasional deployment of undercover state security personnel for purposes of surveillance and intelligence-gathering in and around the neighbouring villages.[8]

3.3 Broken Promises

Apart from the land question, by 2013 the villagers had also become frustrated with the mine's negative environmental impacts. There were concerns over excessive dust from coal trucks and noise from blasting activities, while the contamination of two streams, which are the major local sources of water for domestic and irrigation activities, raised further tensions (Maganga and Jacob, 2016). In an interview in 2015, TANCOAL officials denied that the company was responsible for the contamination.[9] Villagers' complaints about water pollution were later confirmed by an independent water-quality laboratory test conducted by experts from the Ministry of Water and Irrigation in July 2016. The report concluded that water from the two main streams (Nyakatunda and Nyamaviva) and from TANCOAL's campsite in Ngaka was highly contaminated, had low oxygen-solution levels and did not meet the required standards due to the discharge of coal effluent from the mine. The report recommended that villagers should immediately stop consuming water from the two streams, which was found to be unsuitable for human consumption. The report also recommended the regular monitoring of water quality and advised TANCOAL to provide an alternative source of clean water for the villagers' use (URT, 2016).

Following the recommendations in the water-quality report, TANCOAL responded by installing three water tanks to supply 'clean' water. This was initially seen as an important contribution to the community on the part of the mine because local women and schoolgirls were walking long distances to fetch water from the streams.[10] Two months after the tanks had been installed, villagers discovered that the water they contained came from the TANCOAL camp site, which had also been found to be contaminated by the water-quality test. These revelations further increased the tensions between the villagers and the investors. In 2017 TANCOAL was collaborating with the Mbinga District Council to finance a new water project to supply clean water to the area.

4.   THE LOCAL STATE AND A CHANGING POLITICAL LANDSCAPE

As a result of local frustrations over unfulfilled promises, the CCM leaders suddenly saw some of their support draining away to the opposition parties. This was new to local CCM leaders in Mbinga, who have dominated local politics since democratization in the 1990s with the backing of traditional grassroots institutions emanating from the 1960s Ujamaa process, such as local farmer associations and smallholder and community structures adjacent to the Ngaka coal mine. The opposition has been eager to capitalize on the worsening relations between the CCM and its traditional constituencies. Regional and district opposition leaders have exploited the frustrations of the local population over the Ngaka investment and the security and pollution incidents by sending a clear message that the CCM has 'forgotten them' and 'betrayed them', having decided instead to associate itself with the multinational companies. As a senior district official for the opposition party Chama cha Demokrasia na Maendeleo (CHADEMA) stated in an interview in 2016:

> Our campaign in the last election was centred around the coal mine issue, and particularly promises broken by the government and their foreign partners. We used the violent events of 2012 and 2013 to demonstrate the extent to which the CCM government had betrayed local people and its members. The strategy worked well and enabled us to gather substantial votes, and hopefully we can build on this momentum in the next election. (Interview with opposition representative in Mbinga, July 2016)

This claim of recent electoral success was backed up in a separate interview with a group of villagers who stated they had moved to the opposition recently. A representative who spoke on behalf of the group summarized their sentiments as follows:

> We used to see the CCM as our strong hope in promoting local development and fighting oppression for poor people like us, but after what happened in Ngaka, many of us see CCM leaders and their NDC collaborators to be as oppressive as foreign companies. (Account from focus-group discussion in Ntunduwaro village, July 2016)

It was clear that poor compensation and the consequences of what was perceived to be the insufficient fulfilment of promises and expectations became a tool to fuel local opposition and dissent, which had political ramifications for electoral politics locally.

Although the ruling CCM party remains dominant, in the 2010 local and national elections its share of the vote at the district level fell, and the Mbinga MP for the ruling CCM party was defeated in his re-election bid at the party primaries.[11] According to the CCM's Ruvuma regional secretary, the MP lost the primary following accusations that he supported the coal investors and had ignored local grievances over compensation. He added that:

> The ex-MP had become very unpopular, especially in areas surrounding the coal mine. It was clear the CCM was going lose the seat, and the party regional and central committee had to find someone fresh and credible to replace him.[12]

The eventual winner of the CCM primary and the current MP ran on the promise of confronting TANCOAL and delivering on pressing issues such as compensation and community benefits. Also, for the first time since the introduction of multiparty politics, the local CCM ward councillor was defeated by the opposition candidate, a sign of the CCM's declining support base due to the way it had dealt with the investment. Both events were linked to disputed compensation payments and unfulfilled economic and pollution-related promises, which dominated political campaigns in the villages close to the mine, as well as in Mbinga District more generally.

4.1 Towards a Reciprocal Exchange Deal?

In response to the initial community backlash between 2011 and 2013, the NDC and its foreign partner began to explore various options to engage local communities in efforts to diffuse tensions and improve community relations. In the words of the NDC's head of community relations, the state-owned firm and its partner had realized that they could no longer rely on private and government security forces to protect their coal operations in Ngaka and ensure their smooth running. The NDC representative emphasized that: 'Even though coal-mining was progressing, we felt something was not right, and there was an urgent need to rebuild trust with the surrounding villages'.[13]

The NDC and its Australian partner became increasingly concerned with the potential reputational risks of local resistance, despite constant reassurance from the state-backed NDC that the protest was not serious. In an interview with a senior IEC representative, the latter indicated that it was pressure from the IEC that stimulated its joint-venture partner, the NDC, to rethink their joint strategy and start exploring corporate social responsibility (CSR) initiatives in order to benefit local communities and minimize conflicts.[14]

The pressure the Australian IEC placed on the NDC is in line with recent empirical evidence showing that companies, especially if listed on stock exchanges, are more likely to pursue various CSR strategies to offset potential reputational damage to themselves (Trebeck, 2007; Van Tulder et al., 2009; Muller and Kräussl, 2011; Kotchen and Moon, 2011). More recently, other scholars have argued that the potential reputational damage to investors because of their actions does offer local communities a degree of leverage in their engagement with investors, although they also caution that the type of investor determines the degree of leverage (Rutten et al., 2017). Various CSR initiatives in Ngaka can be seen as part of what Buur et al. (2020) call efforts to establish reciprocal exchange deals to ensure that local populations are directly engaged with the coal-mining economy on the one hand and that attempts are made to legitimize investments on the other, as research from other parts of the world has shown (Bebbington, 2010).

Between 2011 and early 2015, securitization was the main source of holding power the state-owned enterprise (NDC) and its foreign partner (IEC) deployed in dictating community engagement. A combination of the state security apparatus and private security contractors was used to impose a culture of fear, suppress local opposition and resistance, and ensure that coal was extracted even at the expense of the legitimate rights of the local population to receive compensation and due process in the form of consultation. This holding power was based on the compatibility of interests between the ruling elites and the foreign investor and was initially demonstrated through violence and constant threats directed at the local population and smallholder farmers by the security forces. Although the villagers managed to disrupt operations temporarily in 2013, it can be argued that before the 2015 general election they had lacked the ability to influence the behaviour of the state and its corporate partners with respect to coal investments.

This situation changed in the run-up to the 2015 general election, when coal mining emerged as an important electoral issue and a tool for political mobilization, especially in the hands of the newly emerging political opposition in Mbinga. The opposition made various claims, its main accusation being that deep patronage networks had developed between local CCM politicians and coal investors to the detriment of local communities, particularly local landowners, who were subject to the controversial compensation scheme that had been imposed by the state through the NDC on behalf of its corporate partner. The fierce campaigns, local mobilization and the subsequent election of the first opposition party councillor in October 2015, coupled with the relative decline in the CCM's popularity in the coal-mining area, were indications that local communities and smallholders constituted an important voting bloc and possessed the capacity to inflict significant political damage on the dominant CCM's power base. The opposition election victory in the Ruanda ward, a coal-mining area, was important, albeit preliminary evidence that local communities had acquired some power, suggesting a shift in the holding power of the villagers against the state and its multinational partner.

Initiatives aimed at upgrading community infrastructure, such as the renovation of a local primary school and health clinic in Ntunduwaro village, were positively received and considered important in repairing the tense relationship between community members and the investors. They also repaired the lack of recognition on the part of the local population, which was replaced by something approaching mutual recognition between it and the ruling elite. The next turning point came with the arrangement for the mine and a local organization to provide a local food-procurement and catering service. The provision of economic opportunities can be considered highly important in moving the investment towards something approaching a reciprocal exchange deal.

In mid-2011, TANCOAL officials, pushed by the Australian IEC when it became clear that there was considerable resistance to the investment, began fearing that the tensions and conflicts could undermine the investment. They started consultations with local politicians and community leaders from Ruanda, the Ntunduwaro villages and Mbinga District officials to discuss various options for strengthening community engagement in order to make the local communities more positive towards the coal investment. The discussion led to the establishment of the Mbalawala Women's Group (MWG) in late 2011 and its registration as a local NGO in 2012.[15] The Women's Group established a number of activities, including catering at the mine, vegetable farming, a tree nursery, pottery making and a charcoal briquette business. The MWG's initial activities and equipment were entirely funded by TANCOAL and later supplemented by a $28,500 grant from the Australian government in 2012. Most of these activities have been set up as independent small businesses owned and managed by MWG members (Fieldwork Notes, July 2017).

Of all the group's activities, providing food-procurement and catering services to TANCOAL's Ngaka mine stands out. According to TANCOAL officials, the company was approached by a number of reputable foreign catering-service providers from Africa and Europe, but they opted to contract the local women's group to supply locally grown foodstuffs and catering instead. One TANCOAL senior official described the decision to procure the food locally as part of an approach which 'is not based on providing charity but to offer sustainable partnership opportunities and promote communities' self-reliance'.[16] TANCOAL views the procurement deal as a catalyst to accelerate backward linkages that could benefit the local population, which it believes will contribute to boosting the incomes of the communities that live adjacent to the coal mine. Literature on linkages in extractive industries demonstrates that local procurement can generate positive impacts for communities and the host country more generally, especially when goods and services are procured locally or sub-nationally (Morris et al., 2012; White, 2017).

Through the procurement deal, MWG members have received training in the form of capacity-building workshops in entrepreneurial skills and financial management. TANCOAL has also arranged mentoring programmes for women. Although the procurement deal has helped change the overall perceptions of the mine among the local population to some extent, villagers are not happy that only a specific group of women are receiving this training.[17] In Ntunduwaro, villagers complained that only a few of them, namely those who are believed to be connected with the MWG leadership, which was seen as close to local CCM leaders, were selected to attend training in entrepreneurship.

TANCOAL officials claim that the procurement project was not imposed on the local community, as they offered avenues for local leaders to participate and make a contribution, leading to acceptance and positive attitudes towards the project and the investors. But interviews with community members indicate that there were limited formal spaces for dialogue and that only the local elites, most of which were seen as aligned to CCM, were involved. This limited engagement raises the question of whether local populations can actually influence and benefit from investments where the state has a double role as both investor in partnership with a foreign investor and custodian or final arbiter of different rights.

The IEC's efforts are an example of a multinational company that, while receiving the backing of the state, also realized that there was a need to legitimize its operations locally when the state's and ruling CCM elite's legitimacy was challenged. In this case, the IEC pushed TANCOAL into an alliance with a local NGO, the MWG, to improve its reputation. Through the NGO, TANCOAL, and thus the IEC and the NDC, attempted to win the support of those living near the coal mine. Interactions between corporations and NGOs can therefore play a critical role in settling differences between investors and local communities.

5.   CONCLUSION

This chapter has discussed the double role of the state as both an investor in partnership with a foreign investor and the custodian or final arbiter of different rights. Its double role allowed the coal investments to move forward by drawing on the state's ability to access and distribute land, control local populations and enforce decisions. The double role of the state also created problems for the foreign investor as the longer history of state-society relations came with a history of mistrust and violence. This created resistance when compensation was limited and the promised local investments were not forthcoming.

This suggests that the double role of the state as both state and investor creates its own problems. It thus responds to a call for empirical evidence regarding the complex relations between investors, ruling elites and local populations (Buur et al., 2017). The chapter shows that extractive investments involving SOEs tend to take the state's legitimacy for granted and that this overrules the need to adhere to due process and compensation. This was simply not considered necessary, at least not initially. The failure to seek consent and enter into reciprocal exchange deals with local populations came with a heavy price that forced the foreign investor to push for a different approach than that of the state as conflict escalated.

The findings from Ngaka reveal the complexity of the interactions between the state, the foreign investor and the local population. With the backing of the state, TANCOAL managed to ignore community opposition and its members' right to timely and adequate compensation and went ahead with coal extraction anyway. However, following years of hostilities with surrounding communities after the failure to meet expectations and honour its promises, the state-owned company and its private partner, a foreign investor, have gone through a lengthy process characterized by several attempts to conclude something that resembled a reciprocal exchange deal. These efforts, which are aimed at securing local support and defusing conflict and open opposition, include a number of CSR initiatives and local procurement deals. The latter, which is seen as a success story by both the company and local populations, is nonetheless greatly contested by other parts of the community, who remain unconvinced of its virtues, as it benefits a particular segment of the population that appears to be aligned with the local CCM/state elite.

The chapter also found that, for private companies involved in joint ventures with SOEs like IEC in Ngaka, the presence of the state as part of the shareholding set-up helps to minimize the political and investment risks and offers stability and protection for the investment. The compatibility of interests between the ruling elite and the investor clearly facilitated the first phase of the investment and screened it from the hostility of local populations. Similar trends have been documented by a recent study of standards of land acquisition by mining and petroleum investments involving state actors in Tanzania (Pedersen and Jacob, 2017).

However, under pressure from IEC, the foreign investor, the contested nature of the first phase of implementation initiated by TANCOAL, in which the repressive security apparatus was used to force through the investment, was changed due to public pressure and the fear of reputational risks. Despite assurances from the state, private companies can to some degree influence their state partners to operate in ways that reflect the interests and demands of a publicly listed company subject to the pressures of accountability, transparency and the international soft-law expectations of investors and other stakeholders.

The Ngaka case is a clear example of intra-elite conflict, given especially the infighting between national-level and sub-national elites. Regional, district and village-level elites in Ruvuma, on the other hand, are faced with a delicate balancing act between safeguarding the land rights and livelihoods of their local populations for their own political survival on the one hand, while ensuring the smooth running of these state-backed investments on the other. This calls for a further unpacking of elites and for greater attention to be paid to the role of sub-national elite actors.

Finally, as described throughout, this case study illustrates the potential leverage available to local villagers as a result of mobilizing and demonstrating their opposition. Local opposition and dissent over the benefits of coal extraction enforced by the state and the SOE has had impacts on the local political landscape. While the local political elites, the SOE and the foreign investor initially downplayed and suppressed local dissent, the conflict and outcome of the local elections changed the political dynamics of the situation. While there is not enough evidence to suggest that the NDC as the SOE will review its practices, Tanzania's shift towards a stronger focus on resource nationalism (see Jacob, 2020), coupled with its strong requirements for state participation in mineral extraction through SOEs, means that the role of the state has changed. The state is no longer just protecting foreign capital investments and playing a brokerage role, as was the case under liberalization, it is also safeguarding its own share of the investments through SOEs. This trajectory could suggest that sub-national regions endowed with natural resources are increasingly becoming sites of strategic importance to the Tanzania state and that conflicts are more likely to erupt between SOEs and local communities and potentially with local ruling elites due to the state's double role.

NOTES

1. In 2008 the Sydney-based Intra Energy Corporation (IEC) formed a joint venture with Tanzania's National Development Corporation (NDC) to create TANCOAL. Under the terms of the joint venture, the Tanzanian government owns 30 per cent of TANCOAL through the NDC, and the IEC owns the remaining 70 per cent.
2. This is based on the argument that the state is accountable to its own citizens, while corporations and private businesses are accountable to their shareholders.
3. The same is the case in much of the literature on the social license to operate (SLO) (Moffat and Zhang, 2014; Conde and Le Billon, 2017; Ehrnström-Fuentes and Kröger, 2017), which focuses mainly on private investments. This emphasis on the links between private investments and SLOs is also found in a recent study

looking at the various efforts foreign mining companies and international oil companies in Tanzania have made to acquire an SLO (Kessy et al., 2018).
4.   In 1976 Tanzania's population was 16,493,435.
5.   Notable cases of evictions influenced by neoliberal reforms include the 1988 eviction of pastoralists in the then Mkomazi game reserve (Brockington, 2002), evictions of Maasai pastoralists in Loliondo, adjacent to the Ngorongoro National Park in 1999 (Kamata, 2012), evictions of Sukuma agropastoralists from the Ihefu valley in the Usangu basin in 2006 (Walsh, 2012), and the eviction of villagers on Mafia Island from marine park conservation (Benjaminsen and Bryceson, 2012).
6.   This view was widely shared by other villagers during focus-group discussions.
7.   The meeting was held in Ntunduwaro village on 27 January 2011 and was attended by 96 village members. According to village leaders, the turnout was historic, since village general assembly meetings are usually poorly attended.
8.   Interview with TANCOAL's senior official, Ngaka, August 2015.
9.   Interview with TANCOAL mining manager in Ngaka, August 2015.
10. Information from focus-group session in Ntunduwaro, August 2015.
11. The then Mbinga East constituency was split into the Mbinga Rural and Mbinga Urban constituencies in the run-up to the 2015 general elections. The CCM candidate for Mbinga Rural received 68 per cent of the votes, compared to over 90 per cent obtained in 2010. The 2010 electoral data come from party sources.
12. Interview with the CCM's Ruvuma regional secretary, Songea, September 2017.
13. Interview with NDC's head of community relations, Ngaka, 2016.
14. Interview with IEC representative, Ngaka, 2016.
15. Although the NGO was registered in 2012, activities commenced in 2013.
16. Interview with TANCOAL official in Ngaka, 2016.
17. Information from focus-group discussion, Ntunduwaro, 2016.

REFERENCES

Ayers, A.J. (2013) 'Beyond myths, lies and stereotypes: the political economy of a "New Scramble for Africa"', *New Political Economy*, 18(2), 227–57.
Bebbington, A. (2010) 'Extractive industries and stunted states: conflict, responsibility and institutional change in the Andes' in Raman, R. and Lipschutz, R. (eds) *Corporate Social Responsibility: Comparative Critiques*, London: Palgrave Macmillan, pp. 97–115.
Behuria, P., Buur, L. and Gray, H. (2017) 'Studying political settlements in Africa', *African Affairs*, 116(464), 508–25.
Benjaminsen, T.A. and Bryceson, I. (2012) 'Conservation, green/blue grabbing and accumulation by dispossession in Tanzania', *Journal of Peasant Studies*, 39(2), 335–55.
Boesen, J., Storgaard Madsen, B. and Moody, T. (1977) 'Ujamaa: socialism from above', Scandinavian Institute of African Studies, Uppsala, Sweden.
Brockington, D. (2002) *Fortress Conservation: The Preservation of the Mkomazi Game Reserve*, African Issues Series, Oxford: James Currey.
Buur, L. and Nystrand, M.J. (2020) 'Mediating bureaucrats: embedded economic action in the Mozambican sugar industry', *The Journal of Modern African Studies*, 58(3), 337–60.

Buur, L., Nystrand, M. and Pedersen, R.H. (2017) 'The political economy of land and natural resources in Africa: an analytical framework', no. 2, DIIS Working Paper.

Buur, L., Pedersen, R.H., Nystrand, M.J. and Macuane, J.J. (2019) 'Understanding the three key relationships in natural resource investments in Africa: an analytical framework', *The Extractive Industries and Society*, 6(4), 1195–204.

Buur, L., Pedersen, R.H., Nystrand, M.J., Macuane, J.J. and Jacob, T. (2020) 'The politics of natural resource investments and rights in Africa: a theoretical approach', *The Extractive Industries and Society*, 7(3), 918–30.

Carmody, P. (2013) *New Scramble for Africa*, Cambridge: Polity Press.

Collins, D. (2009) 'The failure of a socially responsive gold mining MNC in El Salvador: ramifications of NGO mistrust', *Journal of Business Ethics*, 88(2), 245–68.

Conde, M. and Le Billon, P. (2017) 'Why do some communities resist mining projects while others do not?', *The Extractive Industries and Society*, 4(3), 681–97.

Cotula, L., Vermeulen, S., Leonard, R. and Keeley, J. (2009) 'Land grab or development opportunity? Agricultural investment and international land deals in Africa', London and Rome: Food and Agriculture Organization of the United Nations, International Fund for Agricultural Development and International Institute for Environment and Development.

Coulson, A. (1982) *Tanzania: A Political Economy*, Oxford: Oxford University Press.

Daniel, S. and Mittal, A. (2009) *The Great Land Grab Rush for World's Farmland Threatens Food Security for the Poor*, Oakland, USA: Oakland Institute.

Edwards, D. (2003) 'Settlement, livelihoods and identity in Southern Tanzania: a comparative history of the Ngoni and Ndendeuli', PhD thesis, University of Edinburgh.

Ehrnström-Fuentes, M. and Kröger, M. (2017) 'In the shadows of social licence to operate: untold investment grievances in Latin America', *Journal of Cleaner Production*, 141, 346–58.

Emel, J., Huber, M.T. and Makene, M.H. (2011) 'Extracting sovereignty: capital, territory, and gold mining in Tanzania', *Political Geography*, 30(2), 70–79.

Fimbo, G.M. (2004) *Land Law Reforms in Tanzania*, Dar es Salaam, Tanzania: Dar es Salaam University Press.

Hall, D. (2011) 'Land grabs, land control, and southeast Asian crop booms', *Journal of Peasant Studies*, 38(4), 811–31.

Holterman, D. (2014) 'Slow violence, extraction and human rights defence in Tanzania: notes from the field', *Resources Policy*, 40, 59–65.

Jacob, T. (2017) 'Competing energy narratives in Tanzania: towards the political economy of coal', *Africa Affairs*, 116(463), 341–53.

Jacob, T. (2020) 'The return of the state: a political economy of resource nationalism and revived state owned enterprises in Tanzania's coal sector', PhD thesis, Roskilde University, accessed 14 November 2022 at https://forskning.ruc.dk/en/publications/the-return-of-the-state-a-political-economy-of-resource-nationali.

Jacob, T. and Pedersen, R.H. (2018) 'New resource nationalism? Continuity and change in Tanzania's extractive industries', *The Extractive Industries and Society*, 5(2), 287–92.

Jacob, T., Pedersen, R., Maganga, F. and Kweka, O. (2016) 'Rights to land and extractive resources in Tanzania (2/2): the return of the state', DIIS Working Paper, Copenhagen, Denmark.

Jennings, M. (2002) '"Almost an Oxfam in itself": Oxfam, Ujamaa and development in Tanzania', *African Affairs*, 101(405), 509–30.

Jennings, M. (2008) *Surrogates of the State: NGOs, Development, and Ujamaa in Tanzania*, Bloomfield, CT, USA: Kumarian Press.

Kamata, N.W. (2012) 'The economic diplomacy of Tanzania: accumulation by dispossession in a peripheral state', *Agrarian South: Journal of Political Economy*, 1(3), 291–313.

Kelly, A.B. and Peluso, N.L. (2015) 'Frontiers of commodification: state lands and their formalization', *Society & Natural Resources*, 28(5), 473–95.

Kessy, F., Melyoki, L. and Nyamrunda, G. (2018) *The Social License to Operate in Tanzania: Case Studies of the Petroleum and Mining Sectors*, Dar es Salaam: Uongozi Institute.

Khan, M. (2010) 'Political settlements and the governance of growth-enhancing institutions', SOAS Working Chapter, School of Oriental and African Studies, London.

Kotchen, M.J. and Moon, J.J. (2011) 'Corporate social responsibility for irresponsibility' *The BE Journal of Economic Analysis & Policy*, 12(1), 1–23.

Lange, S. (2008) *Land Tenure and Mining in Tanzania*, Norway: Michelsen Institute Bergen.

Lange, S. (2011) 'Gold and governance: legal injustices and lost opportunities in Tanzania', *African Affairs*, 110(439), 233–52.

LEAT (2002) 'Assessment summary of the complaint regarding MIGA's guarantee of the Bulyanhulu mine, Tanzania', Lawyers' Environmental Action Team (LEAT), Dar es Salaam.

Lee, M.C. (2006) 'The 21st century scramble for Africa', *Journal of Contemporary African Studies*, 24(3), 303–30.

Maganga, F. and Jacob, T. (2016), 'Defying the looming resource curse with indigenization? Insights from two coal mines in Tanzania', *The African Review: A Journal of African Politics, Development and International Affairs*, 43(2),139–160.

Makene, M.H., Emel, J. and Murphy, J.T. (2012) 'Calling for justice in the goldfields of Tanzania', *Resources*, 1(1), 3–22.

Moffat, K. and Zhang, A. (2014) 'The paths to social licence to operate: an integrative model explaining community acceptance of mining', *Resources Policy*, 39, 61–70.

Monson, J. (1998) 'Relocating Maji Maji: the politics of alliance and authority in the southern highlands of Tanzania, 1870–1918', *Journal of African History*, 39(1), 95–120.

Morris, M., Kaplinsky, R. and Kaplan, D. (2012). '"One thing leads to another": commodities, linkages and industrial development', *Resources Policy*, 37(4), 408–16.

Muller, A. and Kräussl, R. (2011) 'Doing good deeds in times of need: a strategic perspective on corporate disaster donations', *Strategic Management Journal*, 32(9), 911–29.

Nambiza, W.P. (2007) 'Whose development counts? Political ecology of displacement of Bulyanhulu Mining Community in Tanzania', Master's thesis, Norges teknisk-naturvitenskapelige universitet.

Neumann, R.P. (2001) 'Africa's "last wilderness": reordering space for political and economic control in colonial Tanzania', *Africa*, 71(4), 641–65.

Nystrand, M. (2015) 'The rationale of taking social responsibility: social embeddedness of business owners in Uganda', Doctoral thesis, Gothenburg University, accessed 14 November 2022 at https://gupea.ub.gu.se/handle/2077/38753.

Odgaard, R. (1986) 'Tea: does it do the peasant women in Rungwe any good?' in Boesen, J., Havnevik, K.J., Koponen, J. and Odgaard, R. (eds) *Tanzania in Crisis and Struggle for Survival*, Uppsala: Africana, pp. 207–24.

Pearce, F. (2016) 'Common ground: securing land rights and safeguarding the earth', Policy chapter, Land Coalition, Rights and Resources Initiative, Oxfam International, Oxford, UK.

Pedersen, R.H. and Buur, L. (2016) 'Beyond land grabbing: old morals and new perspectives on contemporary investments', *Geoforum*, 72, 77–81.

Pedersen, R.H. and Jacob, T. (2017) 'Reconfigured state-community relations in Africa's extractive sectors: insights from post-liberalisation Tanzania', *The Extractive Industries and Society*, 4(4), 915–22.

Pedersen, R., Jacob, T., Maganga, F. and Kweka, O. (2016) 'Rights to land and extractive resources in Tanzania (1/2): the history', DIIS Working Paper, Copenhagen, Denmark

Raikes, P. (1986) 'Eating the carrot and wielding the stick: the agricultural sector in Tanzania' in Boesen, J., Havnevik, K.J., Koponen, J. and Odgaard, R. (eds) *Tanzania: Crisis and Struggle for Survival*, Uppsala: Africana, pp. 105–42.

Rutten, R., Bakker, L., Alano, M.L., Salerno, T., Savitri, L.A. and Shohibuddin, M. (2017) 'Smallholder bargaining power in large-scale land-deals: a relational perspective', *Journal of Peasant Studies*, 44(4), 1–27.

Schneider, L. (2006) 'Colonial legacies and postcolonial authoritarianism in Tanzania: connects and disconnects', *African Studies Review*, 49(1), 93–118.

Schroeder, R.A. (2010) 'Tanzanite as conflict gem: certifying a secure commodity chain in Tanzania', *Geoforum*, 41(1), 56–65.

Scott, J.C. (1998) *Seeing Like a State: How Certain Schemes to Improve the Human Condition Have Failed*, New Haven: Yale University Press.

Shivji, I.G. (1998) *Not Yet Democracy: Reforming Land Tenure in Tanzania*, London: International Institute for Environment and Development (IIED).

Trebeck, K. (2007) 'Tools for the disempowered? Indigenous leverage over mining companies', *Australian Journal of Political Science*, 42(4), 541–62.

United Republic of Tanzania (2016) *Laboratory Analytical Water Quality Report*, Songea: Ministry of Water and Irrigation.

Van Tulder, R., Van Wijk, J. and Kolk, A. (2009) 'From chain liability to chain responsibility', *Journal of Business Ethics*, 85(2), 399–412.

Von Freyhold, M. (1979) *Ujamaa Villages in Tanzania: Analysis of a Social Experiment*, London: Heinemann.

Walsh, M. (2012) 'The not-so-Great Ruaha and hidden histories of an environmental panic in Tanzania', *Journal of Eastern African Studies*, 6(2), 303–35.

White, S. (2017) 'Regulating for local content: limitations of legal and regulatory instruments in promoting small scale suppliers in extractive industries in developing economies', *The Extractive Industries and Society*, 4(2), 260–66.

Wolford, W., Borras Jr, S.M., Hall, R., Scoones, I. and White, B. (2013) 'Governing global land deals: the role of the state in the rush for land', *Development and Change*, 44(2), 189–210.

4. Riding the waves of change: changing relations in the Ugandan sugar sector

Malin J. Nystrand, Arthur Sserwanga and Brenda Kyomuhendo

1. INTRODUCTION

The sugar industry in Uganda is of longstanding, the first sugar mills having been set up in the 1920s. The industry has for a long time been dominated by a few large investors, of which Kakira Sugar Works (Kakira), located in the Busoga[1] region east of Kampala, is the largest. Over time, Kakira has developed a comprehensive relationship with different parts of the local population, including formal relations with both outgrowers and industrial workers through the facilitation of farmers' associations and trade unions, as well as the provision of a range of services for the broader community, such as schools, health centres and road maintenance. Above all, Kakira's long-term facilitation of sugarcane farming and the presence of a relatively stable market for sugarcane has created the conditions for sugarcane farming becoming the most important income-generating activity in the region. These stable relations with the local community have also been fundamental to Kakira's success as a business, as its production chain depends on a steady supply of sugarcane from its outgrowers. This clearly resembles what Buur et al. (2020) call reciprocal exchange relations between investors and local populations, and has apparently been stable for a long time.

However, during the last decade, several new sugar mills have emerged, challenging established relations within and around the sugar industry with consequences for Kakira and its long-term exchange relations with various local population groups.

The tensions in the sugar sector in Busoga erupted into a regular price war in 2016 and 2017. A group of new millers who had set up mills in the region raised the price paid to farmers for sugarcane, thereby outcompeting Kakira on price. Farmers responded by selling more to new millers and less to Kakira, harvesting earlier (thus reducing the quality of the canes) and renting more land for sugarcane production, which also increased the cost of renting land.

One consequence was that 2017 became the worst year in 30 years for Kakira according to Mr Barungi, Assistant to the General Manager, Kakira (Interview, 4 October 2018). Kakira produced at half its usual capacity for both sugar and electricity due to the high price and low availability of quality sugarcane. After half a year the new millers reduced the price, but to a level that was still higher than before 2016. Expectations had now changed. Farmers expected the high price to come back, while Kakira thought the price level was still too high.

New legislation for the sugar sector, namely the Sugar Bill, which had been discussed for a decade, was tabled again, but Uganda's President and Parliament had difficulties in agreeing on the content. The Bill was sent back and forth between them several times before the President signed it on 23 April 2020 (The Republic of Uganda, 2020), and it was a standing issue in media debates in Uganda for about two years. The debate around the Sugar Bill high-lighted many of the tensions in the industry, where Kakira and the farmers in Busoga, represented by the Busoga Sugarcane Growers Association (BSGA), now tended to be on opposing sides.

The aim of this chapter is to explain how the strong long-term relationship between Kakira and the local community could be undermined when the industry's dynamics, as well as the political economy in which these exchange relations were embedded, changed.

The case of Kakira illustrates how an existing large-scale sugar investment with a long-established reciprocal exchange deal between the investor and the local population was challenged by the entry of new sugar-producing inves-tors. The emergence of the new millers challenged the long-established politi-cal protection of the older group of large sugar investors and demonstrated the increased importance of local populations and sugarcane farmers in local-level politics.

The analysis in this chapter makes use of primary data in the form of inter-views with sugarcane farmers and other residents in Busedde sub-county[2] in Jinja district, as well as with representatives of Kakira and other millers, the farmers' association (the BSGA) and government and sugar industry representatives (see attached list of interviews). These data have been comple-mented with secondary material in the form of media reports, sector reports and academic publications. Most of the primary data were collected in 2018 and 2019, though some interviews were conducted earlier, in 2016.

The chapter will proceed with a brief overview of the sugar industry in Uganda, followed by a descriptive analysis of the long-term exchange relation-ship between Kakira and the local population in the Busoga region. Thereafter follows a section analysing how the exchange relationship has changed over time, followed by a brief analysis of how the sugar sector relates to Uganda's changing political economy before the chapter is concluded.

2. OVERVIEW OF THE SUGAR INDUSTRY IN UGANDA

The sugar industry in Uganda has for many decades been dominated by three companies: Kakira, SCOUL (Sugar Cooperation of Uganda Ltd) and Kinyara Sugar Works. Kakira and SCOUL were both started in the 1920s by Ugandan-Asian families that still control them (Ahluwalia, 1995). Both are located east of Kampala: Kakira near Jinja town, approximately 100 km east of Kampala; and SCOUL in Lugazi, about 50 km east of Kampala. Kinyara Sugar Works started in the 1960s and was originally state-owned but is currently owned by the Mauritian Rai Group. It is located in Masindi district, approximately 200 km northwest of Kampala. Uganda's traditional sugar-producing areas are therefore concentrated in two main areas: east of Kampala towards Jinja, and further northwest around Masindi.[3]

In 2011 the government licensed several new sugar producers in different parts of Uganda (Sanya, 2011). The licensing of new sugar mills came about due to the adoption of a Sugar Policy in 2010 (Ministry of Tourism Trade and Industry, 2010). The policy called for government licensing of sugar mills in response to complaints from established millers about the increasing number of small sugar mills (so-called 'jaggery mills'), which were seen as diverting sugarcane supply to less productive ends and as disturbing the value chain of industrial sugar production. An important part of the Sugar Policy was the principle of 'zoning', that is, that there should be a geographical distance between mills of at least 25 km to facilitate the development of backward linkages between millers and sugarcane farmers or outgrowers and to allow enough land for the sugar mill to expand production.

Three of the new mills licensed in 2011, Sugar and Allied Industries Ltd (Kaliro), Kamuli Sugar Ltd (Kamuli) and Mayuge Sugar Industries (Mayuge), are located in the Busoga region, that is, not far from Kakira. The location and licensing of these firms, in particular Mayuge, located only 17 km from Kakira, in direct contradiction of the Sugar Policy,[4] has become a sensitive issue in the Busoga region. It also played into Ugandan sugar politics in general, especially in relation to the controversies surrounding the adoption of the 2020 Sugar Bill, that is, the process of turning the Sugar Policy into legislation (for more on this, see below).

The table below shows that the three oldest sugar companies still dominate the industry, accounting for over 75 per cent of Ugandan sugar production. With Kakira, SCOUL, Kaliro, Kamuli and Mayuge all located in the Busoga region, it is clear that this region is the country's sugar-producing centre.

The Ugandan sugar industry produces brown sugar for consumption, and this domestically produced sugar dominates the Ugandan consumer market. In

Table 4.1   *Sugar factories in Uganda*

Sugar factory	Annual production in tonnes in 2018
Kakira	165 031
Kinyara	86 277
SCOUL	77 566
Kaliro	30 000
Kamuli	20 160
Hoima	19 496
Others (Mayuge and four smaller companies)	33 406
Total	433 954

Source: Uganda Sugar Manufacturers Association (USMA), data provided by the association.

most years the Ugandan sugar industry also produces a surplus that is exported regionally, primarily to Kenya. White sugar, which is needed in the soft drinks and pharmaceuticals industries, is imported since it is not yet produced in Uganda, although Kakira reportedly has plans to start its production (The Daily Monitor, 27 May 2020). There is also some importation of brown sugar from elsewhere in the region, particularly from Tanzania, which is also subject to debate and tensions related to the regulation of the trade in agricultural commodities within the East African Community.[5]

Contrasting visions of how the sugar industry in Uganda should be developed underlie debates on the industry. Industry experts and established millers (Kabeho, 2019; Musafiri interview, 2019; Mubiru interview, 2019; Mubiru, 2019) emphasise the importance of consolidating the industry, that is, of improving the organisation and management of existing mills rather than increasing the number of mills. The argument is that, in order for the industry to compete internationally, as well as at home with cheap imports, it has to invest in research on new varieties of cane, develop the production of by-products (electricity, biofuel, ecological trademarks and so on) and not least streamline the production chain between farming and the factory. The current direction of increase in the number of mills, which leads to competition and the oversupply of cane in relation to milling capacity, is seen as going in the opposite direction. Farmers and opinion holders in the media, on the other hand, tend to see competition as beneficial for the industry's economic development. From the farmers' perspective, as we shall see below, competition has given them a better bargaining position with regard to price. In the public debate, free-market arguments have been cited in the media repeatedly and are used by politicians in their arguments against zoning (Nakato, 2019a; Mao, 2019; The Daily Monitor, 2019). This is also in line with the general direction of Ugandan economic policy, which is characterised by a preference for non-intervention from the state, based on the dominant neoliberal market ideology that has strong support among the country's elite (Rubongoya, 2018; Wiegratz, 2016). Hence, the diverging visions are influenced by both different interests and ideology.

In the following sections, we will examine how these tensions within the industry have affected relations between Kakira and the local population and how this can be related to politics in Uganda. However, before analysing how relations have changed, we will explore what has characterised the long-term relationship between Kakira and the local population.

3. KAKIRA AND THE LOCAL POPULATION

Kakira is Uganda's largest sugar producer and one of its oldest, producing 165,000 tonnes per year, corresponding to 38 per cent of total Ugandan sugar production in 2018 (see Table 4.1). The main product is brown sugar for consumption, but the company also produces by-products, including ethanol, bagasse and electricity, both for its own power consumption and for the national grid. Kakira sources sugarcane from its own 10,000-hectare plantation and from around 7,000 outgrower farmers, who produce another 19,000 hectares (Kakira Sugar, 2020). The company employs about 6,000 workers in the factory plus temporary workers in the fields. The company started in 1929 and is owned by the Madhvani Group, Uganda's largest business conglomerate, owned by the Ugandan-Asian Madhvani family. Both the factory and most of the plantations are located in Jinja district in the Busoga region.

Over the years, Kakira has developed long-term exchange relations with the community around the factory, that is, with employees, farmers and the surrounding communities. The Kakira compound is like a neat town, with well-paved roads, schools, restaurants and health centres around the factory, and it has a strong presence in the Busoga region. Overall, it is a highly organised enterprise, and its role in the community resembles that of the industrial patron in an old-time industrial 'company town' (Garner, 1992).[6]

Although there are now four larger sugar mills in Busoga, Kakira is the oldest, as all the others were licensed as late as 2011. It is therefore safe to say that it is Kakira that has built up the sugar industry in the region. The dominance of Kakira, in terms of both its size and its presence in the community, means that it receives both praise and blame for a variety of issues, including matters outside their control, for example, the sugar tax that was introduced in 2018 (Kyeyune, 2018).

The content of Kakira's exchange deal with various groups within the local community, including the surrounding community itself, employers and sugarcane farmers, will be described below before we analyse how the exchange relationship has come under pressure.

3.1   Kakira's General Exchange Deal with the Surrounding Communities

The presence of the sugarcane industry in general, and not just Kakira, is strongly felt in the communities in Jinja and the surrounding districts. The majority of the population are involved in sugarcane farming in one way or another. Mr Sunday, Agricultural Officer in Busedde sub-county, estimated that 90 per cent of the farmers in the sub-county grow sugarcane. In a study of nine sub-counties in the Busoga region, almost all households were involved in sugarcane production (Waluube, 2013). According to our interviewees in Busedde, sugarcane farming is generally seen as profitable and as creating wealth in the community.

> Sugarcane growing is the order of the day. So, when you do not grow sugarcane, you have no purpose [...] People have built and changed houses. A person who had a small house demolished it and put up a better structure. People have bought motorbikes and cars. The children are being educated using incomes from the sugar cane industry. (Local Council 1 (LC1) chairman, D21)

Furthermore, the sugar industry creates job opportunities, not only at the sugar factory but also temporary work in the fields on both Kakira's plantation and those of the outgrowers. Although the Kakira factory employs over 6,000 workers, many interviewed community members, community leaders and farmers complain that few local people get employment at Kakira, since they mainly employ those who have been educated or trained.

Hence, the main effect in terms of income generation in the community is in the farmers' and outgrowers' relations with Kakira. There is widespread concern, voiced by both community leaders and farmers, with food security due to the dominance of sugarcane farming. The general view, also expressed by the President of Uganda (Kyeyune, 2019), is that those with small plots of land should not go into sugarcane farming, while those who grow sugarcane should always set aside some land for food production. Interviews with LC1 chairmen,[7] who are involved in approving farmers to be registered as suppliers to Kakira, suggested that they do not always approve those applications with plots below a specific size (varying between 1.5 and 3 acres). According to the Agricultural Officer in Busedde sub-county, the extension services provided by the local government's production office are directed towards other crops than sugarcane out of the same concerns for food security. Given the attention being paid to subsistence farming and food security in political circles, Kakira has also brought the food-security issue into their community sensitisation programme.[8]

It is interesting to note that the strong tradition of subsistence farming means that earning money from sugarcane and buying food are seen primarily as problems. One could, of course, argue that this is exactly what is expected and even desired in any process of agricultural transformation. The problem, perhaps unsurprisingly, is that the benefits of sugarcane farming are unevenly divided between different communities. As is shown clearly by both Waluube (2013) and Martiniello (2021), many poorer households in Busoga are not able to reap the benefits, since capital is required to invest in sugarcane farming. Instead, they face pressure to lease out or sell their land, thus increasing their vulnerability. It is also they who do the hardest and lowest paid jobs in the sugarcane fields. This type of differentiation within the community has also been seen in other outgrower schemes (for example, see Jarnholt (2020) on rice in Tanzania and Sulle et al. (this volume) on the sugar sector in Tanzania).

Nonetheless, Kakira has many programmes and activities aimed at benefiting the community at large. The activities that are best known among the interviewed farmers and community members are their maintaining the road network, running schools and health centres, and its scholarship programme.

Most of Kakira's community activities are conducted through their corporate social responsibility (CSR) organisation KORD (Kakira Outgrowers Rural Development Fund). KORD was initiated by Kakira and is funded by both it and its sugarcane suppliers. Contributions to KORD are deducted when sugarcane is delivered, Kakira contributing UGX 125 per tonne and the farmer UGX 250 per tonne.[9] Some of KORD's funds are used to finance the farmers' association (BSGA), and other funding is used for CSR activities suggested by the BSGA. KORD also has a project committee that formally decides on the activities to be undertaken and monitors implementation. The activities KORD has financed include road rehabilitation, the construction of health and school facilities and paying the school fees of vulnerable children. They also partner with international NGOs and organisations, such as the German GIZ (Gesellschaft für Internationale Zusammenarbeit) and the American USAID, for specific projects, for example, related to the environment or targeting vulnerable groups (KORD, 2020).

In addition to its activities through KORD, Kakira runs an extension service programme and sensitisation activities for its outgrowers, as well as providing different kinds of benefits for their employees, as discussed below.

Furthermore, according to Mr Barungi (4 October 2018), Kakira runs a social assistance budget of UGX 50 million (Ugandan shillings) a month (approximately USD 13,000), which is used to respond to requests from individuals or groups for churches, libraries, schools, weddings and so forth. Mr Barungi also suggested that Madhvani does not talk about this and that most people, including KORD, might not even get to know about it.[10]

In our interviews with community members, leaders and farmers, some complained that it was hard to get scholarships and that the schools are mainly for employees of Kakira. However, it is generally recognised that Kakira does have a special status in the community.

> Kakira has helped us so much to improve on our standards of living. They have constructed some schools, they have constructed health units, and they have also rehabilitated our roads, though we still have more that need rehabilitation. So that relationship has been good, so we feel we should support them. (Sugarcane farmer, D32)

Road maintenance is a huge cost for Kakira and KORD,[11] but it is also the activity that is most recognised by community members. Moreover, this activity has both a business and a social rationale since it facilitates the transport of sugarcane, as well as benefiting the community more broadly. Formally, it should be the government's responsibility to maintain the roads, a government responsibility that Kakira takes on 'voluntarily'.

The new millers are not as involved in community work as Kakira, although some have started to venture into this sphere. Both Kamuli and Kaliro support road maintenance around their factories, not by doing it themselves, but by providing fuel to the local government's road maintenance programme. They also engage in one-off charity activities, such as the construction and renovation of schools, and organise annual health camps.[12] In essence, they have understood the need to involve themselves in the community, but so far their activities are not of the same scope or level of organisation as Kakira's, although it might just be a matter of time before they catch up.

In general, directly or indirectly Kakira takes on a considerable number of CSR activities in the community, in comparison with other companies in Uganda, and in comparison with its main sugar-producing competitors. However, its long history of providing services, its strong presence in the community and its perceived financial strength give rise to high expectations where what they are already doing is largely taken for granted.

3.2   Kakira's Exchange Deal with Employees

Kakira's employees are naturally an important sub-group within the local community. They are organised in a trade union[13] that negotiates working conditions with Kakira. All workers have to be members, since agreements between Kakira and individual employees are based on the principle of collective bargaining.[14] The union also intervenes in employee matters if there are complaints, for example, related to dismissals. Kakira provides many benefits to its employees, including food for about 10,000 employees and schoolchildren daily; nursery, primary and secondary schools at a reduced cost for the children of employees; health care for employees and their family members; and retirement benefits. Most of these benefits have been in existence since the 1940s, while the trade union started in 1963.[15] Kakira is also concerned with security in the factory for its employees and has a designated office for health and safety issues (Mr Kiwanuka, 4 October 2018).

The benefits above accrue to full- and part-time employees of Kakira, in the factory and in their plantation, as well as technical staff. However, seasonal labourers working in the fields are not covered by these benefits.[16] We do not have any information on the employment conditions of the other millers, except that Kakira's human resources manager, Mr Thenge, mentioned in an interview in 2016 that, due to the opening up of the sugar industry and the emergence of new sugar-producing plants, 'there is poaching of experienced employees', as the new millers try to attract skilled and experienced employees away from Kakira. This forms part of the increasingly competitive environment in the sugar sector in Busoga, in relation to which the relationship and exchange deal between Kakira and its sugarcane producers (and other providers of services) should be understood.

3.3   Kakira's Exchange Deal with Sugarcane Outgrowers

The sub-group within the local community that is most vital for Kakira is the sugarcane outgrowers, another relationship that is highly organised.[17] In order to supply sugarcane to Kakira, an outgrower, or farmer, needs a permit and is registered as a supplier by Kakira. Transporters, in the form of truck owners who transport sugarcane from the fields to the factory, are also registered, and Kakira regulates the prices for transport. Most of the transporters are also outgrowers and therefore sugarcane suppliers themselves.

All registered outgrowers are automatically members of the farmers' association (BSGA). This association has its own governance structure but is facilitated by Kakira, being funded partly by membership fees and partly by Kakira itself. BSGA's membership fees are collected by Kakira through deductions from farmers' payments when they supply sugarcane. BSGA and Kakira have regular meetings to discuss relations between Kakira and the farmers, including pricing. Despite its close connection to and facilitation by Kakira, BSGA's leadership sees the organisation as representing the cane farmers' interest, and they have even organised strikes against Kakira, as will be discussed below.

Registered outgrowers can be 'aided', meaning that they receive seeds and chemicals from Kakira on credit. The borrowed amount is deducted when the cane is supplied at 18 per cent interest[18] (as per 2018) and in instalments. Furthermore, registered farmers can access bank loans for agricultural purposes from Tropical Bank with a recommendation from Kakira, the sugarcane supply to Kakira constituting security for the bank. Farmers who are aided or have loans are obliged to supply only to Kakira, as that is one of the conditions for receiving credit and loans. Unaided cane producers are free to supply other plants, like Mayuge, besides supplying Kakira, even if they are registered with Kakira. All the interviewed farmers in Busedde sub-county supply Kakira, either directly or indirectly via middlemen, and a few of them supply both Kakira and Mayuge.[19] In the study by Waluube (2013), 70 per cent of interviewed households in the Busoga region supplied Kakira, and 25 per cent Mayuge.

All farmers who are registered with Kakira have bank accounts, and payments are made directly into their accounts within a month of their supplying the cane. Part of the payment to farmers is paid by the end of the year. The farmers refer to this as 'bonus'; Kakira calls it 'arrears', although it is, in fact, a deferred payment or a form of forced saving. Some farmers mention this as a benefit of supplying Kakira. If a farmer wants payment directly at delivery, he can apply for an 'advance' and get paid in cash.

In order to be approved as a cane supplier for Kakira, a farmer has to be recommended by the local government representative at the village level (LC1 chairman), and in order to be approved for a loan or to be aided, the LC1 chairman and neighbours have to confirm the farmer's ownership of land.

Before approving a farmer as a supplier, Kakira's staff members measure the farm using the Global Positioning System (GPS). Kakira repeatedly monitors the farms of its registered suppliers to know how much is supplied for production and payment purposes. If the harvest goes wrong for an aided farmer, Kakira will postpone the repayment of the loan until the next harvest and continue monitoring the farm. In the Busoga region, sugarcane normally takes around 18 months to mature.

Kakira's monitoring of the sugarcane plantations is done for the purposes of industrial planning, production and the recovery of credit, but Kakira also has a programme for outgrower development. Its sensitisation activities focus on health and safety and on mitigating the adverse environmental and social effects of sugarcane farming, including food security, child labour, deforestation and water use. Kakira maintains a presence in the communities through local headquarters at the sub-county level and field assistants at the village level, one for every three villages. These structures are used for both monitoring and awareness campaigns.

Concerning the new millers, Kaliro appears to have applied some of the same principles as Kakira in its relationship with the sugarcane farmers.[20] It has a programme for registering farmers who become 'aided' and therefore receive seedlings, fertiliser and help with ploughing their land on credit. The credit is interest-free and is deducted when the cane is supplied. Kaliro also provides transport for the cane to these farmers. It interacts with farmers' associations, but has not taken the initiative to organise them as Kakira has. Although it has meetings with farmers, these are organised through the LC1 chairmen, and they interact with local government officials on matters related to agriculture.

Kamuli has a similar deal with the farmers close to their factory, offering tractor assistance for ploughing, seedlings and fertilisers on credit at modest rates of interest. Kamuli says that its sugarcane suppliers have a farmers' association that they interact with, but it is not very strong as yet, since its factory is relatively new.

We did not manage to interview anyone from Mayuge.[21] However, according to the farmers we did interview, Mayuge does not offer the same type of services and interactions with farmers as Kakira but seems to compete primarily on price.

The farmers we interviewed generally recognise that Kakira is more organised, more trustworthy and provides more for the community and the farmers than other millers.[22]

> Kakira has a heart of helping its farmer, by ploughing for them, repairing our roads. However, Mayuge millers do not do that. (Sugarcane farmer, D50)

Beneath this highly structured formal relationship between cane suppliers and Kakira lies a myriad of informal local relations. Many sugarcane outgrowers are not registered suppliers of Kakira's but supply through farmers who are registered. In particular, those who are transporters often act as middlemen for the unregistered farmers. Due to these more informal ways of supplying Kakira, the company influences the use of land much more deeply than is revealed by only looking at the relationship between Kakira and the registered cane suppliers. This has consequences for transport, the harvesting of sugarcane, field labour and the supervision of the latter.[23]

In summary, Kakira has built up the sugar industry in the Busoga region since the 1930s in an impressive fashion. The company has made efforts to build a strong relationship with the local population that in many ways resembles a reciprocal exchange deal, both with its employees and sugarcane suppliers, and with the community in general. Kakira has created income-generating opportunities through sugar outgrowing that involves almost all households in Busoga and job opportunities in both the factory and the field. It also provides social services in the form of schools, health centres and road maintenance, as well as facilitating the organisation of both farmers and labour. These benefits are recognised by labour, community members and sugarcane farmers. In return, Kakira has had a stable supply of sugarcane for its production and generally peaceful relations with the community surrounding the factory. However, as we will describe in the next section, the entry of new millers in the region introduced competition over the sugarcane supply, thereby changing the balance in this relationship and threatening the status quo.

4. EXPECTATIONS, PRICE AND CHANGING RELATIONS

Despite the sugarcane farmers recognising the benefits from their relationship with Kakira, there were also a range of conflictual issues, price being the most crucial. At the time of our research in November 2018, the price Kakira offered was UGX 128,000 per tonne, while the Mayuge plant offered UGX 130,000 per tonne. Some farmers who could (i.e. who were not aided) therefore supplied Mayuge in addition to supplying Kakira. The main reason given for supplying Mayuge was that the price was higher. In some cases, the location of the farmer's plantation in relation to the miller's factory, in other words the transport costs, also played a role.[24]

Price was not only the main factor determining who farmers supplied to, in particular for unaided farmers; it was also the first problem the farmers brought up when asked about their relationship with the millers. The issues concerning the pricing of sugarcane were several.

Firstly, many farmers mentioned that the price had been reduced and saw this as destroying the relationship between themselves and the millers: 'The price reductions spoil our relationship' (Sugarcane farmer, D27). If one looks more closely at what underpins this statement, it has to do with expectations. At one point, when Mayuge and other millers tried to outcompete Kakira on price, the price of sugarcane went up to UGX 175,000 per tonne. Although the price was only that high for a few months in 2017, it created expectations among some farmers that the price would remain at that level or increase. Any reductions since then they have taken as a disappointment.

Expectations can have clear economic outcomes when people act on them, as has been seen in other situations (see Frynas and Buur, 2020). In this case, the underlying factor affecting the farmers' profitability is the cost of renting land. When sugarcane prices were high, many farmers decided to go into sugarcane and rented land for this purpose. Much of the land the farmers use for sugarcane is rented (approximately 80 per cent according to Kintu, Interview November 2018), often from other small-scale farmers in the community. The increased demand for renting land meant that the cost of doing so increased. As the lease agreements for land are usually for several years and the gestation period for sugarcane is 18 months, farmers who rented land when leases were high found themselves stuck in an unprofitable situation when the price of sugarcane fell just a few months later.

The problem is thus that the high prices in 2017 gave rise to expectations of continued higher prices and changed farmers' behaviour in accordance with this expectation. Disappointment with the subsequent level of the sugarcane price is not likely to disappear until this underlying issue of land cost is solved, with time or state interventions.

The second issue with price, apart from the price level, was market volatility with price fluctuations. Market prices will always fluctuate, but since sugarcane has a long gestation period (18 months), the farmers bear a large part of the risk in the production chain. As one sugarcane farmer argued:

> Sometimes you calculate when the market price is 128,000 shs, and you might find that by the time you harvest, the price has decreased. (Sugarcane farmer, D31)

Many farmers interviewed complained about this and wanted to have a price set for each season, or even for several years ahead. They have not achieved this so far, although a minimum for the farmers' share in the price (50 per cent) is laid down in the new Sugar Act.[25]

The third major complaint from the farmers about prices was that they were not consulted when cane prices were set, that is, that the prices were just given to them by the millers based on their calculations of sugar content, weight and market prices. This means that all holding power rests with the millers:[26]

> It is a business relationship; however, farmers are not consulted when setting prices. The millers sit and pass new price schedules, and we cannot dispute it since it is already passed. Even when we are called for meetings on these issues, they are just informative and not consultative. (Sugarcane farmer, D5)

Essentially, the farmers felt that they did not have any bargaining power. A local leader who was also a sugarcane farmer expressed this clearly when he was asked what the main challenges were in the relationship between the farmers and the millers:

> Unstable price. Farmers do not have bargaining power in respect to the price paid by the millers. (Sugarcane farmer and LC3 local leader, D49)

The cane producers organised in BSGA tried to promote the farmers' interests and campaign for a minimum price. They brought up this issue repeatedly in meetings with Kakira and government representatives, but also organised strikes in attempts to affect prices. One strike was organised for two weeks in November 2017, meaning that the farmers refused to supply cane to Kakira.[27] The BSGA leadership talked about the strike as successful, as it resulted in the price being stabilised after a period of large fluctuations. However, the farmers expressed disillusionment with the strike:

> In the association, they have no power. When the factory reduces the price, they may organise a strike, but still, nothing is achieved. Farmers are losing confidence in BSGA. (Sugarcane farmer, D7)

The result of the strike seems to be that many farmers lost hope in BSGA's ability to influence the situation. The solutions that interviewed farmers were calling for were for the government, Members of Parliament (MPs) and the President to intervene in the price-setting. They also wanted millers to be allowed to compete over the cane supply. These suggestions correspond precisely with the contested issues in the Sugar Bill.

Some farmers were very clear that the competition between the millers had benefited them:

> It is good that we have other millers than Madhvani.[28] If it were not for competition, Madhvani would squeeze us at every step. The millers generally have more power, but competition curbs that power (Sugarcane farmer, D16)

Although they were still dissatisfied with the price level, their concrete experience was that the entry of new millers in the region put upward pressure on the prices they got for the sugarcane, something they could not achieve through the BSGA. As another farmer suggested:

> Madhvani was alone, but now we got other millers in Mayuge, Kaliro and Kamuli. This brings about competition and better prices for the farmers. (Sugarcane farmer, D49)

In sum, Kakira was put under pressure by the increased competition over the sugarcane supply following the entry of new millers in the region, despite Kakira providing more benefits for the community than its competitors. The increased competition also changed the market in land by increasing rents, and thus increasing the costs of production for the farmers. Farmers were expecting higher prices and were also dissatisfied with their bargaining position in relation to Kakira, which reduced their loyalty to it. The long-term relationship between the local population and Kakira was challenged, and both parties were calling on the government and political leaders to intervene and regulate the relationship.

The farmers wanted prices to be regulated, while Kakira, like the other old millers in Uganda, wanted competition to be regulated. As mentioned above, the President tended to side with the old millers, while Parliament sided with the farmers, which led to the Sugar Bill being stuck between President and

Parliament for several years. The next section will explain in brief how the tensions in the sugar sector were related to broader changes in Uganda's political settlement (for a more thorough analysis of this, see Nystrand et al., 2023 forthcoming).

5. CHANGING POLITICAL ALLIANCES

The three major actors in the Ugandan sugar industry, Kakira, SCOUL and Kinyara, have all enjoyed close relations with the ruling party, the National Resistance Movement (NRM), and President Museveni. Kinyara used to be state-owned but was later sold to a Mauritian company. Both Kakira and SCOUL are owned by Ugandan-Asian families, who came to the country in the early twentieth century and gradually built what became large business conglomerates. These families were expelled by President Idi Amin in 1972 but were invited back to Uganda by Museveni in the late 1980s, when the NRM government also facilitated an infusion of capital enabling them to restart their businesses. The return of Asian capital to Uganda in the early days of Museveni's regime has been seen as important for the revival of the economy, both in a direct sense through the business activities, but also indirectly, by creating confidence so that foreign capital would return to Uganda (Babiiha, 2015; Olanya, 2014). The Madhvani Group, of which Kakira is a part, is Uganda's largest business conglomerate, and its sheer size means that the Madhvani family's importance to the Ugandan economy in general and thereby their influence on politics has been quite substantial. On the other hand, and in light of the precarious role of Ugandan-Asians in the history of Uganda, they also need political protection. Hence, the relationship between the large sugar producers and the Museveni regime has long been characterised by what Buur et al. (2020) refer to as compatible interests where investors and ruling elites mutually support each other.

The increase in the number of mills from 2005 onwards changed this dynamic. Most importantly, the increased competition tilted the balance of power between the large millers and the sugarcane farmers, as we have seen in the case of Kakira and its sugarcane suppliers. The Sugar Policy and the subsequent Sugar Bill attempted to restore the balance by restricting the geographical distance between sugar mills and thereby strengthening the integration between the sugar factories and the surrounding sugarcane farmers. From the industry's perspective, reduced competition and control over the production chain from farmer to mill was needed to consolidate the Ugandan sugar industry and compete internationally. It was also argued that the main sugar-producing countries in the world, such as Brazil and India, also have sugar sectors that are regulated and protected (Madhvani, 2020; see also Buur et al., 2012). The sugar farmers in Busoga, on the other hand, were strongly in favour of competition between millers, as they saw positive effects on their bargaining position, in particular concerning price, as described above.

The calls for regulation meant that the tensions in the sugar industry entered into domestic politics. The licensing of Mayuge, in contradiction with the Sugar Policy, made it clear that the policy was insufficient as a way of regulating the sugar industry, and the process of transforming the policy into law was initiated in 2011 by the President, after lobbying by the major sugar industry actors. This process had been stuck for many years, but after the turmoil in the Busoga region in 2016–17, the Sugar Bill was tabled again.

The President and the majority of MPs took different positions on the Sugar Bill, in particular on the issue of zoning, which meant that it was sent back and forth between the President and the Parliament for several years before eventually being promulgated into law in April 2020. The President argued for zoning to be included in the Bill, in line with the interests of major well-established industry actors like Kakira,[29] while MPs, particularly from the Busoga region, argued for its removal, in line with the interests of the sugar farmers. The whole Sugar Bill saga itself became a major topic in Ugandan politics and media for several years. However, as the Bill as finally adopted did not include the zoning clause, it was more in line with the interests of the sugarcane farmers and the MPs, who argued for competition between millers.

Why, then, after several years of debate and political positioning, did President Museveni give in and sign the Sugar Bill without the zoning clause? We argue that this is because of the role electoral politics plays in Uganda, despite the imperfections of the democratic system. Firstly, the Sugar Bill saga clearly shows that there is some division of power within the political system in Uganda, where the Parliament is sometimes able to get its way and overrule the President. Secondly, President Museveni cares about the legitimacy of his power. Although he certainly does not always play by democratic rules, particularly when it comes to dealing with political opposition, elections play a role in legitimising his position. As Golooba-Mutebi and Hickey (2016) point out, Museveni is known to use both hard and soft forms of power to maintain the regime's stability. The sugarcane farmers in Busoga are voters, and with an upcoming election in 2021, Museveni had to pay attention to popular opinion. Thirdly, most of the MPs in Uganda are elected on the basis of a direct mandate from their constituencies. These elections are often highly competitive, and MPs who have disappointed their voters are regularly voted out, regardless of party affiliation. Hence, MPs who want to keep their positions have to pay attention to sentiment within their constituency. When the party position or the position of the President diverges from the local voters' views or interests, the MPs have to balance competing interests. It will be in their interests to try to influence decisions in Parliament in line with the interests of their voters (for further analysis of the politics around this issue, see Nystrand et al., 2023 forthcoming).

6. CONCLUSION

The case of Kakira and Uganda's sugar politics shows how a seemingly stable long-term relationship between investor and the local population resembling what Buur et al. (2020) term a reciprocal exchange deal can be challenged when the political situation in which this relation is embedded changes. Looking at the balance between and characteristics of the three relationships based on Buur et al.'s (2020) analytical framework, we can see that in this case the relationship between Kakira and the President, which was characterised by compatible interests and long-term stability, was trumped by the increasing need for both President and MPs to pay attention to their relationships with local populations as voters, thus honouring the mutual recognition this relationship demands.

The main beneficiaries of these changes seem to be the sugarcane farmers, who have improved their bargaining position in relation to the millers and possibly the price they get for their sugarcane, and they have also demonstrated that they could affect national politics. In Khan's (2010) terms, their holding power seems to have increased.

However, if the industry experts are correct, the industry's fragmentation might undermine the economic feasibility and international competitiveness of the large sugar companies and thus undercut the sugar industry, including the sugarcane farmers, in the long run. Another possibility is that the large sugar millers gradually withdraw from outgrower schemes and increase their own sugar plantations to maintain control over the production chain,[30] which would also reduce the economic viability of the small-scale sugarcane producers. However, this development would include the acquisition of land. Given the current sensitivity over land issues in Uganda, such a move would expose the sugar companies to serious criticism and a backlash from both the ruling elites and local populations.[31] Only the future will tell whether the sugar industry as a whole will suffer or thrive from the increased competition.

NOTES

1.   Busoga is not a formal region, but a traditional Bantu kingdom and one of five constitutional monarchies in Uganda. It includes the districts of Jinja, Kamuli, Iganga, Bugiiri, Mayuge, Luuka, Kaliro, Busiki, Buyende, Namutumba and Namayingo (The Ugandan, 2020). Sugar production is strongly prevalent in all these districts.
2.   Busedde sub-county was chosen as a location for the interviews because of its intensified sugarcane cultivation and its strategic location, which enables farmers

to supply sugarcane to both Kakira and other millers, namely Kaliro, Kamuli and Mayuge. Busedde is located approximately 25 km from Kakira's factory and at about the same distance from Mayuge. However, the majority of sugar farmers we interviewed owned sugarcane plantations in more than one sub-county.

3. A new sugar region is emerging in northern Uganda, most concretely in the form of a new sugar factory and plantations being set up in Atiak in Amuru district (which was not yet producing any sugar as of July 2020). Furthermore, the Madhvanis and the government have for many years tried to set up a sugar industry in Amuru district, but this venture has been met with fierce local resistance and has not yet taken off (see Buur et al., 2019, for a short history of Amuru Sugar Works).

4. The licensing of Mayuge in 2011, in contradiction with the Sugar Policy of 2010, was a mistake, according to industry experts (Musafiri interview, 2019; Mubiru interview, 2019). The licensing authority at the time was the Uganda Investment Authority, which came under the Ministry of Trade, Industry and Cooperatives. According to Musafiri (interview, 2019) they did not have the technical knowledge to understand the consequences of this decision. Since Mayuge was licensed to place the factory in the location it is, the government has to compensate it if it decided it had to move, which is one of the problems put forward in the debate (Mubiru interview, 2019), although it was solved in the draft Sugar Bill from 2016 by exempting existing mills from the zoning clause (Ministry of Trade, Industry and Cooperatives, 2016).

5. Since this chapter is primarily concerned with relations within Uganda's domestic sugar industry, the debate and conflicts around sugar regulation and trade in the East African Community will not be dwelled on further here.

6. Garner (1992) defines a 'company town' as a 'settlement built and operated by a single business enterprise'. These were common in the early Industrial Revolution in Europe. In Sweden these towns were called *bruksorter*, which sprawled around the mills that grew up in the seventeenth and eighteenth centuries. Österbybruk, founded in the seventeenth century, is one such example.

7. LC1 chairman (Local Council 1) is the village-level local government representative.

8. A study commissioned by Kakira and State House jointly (Waluube, 2013) focused specifically on food security in relation to sugarcane farming.

9. The total budget of KORD is approximately UGX 300 million per year (2016), according to Michael Kintu, Project Manager at KORD, interviewed on 23 November 2016. In addition, Kakira provides KORD with an office, outside the budget.

10. We can only speculate as to the reason why Madhvani would not talk about this assistance, but it fits in with the morality, common to many religions, that the value of 'doing good' decreases if it is flaunted publicly (Graeber, 2011). According to this morality, good deeds should be done out of a moral imperative, not in order to gain something.

11. Road maintenance cost USD 1 million per year, according to Mr Barungi, 4 October 2018. They maintain the road network within a 35-km radius of the factory. Part of this cost is included in the KORD budget.

12. This information from the Kamuli representative is confirmed by media reports; see Wafula, 2019d.

13. The trade union is the National Union of Plantation Agricultural Workers Uganda, Kakira branch.

14. The number of members in the union was 7,861 as of 23 November 2016, while the total number of employees, full- and part-time, was 8,911, including both factory workers and workers in the plantations (Kakira's human resources manager, Mr Thenge, and the union (NUPAW) Kakira branch chairman, Mr Awile, interviewed on 23 November 2016).

15. The information on employee benefits and the trade union is based on interviews with Kakira's human resources manager and representatives of the trade union on 23 November 2016; see list of interviews.

16. The seasonal labourers work for both Kakira and for the outgrowers supplying Kakira with cane. Many of them are migrant workers from other regions in Uganda, and there are many stories of their hard working conditions, see Martiniello (2021) for the most recent account.

17. The description of relations between Kakira and its outgrowers is based on interviews with farmers, as well as with Kakira and BSGA representatives.

18. This might sound like a high rate of interest, but average interest rates have remained at around 20 per cent in Uganda for a long time (Mugume and Rubatsimbira, 2019).

19. Of the 24 interviewed farmers, 12 supply only Kakira, out of which 7 are aided, i.e. bound to supply only Kakira. Another 8 farmers supply both Kakira and Mayuge, while 4 farmers supply via middlemen (primarily to Kakira).

20. Information on Kaliro's and Kamuli's interaction with farmers is based on interviews with representatives of Kaliro and Kamuli millers, see list of interviews.

21. We collected our empirical data at a time when relations within the sugar industry were high on the agenda in both politics and the media. Given that Mayuge's location was seen as the main problem in relation to the regulation of sugar, it is understandable that they were reluctant to participate in the study.

22. There are complaints about millers cheating at the weighbridge when sugarcane is supplied. However, the perception seems to be that this does not apply to Kakira. The fact that their payment and registration system is computerised is also mentioned as contributing to Kakira's trustworthiness.

23. According to our interviews, the informal exchange relations that exist within communities are ones of solidarity and cooperation, as well as involving the challenges of power relations, cheating, theft and sabotage (burning of cane), but these relationships will not be dwelled on here, as the focus is on the relationship with Kakira. Martiniello (2021) provides a recent account of the different effects on access to land and the unequal valuation of labour within different communities in Busoga.

24. The transport costs varied between UGX 14,000 and 27,000 per tonne, depending on the distance. Kakira regulates the transport costs for its registered transporters and handles the payments between farmers and transporters through its payment system. However, some farmers mentioned that, when fuel prices are high, the transporters charge extra, on top of Kakira's stipulated price.

25. The sugar price paid to suppliers is determined based on a formula stipulated in the Sugar Act (2020). It is based on the average market price for sugar multiplied by the rendement (i.e. the sugar content), the sugar weight and a percentage agreed between the parties, which should be a minimum of 50 per cent. This percentage has been gradually increased in negotiations from about 20 per cent in the late 1990s (Musafiri interview, 2019).

26. The concept of 'holding power' comes from Mushtaq Khan, who defines it as 'the capability of an individual or group to engage and survive in conflicts' (Khan, 2010, p. 6).
27. Another strike was organised in July 2019 (Nakato, 2019b), but that was after our interviews with the farmers and BSGA representatives in Busoga, which took place in October and November 2018.
28. The Madhvani family are the owners of Kakira, and farmers often refer to them rather than to the company.
29. The President's position was most likely based not only on the alliance with the main sugar actors, but also on ideology. President Museveni has often expressed a genuine interest in the industrialisation and modernisation of the Ugandan economy, and it is clear from his arguments around the Sugar Bill that he agrees with the industry experts that the fragmentation of the industry is hampering industrialisation of the sugar sector (Kyeyune, 2019).
30. This argument has been put forward by both industry experts and President Museveni (Wafula, 2019b).
31. The Madhvanis have most likely already 'burnt their fingers' in the decade-long conflict over their attempt to set up a sugar factory in Amuru district in northern Uganda (see Buur et al., 2019, for an explanation of this conflict).

REFERENCES

Ahluwalia D.P.S. (1995) *Plantations and the Politics of Sugar in Uganda*, Kampala: Fountain Publishers.

Babiiha S.M. (2015) 'International Capital, Inclusive Planning and Post-War Recovery: The Case of Acholi Land, Northern Uganda', *Journal of Governance and Development*, 11(1), 1–16.

Buur L., Mondlane C. and Baloi O. (2012) 'The White Gold: The Role of Government and State in Rehabilitating the Sugar Industry in Mozambique', *Journal of Development Studies*, 48(3), 349–62.

Buur L., Pedersen R.H., Nystrand M. and Macuane J.J. (2019) 'Understanding the Three Key Relationships in Natural Resource Investments in Africa: An Analytical Framework', *The Extractive Industries and Society*, 6(4), 1195–204.

Buur L., Pedersen R.H., Nystrand M., Macuane J.J and Thabit J. (2020) 'The Politics of Natural Resource Investments and Rights in Africa: A Theoretical Approach', *The Extractive Industries and Society*, 7(3), 918–30.

Frynas G. and Buur L. (2020) 'The Presource Curse in Africa: Economic and Political Effects of Anticipating Natural Resource Revenues', *The Extractive Industries and Society*, 7(4), 1257–70.

Garner J.S. (1992) *The Company Town: Architecture and Society in the Early Industrial Age*, New York: Oxford University Press.

Golooba-Mutebi F. and Hickey S. (2016) 'The Master of Institutional Multiplicity? The Shifting Politics of Regime Survival, State-Building and Democratisation in Museveni's Uganda', *Journal of Eastern African Studies*, 10(4), 601–18.

Graeber, D. (2011) *Debt: The First 5,000 Years*, Brooklyn NY: Melville House Publishing.

Jarnholt E.D. (2020) 'Contract Farming Schemes in Rice and Sugar in Tanzania: The Implications for Exchange Relations, Power Distribution and Differentiation', PhD Thesis, Roskilde University.

Khan M. (2010) 'Political Settlements and the Governance of Growth-Enhancing Institutions', Research Paper Series on Governance for Growth, School of Oriental and African Studies, University of London, accessed 20 November 2022 at https://eprints.soas.ac.uk/9968/1/Political_Settlements_internet.pdf.

Martiniello G. (2021) 'Bitter Sugarification: Sugar Frontier and Contract Farming in Uganda', *Globalizations*, 18(3), 355–71.

Nystrand M.J., Sserwanga A. and Kyomuhendo B. (2023) 'The Sugar Bill and the Politics of Sugar in Uganda', SECO Working Paper 2023, Roskilde University forthcoming.

Olanya D.R. (2014) 'Asian Capitalism, Primitive Accumulation, and the New Enclosures in Uganda', *African Identities*, 12(1), 76–93.

Rubongoya J.B. (2018) '"Movement Legacy" and Neoliberalism as Political Settlement in Uganda's Political Economy', in Wiegratz J., Martiniello G. and Greco E. *Uganda: The Dynamics of Neoliberal Transformation*, London: Zed Books.

Wiegratz J. (2016) *Neoliberal Moral Economy: Capitalism, Socio-Cultural Change and Fraud in Uganda*, London and New York: Rowman and Littlefield.

Official Documents

Ministry of Tourism Trade and Industry (2010) 'National Sugar Policy: A Framework for Enhancement of Competitiveness, Public-Private Partnerships, and Social Transformation', The Ministry of Tourism Trade and Industry, Government of Uganda, November 2010.

Ministry of Trade, Industry and Cooperatives (2016) 'The Sugar Bill, 2016', UPCC, Entebbe, by Order of the Government.

Mugume A. and Rubatsimbira D.K. (2019) 'What Explains High Interest Rates in Uganda?' Working Paper No 06/2018, Bank of Uganda.

The Republic of Uganda (2020) 'The Sugar Act'.

Waluube M.F.K. (2013) 'Sugarcane Cash and Food Insecurity in Busoga Region of Uganda: A Qualitative Investigation', State House of Uganda and Kakira Sugar Ltd.

Media and Online Sources

The Daily Monitor (2019) 'Sugar Mills Zoning Negates Demand and Supply Forces' Editorial, *The Daily Monitor*, 1 May 2019.

The Daily Monitor (2020) 'Uganda to Start Manufacturing Pharmaceutical Sugar' Editorial, *The Daily Monitor*, 27 May 2020.

Kabeho J.M. (2019) 'It's Wrong to Have Sugar Factories near Each Other', *The Daily Monitor*, 15 May 2019.

Kakira Sugar (2020) 'Kakira at a Glance', accessed 10 March 2020 at http://www.kakirasugar.com/?q=content/kakira-glance.

KORD (2020) 'What We Do', accessed 5 May 2020 at http://www.kordfund-ug.org/what-we-do/.

Kyeyune M. (2018) 'Sugarcane Growers Protest New Tax, Demand Sugar Law', *The Daily Monitor*, 24 July 2018.

Kyeyune M. (2019) 'Museveni Rejects Sugar Bill, Warns of Turmoil in Industry', *The Daily Monitor*, 4 April 2019.

Madhvani K.M. (2020) 'Hard Facts about Sugar Industry in Uganda', *The New Vision*, 14 January 2020.

Mao N. (2019) 'Resisting Government Intrusion: From Rent, Sugar to Religion – Part I', *The Daily Monitor*, 22 September 2019.

Mubiru W. (2019) 'Sugar Bill Will Stabilise the Industry', *The Daily Monitor*, 12 November 2019.

Nakato T. (2019a) 'Sugar Bill Should be Fair to All Players – Busoga MPs', *The Daily Monitor*, 16 May 2019.

Nakato T. (2019b) 'Busoga Cane Farmers Strike over Low Prices', *The Daily Monitor*, 3 July 2019.

Sanya S. (2011) 'Eight Firms Join Sugar Production', *The New Vision*, 22 November 2011.

The Ugandan (2020) 'The History of Busoga Kingdom, accessed 15 March 2020 at https://www.theugandan.info/the-history-of-busoga-kingdom/.

Wafula P. (2019a) 'Sugar Bill: Farmers Vow to Vote out People who Initiated It', *The Daily Monitor*, 3 June 2019.

Wafula P. (2019b) 'Museveni Urges Millers to Grow Own Sugarcane', *The Daily Monitor*, 12 July 2019.

Wafula P. (2019c) 'We no longer Make Money from Sugar – Madhvani', *The Daily Monitor*, 20 August 2019.

Wafula P. (2019d) 'Kaliro Residents Get Free Check-up, Treatment', *The Daily Monitor*, 12 December 2019.

List of Interviews

a)   *Farmers and community members in Busedde sub-county (39 interviews)*

Atlas ID	Occupation/position	Time of interview
D1	Sugarcane farmer, Busedde sub-county	Nov 2018
D3	Sugarcane farmer, Busedde sub-county	Nov 2018
D4	Sugarcane farmer, Busedde sub-county	Nov 2018
D5	Sugarcane farmer, Busedde sub-county	Nov 2018
D6	Sugarcane farmer, Busedde sub-county	Nov 2018
D7	Sugarcane farmer, Busedde sub-county and work with various NGOs	Nov 2018
D8	Sugarcane farmer, Busedde sub-county	Nov 2018
D11	Sugarcane farmer, Busedde sub-county and retired Agricultural Officer	Nov 2018
D12	Sugarcane farmer, Busedde sub-county	Nov 2018
D13	Sugarcane farmer, Busedde sub-county	Nov 2018
D14	Sugarcane farmer, Busedde sub-county	Nov 2018
D16	Sugarcane farmer, Busedde sub-county	Nov 2018
D27	Sugarcane farmer, Busedde sub-county	Nov 2018
D28	Sugarcane farmer, Busedde sub-county	Nov 2018
D29	Sugarcane farmer, Busedde sub-county	Nov 2018
D30	Sugarcane farmer, Busedde sub-county	Nov 2018
D31	Sugarcane farmer, Busedde sub-county	Nov 2018
D32	Sugarcane farmer, Busedde sub-county	Nov 2018
D46	Sugarcane farmer, Busedde sub-county	Nov 2018
D47	Sugarcane farmer, Busedde sub-county	Nov 2018
D48	Sugarcane farmer, Busedde sub-county	Nov 2018
D49	Sugarcane farmer and LC3 chairman, Busedde sub-county	Nov 2018
D50	Sugarcane farmer, Busedde sub-county	Nov 2018
D51	Sugarcane farmer, Busedde sub-county	Nov 2018
D9	Community member, Busedde sub-county, retailer and farmer	Nov 2018
D22	Community member, Busedde sub-county, farmer and businesswoman	Nov 2018
D23	Community member, Busedde sub-county, farmer and builder	Nov 2018
D24	Community member, Busedde sub-county, farmer and motorbike rider (boda-boda)	Nov 2018
D25	Community member, Busedde sub-county, farmer and deal in bananas	Nov 2018

Atlas ID	Occupation/position	Time of interview
D26	Community member, Busedde sub-county, farmer	Nov 2018
D2	Islamic leader and farmer, including sugarcane	Nov 2018
D10	Imam (chairman of the mosque), farmer and businessman	Nov 2018
D15	Senior Assistant Secretary/Sub-county Chief, Busedde sub-county, and sugarcane farmer	Nov 2018
D17	Agricultural officer, Busedde sub-county, and sugarcane farmer	Nov 2018
D18	LC1 chairman, Bulondo village, Busedde sub-county, and sugarcane farmer	Nov 2018
D19	LC1 chairman, Bukobya village, Busedde sub-county, and sugarcane farmer	Nov 2018
D20	LC3 chairman, Busedde sub-county, and sugarcane farmer	Nov 2018
D21	LC1 chairman, Namazingili village, Busedde sub-county, and sugarcane farmer	Nov 2018
D33	Chairperson for elders, Busedde sub-county, and sugarcane farmer	Nov 2018

b)   *Representatives of millers*

Kintu Michael	Project Manager, KORD (Kakira Outgrowers Rural Development Fund)	23 Nov 2016 and 4 Oct 2018
Barungi Kenneth	Assistant to General Manager, Kakira Sugar Works	4 Oct 2018
Kiwanuka George	Health and Safety Supervisor, Kakira Sugar Works	4 Oct 2018
Abbys Balah	Agricultural Production Manager, Sugar and Allied Industries Ltd (Kaliro)	12 Dec 2019
Rajesj Menjit	Production Manager, Kamuli Sugar Ltd	17 Dec 2019

c)   *Human resource and union representatives, Kakira (group interview)*

Thenge Moses H	Human Resources Manager, Kakira Sugar Works	23 Nov 2016
Wamboka Ronald	Senior Industrial Relations Officer, Kakira Sugar Works	23 Nov 2016
Awile Stephen	Chairman, The National Union of Plantation Agricultural Workers Uganda (NUPAW), Kakira branch	23 Nov 2016
Mugweri Mustafa	Vice Chairman, NUPAW, Kakira Branch	23 Nov 2016
Wamadri Harry	Branch Secretary, NUPAW, Kakira Branch	23 Nov 2016
Ofutra Muhammad	Organising Secretary Plantation, NUPAW, Kakira Branch	23 Nov 2016
Bwire Jackson Charles	Representative, NUPAW, Kakira Branch	23 Nov 2016

d) *Farmers' association representatives*

Isa Budhugo	Chairman, BSGA (Busoga Sugarcane Growers Association)	4 Oct 2018
Bamwise Herbert	General Secretary, BSGA (Busoga Sugarcane Growers Association)	4 Oct 2018
Naitema Godfrey	Publicity Secretary, BSGA (Busoga Sugarcane Growers Association)	4 Oct 2018

e) *Industry and government representatives*

Mubiru Wilberforce	Secretary, Uganda Sugar Manufacturers Association (USMA)	13 Sept 2019
Musafiri Richard	Sugar desk, Ministry of Trade and Industry	23 Sept 2019

5. The politics of the smallholder–investor relationship in the Tanzanian sugar sector

Emmanuel Sulle, Faustin Maganga, Rose Qamara, Evans Boadu, Happiness Malle and Onesmo Minani

1. INTRODUCTION

In Tanzania, as in many other developing countries, the government and development partners promote partnerships that bring together investors (agri-businesses) and local small-scale producers (Southern Agricultural Growth Corridor of Tanzania (SAGCOT, 2012; United Republic of Tanzania (URT, 2013) in order to create potential win-win outcomes. Yet, the outcomes of land-based investments are context-specific, with highly differentiated results between winners and losers (Hall et al., 2015; Pedersen and Buur, 2016; Dubb et al., 2017; Sulle, 2017b) in different configurations. These differentiated outcomes of land-based investments and the politics of the investor–smallholder relationship are poorly understood in the current literature. The creation of a conducive environment for large-scale farming through the ongoing land reforms to facilitate land acquisition for small-producers and investor companies are likely to result in new relationships between large-scale farmers, smallholder farmers, labour, agribusiness and the state (Scoones et al., 2018).

Relationships between local populations and large-scale investments in Africa are nothing new. The colonial and post-colonial eras in Africa have shown that land-based investment tends to displace local people from their lands and livelihoods. The historical track record of conflictual and even hostile relationships between smallholder farmers who have been displaced from their land and foreign investors continues to shape large-scale investment processes at the present day (Buur et al., 2017, p. 6). Tanzania's current land-based investment policies, coupled with international standards and approaches, are influencing the relationship between smallholder farmers and investors. While some local landowners are voluntarily selling their land to investors, as well as to other buyers, some have been coerced by the state and its apparatus to offer their lands for sale against their will (Buur et al., 2017; Hall et al., 2015). Even though scholars have argued that adhering to the proper procedures, where local populations are kept adequately informed and compensated, is sufficient (Veit and Larsen, 2013; Lindsay et al., 2016), this is rarely enough to secure a better relationship between smallholders and investors.

Different approaches have been encouraged to improve relationships between investors and local populations. The most common approaches include Corporate Social Responsibility (CSR), the Social License to Operate (SLO), and Free, Prior and Informed Consent (FPIC), all of which focus on such relationships (Buur et al., 2017, p. 9). However, the involvement of state agencies in these processes alongside smallholders and investors is a prerequisite for the successful implementation of land-based investments. Relationships between these three actors tend to be dynamic and complex in practice due to their adoption of different standpoints with regard to the gains from such deals, which in most cases has marred the relationship between investors and smallholders in particular (Buur et al., 2017, p. 9). We adopt the political economy and natural resources governance approach discussed by Buur et al. (2017; 2019; 2020) to explore the reciprocal exchange deals between local populations and investors, the compatibility of interests between investors and ruling elites, and mutual recognition between local populations and ruling elites in order to analyse the relationship between smallholders and investors and to examine the wider context in which these relations are embedded in respect of land-based investments in Tanzania. Buur et al. (2017) argue that, to understand the relationship between land rights and large-scale resource investments, the triangle constituted by all three relations has to be unpacked.

This chapter does this by also unpacking the external factors related to the politics of the global movement of capital and its ownership. It focuses on understanding sugarcane production in Tanzania, and it answers the following questions: what is the state of the smallholder–investor relationship in Tanzania? Who is benefiting and who is losing out from this relationship? What are the implications of agricultural 'commercialization' and the 'transformation' agenda on the ground? Understanding the historical patterns of the relationships between investors and smallholders on the one hand and investors and the political elites on the other hand is of great importance in analysing land-based investments.

The chapter is based on an in-depth literature review and field interviews with key informants, including sugar-board officials, sugarcane growers, representatives of farmers' groups, other researchers, the officials of the SAGCOT Secretariat, and government officials in national-, regional- and district-level offices. By empirically analysing the case of the Kilombero Sugar Company

Limited (KSCL) and its partnership with outgrowers in Kilombero, Tanzania, the chapter contributes theoretically to the evolving debates on the political economy of land and natural resources.

The rest of the chapter is organized as follows. Section 2 describes the political dynamics of land-based investments in Tanzania. Section 3 provides a historical overview of the Tanzania sugar industry with reference to its past and current trajectories. Section 4 critically unpacks the policies and politics of land and unravels issues of conflict, compensation and outcomes. In the conclusion, the chapter reflects on its findings and analytical framework. We argue that smallholder–investor relationships cannot be detached from their respective relationships with the ruling elites, who shape policies and politics and make election promises related to land-based investments.

2.   THE POLITICS OF LAND-BASED INVESTMENTS IN TANZANIA

In most African countries, land for investments can be acquired either through the state or inheritance under the customary land laws and tenure rights. Tanzania, like the majority of African countries, is faced with similar land problems due to the existence of parallel systems of land acquisition, such as uncertain land rights versus security of tenure. In Tanzania rural or village lands are inherited under customary law. However, these village landowners are mostly confronted with the position of the state, which tends to neglect the customary law and rights of tenure (Peters, 2013; 2016). Indeed, state appropriations of land violating customary laws, in order to provide land for investors, have occurred in rural communities in Tanzania (Kamanga, 2008; Chachage and Baha, 2010; Sulle and Nelson, 2009; 2013). Historically, villages in Tanzania have large areas of arable land that are classified as 'unused' (Purdon, 2013).

Therefore, there is a tendency on the part of the government and private investors to acquire such land without paying compensation, but as the land forms part of rotating systems of land redistribution this can have grave consequences. Coupled with the low rates of compensation for lands thus acquired, there is also a lack of transparency with regard to processes of land acquisition. Purdon (2013) argues that, regardless of whether the compensation rates are low or high, they do not promote smooth processes of land acquisition and would in most cases be rejected by villagers. This creates uncertainty regarding acquisition of village land and its sustainability, even when the land is deemed to be unused. However, in instances where village land has been acquired and transformed into a land-based estate and has benefited from increased investment and production, compensation rates have generated social, political and economic hardship for rural populations (ibid.).

In the late 1980s, Tanzania was hit by a severe socio-economic crisis. In an attempt to curb the debilitating socio-economic situations and to improve economic growth, the government embraced some of the remedies proposed by the Bretton Woods institutions, such as the structural adjustment programmes. Tanzania, like most African countries, altered its institutional arrangements to create a conducive environment for foreign direct investment (FDI) (Massay and Kassile, 2018). To date, Tanzania continues to promote an investment-friendly environment in order to attract international and regional investors into the country.

The move towards agricultural commercialization in Tanzania is aligned with the country's efforts to attract FDI in agriculture. They are also aligned with reforms of the land law, including land-titling and property-formalization initiatives, such as 'Kilimo Kwanza' or 'Agriculture First' and SAGCOT. The Kilimo Kwanza initiative was launched in 2009 as part of the effort to bring about agriculture transformation through a green revolution. Unlike previous initiatives in agriculture and other sectors, Kilimo Kwanza was formulated under the patronage of the Tanzania National Business Council (TNBC),[1] a situation that raises questions about smallholder representation.[2] To implement the Kilimo Kwanza initiative, the country introduced SAGCOT to create 'inclusive, commercially successful agribusinesses that will benefit the region's small-scale farmers, and in so doing, improve food security, reduce rural poverty and ensure environmental sustainability'.[3] SAGCOT has enjoyed widespread support from state and private actors, as well as regional and international organizations.

Even though overall activities within the agricultural sector are guided by the National Agriculture Policy, which came into effect in 2013, a myriad of domestic, regional and international initiatives from both within and outside the agricultural sector influence investment decisions.[4]

Firstly, what is striking about the agricultural sector initiatives mentioned above is that they have fallen behind in meeting their intended goals. Neither the government nor the private sector have come close to realizing the objectives, and at present fewer than 5 large-scale land deals out of the planned 25 in rice and sugarcane had been met by 2015 (URT, 2013).[5] Secondly, another striking aspect of the myriad of policies is that most of the initiatives and strategies seem to contradict each other in terms of priorities. For instance, while Tanzania is implementing the Comprehensive Africa Agriculture Development Programme (CAADP), which focuses on supporting smallholders, the Kilimo Kwanza, SAGCOT and New Alliance initiatives mainly focus on the promotion of large-scale farming, especially of sugarcane and rice (URT, 2013).

In Tanzania, prior to the 1990s land reforms, there have been numerous occasions when domestic or international establishments have acquired land-title deeds on general land for commercial or plantation estates (Sulle,

2017a). Some of these estates, however, have either ceased production or been abandoned since nationalization, attracting nearby villagers to occupy them. This situation led to the privatization of most farms owned by state parastatals in the 1990s. Assessing the process of privatizing the farms owned by the then National Agriculture and Food Corporation (NAFCO), ranches under the National Ranching Company (NARCO) and land belonging to absentee landlords, Chachage and Mbunda (2009, p. viii) observed that the process was 'marred by controversies that have elicited animosities between investors and small-scale producers on the one hand, and between small-scale farmers and pastoralists on the other hand'. In the next section, the chapter provides a brief overview of the Tanzanian sugar industry and its regulatory framework before proceeding to a case study of the partnership between the KSCL and its outgrowers.

3.   THE POLITICS OF THE INVESTOR–SMALLHOLDER RELATIONSHIPS

Understanding how the relationship between investors and smallholders is built over time and what is exchanged between the parties in land-based investments will be explored in depth in the following paragraphs. We first examine how the state's involvement in the agricultural sector both facilitates and obstructs this relationship. To do this, we first examine the history of sugarcane production in Tanzania and the institutional landscape informing investment and cane production. This will be followed by two case studies of sugarcane production partnerships involving large companies and small outgrower producers of cane in Section 4.

3.1   The History of the Sugar Industry in Tanzania

In Tanzania since colonial times, sugarcane production has been a perfect example of investors, the government and political elites working together to ensure that the partnership between investors and outgrowers is built and sustained. For example, sugarcane production in Tanzania can be traced back to the early 1920s, at the time of the colonial administration in what was then Tanganyika. Initially sugarcane was produced in the two major valleys of Kilombero and Mtibwa, where smallholder cane jaggeries[6] were established. It was around the 1920s when, as part of their quest to commercialize Tanzanian sugarcane farming, Indian investors introduced 'better varieties', which they cultivated on their plantations to manufacture brown sugar. African smallholders, conversely, did not take advantage of farming sugarcane to open jaggeries (Baum, 1968, pp. 25–6). Production expanded in the late 1960s when the first commercial sugar factory was established in the village of Msolwa, Kilombero

District, followed by the Mtibwa sugar factory, which was established in 1973, and Ruembe Sugar Factory (Kilombero II), set up in 1976. Later on, in 1982, the government rehabilitated the small Kagera sugar plant, which had been damaged during the Uganda–Tanzania War of 1978. However, since the Arusha Declaration of 1967, the government has nationalized most of the private firms, including the sugar estates and mills.

The nationalized firms were managed by the NAFCO. Subsequently, in 1974, the Sugar Development Corporation (SUDECO) took control with the core aims of developing the national sugar industry, sugar distribution, and sugar exports and imports. Presently, following liberalization, sugarcane is produced by four private large-scale estates collaborating with independent outgrowers. Currently, five sugar estates are producing sugar commercially: Kagera Sugar in Kagera, KSCL and Mtibwa Sugar Estates in Morogoro, Manyara Sugar in Manyara, and the Tanganyika Planting Company (TPC) in Kilimanjaro. Except for Manyara Sugar and the TPC, which depend only on their estates to produce, the remaining companies have a growing number of independent outgrowers. These companies also have different production and efficiency capacities. Of them all, it is only the KSCL that has two medium-sized mills; the remaining companies have just one mill or factory.

Following privatization, sugarcane production by all five companies increased from 98,000 tonnes in 1998 to 304,000 tonnes in 2015 (URT, 2017), making sugarcane the top domestic commercial crop in terms of tonnage produced per year (URT, 2017; Table 5.1). However, this increase has yet to meet the local demand for sugar for both domestic and industrial consumption, which stands at 420,000 and 170,000 tonnes respectively (ibid.). National sugarcane production and policies vary considerably between different African countries. For example, whereas Malawi (Dubb et al., 2017) and Mozambique (Buur et al., 2011; Food and Agriculture Organization (FAO, 2013)) meet their domestic demand and export the surplus, Tanzania has to meet the gap in its domestic demand for sugar, amounting to approximately 286,000 tonnes (URT, 2016), through zero- or reduced-tariff sugar imports (Sulle and Smalley, 2015). In order to increase domestic production, since the 2000s the Tanzanian government has sought to attract new private investment in the sector while encouraging existing producers to increase their output. It has also continued to protect the industry from cheap and poor-quality sugar imports by regulation.

In February 2016, President Magufuli announced restrictions on sugar imports. The presidential order was a response towards the widespread misuse of existing permits and illegal imports of cheap foreign sugar into the domestic market. The sugarcane business is primarily dominated by a sophisticated network of traders, of mostly Asian and Arab origin, with links to ruling elites within the ruling Chama Cha Mapinduzi (CCM) party. These traders finance,

Table 5.1   *Production of main cash crops from 2013 to 2019*

Crop	2013/14	2014/15	2015/16	2016/17	2017/18	2018/19	2019/20
Sugar	294300	300230	293075	329840	324325	353900	298949
Tea	33500	35500	32629	31000	35000	37000	11185
Pyrethrum	7000	7600	2011	2500	2600	2600	1627
Tobacco	100000	113600	60691	60691	55900	54868	70087
Cashew	130124	200000	155416	260000	300000	–	232000
Sisal	37291	40000	42314	42000	43000	15480	35552
Cotton	245831	203313	149445	122000	150000	700000	300000
Coffee	48982	40759	60691	47999	43000	65000	55979

Source: URT (2017, p. 66; 2020).

directly or indirectly, the ruling party, which in exchange offers them tax exemptions or waives customs duties for sugar (Booth et al., 2012; Ronald, 2013; Sulle, 2017b).

Table 5.1 shows that sugar has remained at the centre of the agricultural commercialization strategies of Tanzanian governments since the mid-2000s. In its efforts to spearhead industrial development, the late President Magufuli and his prime minister both made announcements offering land for sugarcane production to investors (Tanzania Daily News, 2016a). In line with Magufuli's ambitions, in the 2016/17 financial year, the Tanzania Investment Centre (TIC) allocated 200,300 ha of land for agricultural activities, including sugarcane production (Majaliwa, 2016). The Ministry of Agriculture, Livestock and Fisheries (MALF) also identified around 294,000 ha of land for sugarcane production in the regions of Kagera, Kigoma, Morogoro, Mara, Mtwara and Pwani na Tanga under the now disbanded Big Results Now (BRN) programme (URT, 2016).[7] The close and intimate relationship between elites and investors in the sugar sector does not stop there, since it has influenced the institutional frameworks (the rules of the game) in the sugar sector.

3.2   Influence on Policy and Institutional Frameworks

After 1995, the sugar industry was largely reshaped by neo-liberal policies implemented by then President Mkapa, who not only spearheaded the legal and institutional framework reforms, but also took serious political decisions in defence of local producers. For example, the Sugar Board of Tanzania (SBT), established by the Sugar Industry Act No. 26 of 2001, regulates all sugar-related activities in the country. Its regulations provide that an outgrower needs a minimum farm size of 0.4 ha within a 40 km radius from a registered miller, to which outgrowers are obliged to sell their sugarcane. This requires outgrowers to be registered by the SBT in their own names or that of the association they belong to, as well as having to enter into a commercial agreement with a sugar factory to which the outgrower has to sell his or her sugarcane (FAO, 2012).

Although the sugar business was formerly liberalized in 1992, the procurement and distribution of locally produced sugar is concentrated in a handful of private companies (Massimba et al., 2013). They collect sugar from producers and store it in their warehouses, mostly in Dar es Salaam in the case of sugar produced in Morogoro. They then distribute it to wholesalers around the country. Given their monopolistic access to sales of sugar and their monopsonistic access to producers, who also favour this system, distributors decide to whom and where to sell or not sell. This arrangement adds to the transportation costs incurred by traders, as they have to purchase sugar from Dar es Salaam and then bring it back to their customers (Massimba et al., 2013). As Massimba et al. (2013, p. 17) further observe, these elements 'cannot simply be undermined in the view of the regulatory frameworks since they are the key drivers that determine and safeguard the interests of all chain actors within the sugar value chain'. It is this local business network, with access permits to import sugar, whose actions significantly affect the industry, especially when the local markets are flooded with cheap sugar.

The current sugar industry's regulatory framework remains inadequate to address all the downstream activities in the sugar sector. This significantly reduces the industry's contributions to rural livelihoods in sugar-growing regions and fails to deal with current contentious issues related to processing capacity, distribution, oligopolies and monopolies, and marketing and distribution (Gabagambi, 2013; Massimba et al., 2013; Smalley et al., 2014; Sulle, 2017a). A clear regulatory framework that safeguards the interests of the outgrowers in the liberalized and yet controlled sugar markets is critical. It is the failure of the regulatory agency, for instance, that hurts most of the poor outgrowers when those who are close to power manipulate import quotas for their own benefit and that of the ruling elites.

Having analysed the regulatory framework that governs the industry, the next section focuses on sugarcane production in the Kilombero Valley through the partnership between the KSCL and outgrowers. The section then goes beyond the KSCL to examine briefly the state of similar relationships between other sugarcane-producing companies in the country.

4.   THE INVESTOR–SMALLHOLDER RELATIONSHIP

Funded by the private-sector investment arm of the World Bank Group, the International Finance Corporation (IFC), the Commonwealth Development

Corporation, Standard Bank and two Dutch financial organizations (Smalley et al., 2014), the Kilombero Sugar Company (KSC) established its first factory in the Msolwa Area in the 1960s. The KSC was later nationalized in 1967 after implementation of the Arusha Declaration, which saw the government reassuming the management of industries of strategic importance to the country. From its inception, the company operated outgrower schemes by leasing about 9,562 ha from the central government, 8,000 ha of which were for sugarcane, while the remaining land was used for factories, offices, housing for staff and social amenities. The company runs two sugarcane crushing and processing facilities on its estate (Illovo, 2014).

4.1   How the Relationship between KSCL and Its Outgrowers was Built and Sustained

In 1998 Illovo, a South African sugar company, acquired the majority shares in the company and then became KSCL. However, at present the Illovo Group is fully owned by Associated British Foods plc, which owns 75 per cent of the total company shares. Nonetheless, the Tanzanian government has retained 25 per cent of the KSCL shares.[8] KSCL has embraced the nucleus estate/outgrower model in order to enhance sugarcane production not only with the estates but with the outgrowers as well, in line with the core aim of SAGCOT.[9] The implementation of the Arusha Declaration in 1967 gave the central government the opportunity to reclaim the management of the company and its commercial value (ibid.).

The company strengthened its relationship with its outgrowers through various arrangements. Firstly, it began to issue cheap loans to outgrowers to increase production. Secondly, the company set up a road maintenance programme on its own estates and outgrowers' fields to facilitate production. Thirdly, it expanded on the provision of health services and supported both primary and secondary schools in the area. The company also mobilized funding to improve outgrowers' productivity from local commercial banks, the World Bank and European Union (Smalley et al., 2014; Sulle, 2017b).

As a result of these incentives, the company was able to lure many outgrowers to put most of their farmland into sugarcane farming. By 2015, KSCL was buying sugarcane from over 8,500 registered farmers cultivating about 12,000 ha with sugarcane and producing nearly 600,000 tonnes of cane (Sulle and Smalley, 2015; Smalley et al., 2014). The KSCL partnership with outgrowers is based on the Cane Supply Agreement (CSA), which is renegotiated and signed by the company and the outgrower associations every three years. The CSA stipulates the division of proceeds between the company and the outgrowers. If neither party is happy, the CSA provides room for amendment every season as needed (Smalley et al., 2014). In 2013–14, the outgrowers received US$35.6 per tonne of delivered sugarcane before adjustments for sucrose levels and actual sales are made. Once all the processed sugar is sold, the company and outgrowers share their proceeds at a rate of 57 per cent for outgrowers and 43 per cent for the company (Smalley et al., 2014).

From July 2017 to date, however, the proceeds-sharing arrangement changed to 40 per cent for outgrowers and 60 per cent for the company. The changes were described by interviewed company officials as resulting from the company surpassing the amount of tonnage produced by outgrower sugarcane. KSCL's partnership with its outgrowers is somewhat different from what is usual with contract farming, where farmers are used to selling only the primary product to the buyer for a given price. The combination of a central major nucleus investment that allows for the clustering of activities around research stations, larger farms with outgrower schemes, infrastructure development (roads and communication), access to irrigation, industrial processing, storage facilities, transport and logistics hubs that impact local communities has made the KSCL, at least on paper, a key investment example that is worth replicating. However, under the KSCL and CSA arrangement, farmers have some space, though limited, to participate in decision-making meetings, including with those who decide on that year's price for sugarcane, but have limited or no access to downstream business decisions regarding sugar (Sulle, 2017b).

Despite the political support KSCL has enjoyed from the beginning of its operation in the country due to the apparent success of its business model of working with local farmers, the company was not able to secure more land to implement its expansion strategies because of the lack of readily available land. Most of the targeted land is village land (Boudreaux, 2012; Sulle, 2015), interfering with which provokes different reactions from both the government and local communities. For instance, in Ruipa and Mpofu villages, the government planned to allocate all the land formerly owned by the SBT to KSCL to replace land it could not recover from villages in the Kilombero Valley (Chachage, 2012).

However, since the SBT did not develop the area for many years and villagers were using and deriving benefit from the land, the only way the SBT could get the land back was to fully compensate the villagers, particularly after they won a court case. As a result of the court case, the SBT conducted a valuation of the area and determined that the cost of compensation would be about TZS11 billion (US$5 million). According to SBT officials, this sum of money prompted the KSCL board to propose incorporating the affected communities into the project as outgrowers.[10] The SBT proposal was in fact first suggested by the then Parliamentary Committee on Public Accounts under the Chairmanship of Honourable Zitto Kabwe back in 2015 (Kabwe, personal communication, 2015). In this way, the model for the local integration of farmers into commercial farming has found its way into policymaking in Tanzania.

4.2   KSCL-Outgrower Model as a Success Story in Tanzania

The KSC is often referred to as a success story in Tanzania's sugar sector. Its model, which combines estates and small-scale outgrowers, has been replicated, as increasing sugarcane production, by using outgrowers, is a core component of SAGCOT's and the Tanzanian government's wider strategy for sugar production (Sulle and Dancer, 2020). The government aimed to incorporate other investors into large-scale agricultural investments by transforming the sector from small-scale production and pastoralism into modern commercial farming. Smallholders were incorporated into the mainstream commercial agribusiness through contract farming and outgrower schemes (Maganga et al., 2016). Around 2011 to 2015, President Kikwete especially encouraged development partners to allocate resources to develop the SAGCOT region. Within SAGCOT, the government and its partners aimed to bring 350,000 ha of land into profitable production to transform 100,000 small-scale farmers into commercial farming, thereby creating 420,000 new employment opportunities that could potentially lift 2 million people out of poverty and generate $1.2 billion in annual farming revenue by 2030 (ERM, 2012).

Despite these grand ambitions, the SAGCOT blueprint notes that most international and domestic investors tend to neglect the agricultural sector for other equally viable sectors due to the high risks involved. The blueprint argues that SAGCOT will therefore need to reduce the anticipated costs and risks for most investors. To minimize investors' costs in the early stages of their investment, the blueprint proposes to grant soft loans to local investors that intend to partner with smallholders and outgrowers in the SAGCOT corridor area (SAGCOT, 2011b). Hence, SAGCOT established its Catalytic Fund, which was extended to the agribusiness that incorporated smallholder farmers into its value chains. The government of Tanzania, its development partners and the private sector are reportedly the main funders of the Catalytic Fund.[11]

In addition, the World Bank (henceforward 'the Bank') manages the basket fund for implementing various SAGCOT projects, including matching grants for funding meant for investors who are willing to partner with or ready to support smallholders. While the Bank initially decided to hold on to its standard principles of compliance in issuing funding to states, including the latter's recognition and protection of the rights of Indigenous Peoples, in early 2016 it abruptly waived this requirement for Tanzania. As a result, on 10 March 2016, the Bank's Board of Directors 'approved $70 million in new financing to support Tanzania's agriculture sector and strengthen it by linking smallholder farmers to agribusinesses for boosting incomes and job-led growth'.[12] Most of the funding has been directed towards implementing SAGCOT (SAGCOT, 2011a).[13]

Three months after securing its investment funds, in June 2016 SAGCOT awarded five local agro-investors US$700,000 to expand their agricultural activities. The first grant beneficiaries of SAGCOT's funds include companies processing and supplying sugarcane, milk and dairy products, and rice in six growth clusters. So far, SAGCOT has set three assessment criteria for companies seeking finance, including the creditworthiness of the proposed business concept (40 per cent), the business's potential to reach more underserved smallholders (35 per cent) and the applicant's prior experience (25 per cent) (SAGCOT, 2012). The SAGCOT initiative builds on existing projects while introducing new ones. Its documents aptly state that it aims to facilitate the development of clusters of profitable agricultural businesses within the SAGCOT corridor. Building on existing operations and planned investments, the clusters are likely to bring together agricultural research stations, nucleated larger farms and ranches with outgrower schemes, irrigated block-farming operations, processing and storage facilities, transport and logistics hubs, and improved 'last-mile' infrastructure for farms and local communities (SAGCOT, 2011b, p. 17). All in all, ideas about agricultural investments mirror the KSCL's organization of a major investment that links outgrower schemes to a whole range of exchanges in relation to finance, input and marketing.

The impacts of the nucleus-outgrower model are context-specific. Dancer and Sulle (2015) analysed the employment data of a large-scale KSCL sugarcane plantation in Kilombero, Tanzania, which is used as the model for nucleus-outgrower schemes in the SAGCOT area (Nshala et al., 2013; Smalley et al., 2014). Their longitudinal analysis comparing 1992 and 2013 employment data shows that many more people were employed by the company in 1992 than in 2013: in 1992 there were 4,503 permanent employees, and only 870 employees in 2013 (see Table 5.2).

Disaggregating the employment data reveals that women are disproportionately and negatively affected by lower employment figures. For instance, while 495 women had permanent positions in 1992 (Mbilinyi and Semakafu, 1995), by 2013 there were only 110 women in permanent positions (Dancer and Sulle, 2015). The decline may be because companies are often interested in having more seasonal and casual labourers than permanent employees (Shivji, 2009). Another explanation is that sugar production is becoming increasingly mechanized, with increasing productivity per employee, combined with the increased use of outsourced labour now employed in outgrower schemes. Indeed, recent studies examining three models of farming: outgrowing, commercial farming and plantations in Ghana, Kenya and Zambia, have demonstrated that plantations create few jobs and that the jobs created are of

Table 5.2　　Longitudinal comparison of workforce employment status in KSCL by gender

	Men		Women		Total	
Year	1992	2013	1992	2013	1992	2013
Permanent	4,008 (44%)	760 (36%)	495 (64%)	110 (27%)	4,503 (45%)	870 (34%)
Seasonal	4,861 (52%)	1,259 (59%)	228 (29%)	250 (61%)	5,089 (51%)	1,509 (59%)
Other non-permanent	344 (4%)	117 (5%)	56 (7%)	49 (12%)	400 (4%)	166 (7%)
Total	9,213 (92%)	2,136 (84%)	779 (8%)	409 (16%)	9,992	2,545

Source: 1992 data from Mbilinyi and Semakafu (1995, p. 68); 2013 data supplied by KSCL Human Resources, April 2014. Percentage figures for men and women represent the proportion of all men and all women working in each category of employment. Percentages in the vertical total column represent the proportion of the workforce working in each category of employment.

low quality, as they are mostly casual jobs. However, other studies show that outgrowing schemes and commercial farming create more local economic links (see the studies presented in Hall et al., 2017[14]) in part because, when new smallholders become involved in the production of sugarcane, it creates new needs such as casual labour in the field, new cane transport and the emergence of cutting companies, among others.

Another set of studies (Smalley et al., 2014; Sulle, 2017b; Dancer and Sulle, 2015) found that sugarcane farming had mixed impacts on households. Despite increased sugarcane production in Kilombero over time, few farmer families that have participated in production have diversified their economic activities. Families that depend on sugarcane production alone remain vulnerable to other potential risks, such as price fluctuations, low records of sucrose levels for sugarcane delivered to the company, and the recorded tonnage delivered. Moreover, as a result of the increasing local demand for sugar, cane production is becoming a lucrative business, attracting wealthy individuals who are currently accumulating poor farmers' land and taking advantage of the business opportunities associated with cane production, such as cane-cutting, loading and transportation.

A critical consequence of sugarcane monocropping in the Kilombero Valley is the declining area of land devoted to food production, which is forcing poor families to commute from their sugarcane-producing villages to near or faraway villages to acquire plots for growing food crops. All these direct and indirect consequences have a hefty impact on families who have to incur travel costs, waste time travelling and find it more difficult to care for their

Table 5.3   *Selected statistics from Tanzanian general elections*

	CCM share of presidential vote (%)	Nearest challenger share of presidential vote (%)	Turnout for presidential election (%)	CCM share of parliamentary vote (%)	CCM share of all parliamentary seats (%)*
2015	58	40	67	59	69
2010	63	27	43	60	74
2005	80	12	72	70	85
2000	72	16	84	65	87
1995	62	28	77	59	80

Source: Adapted from Poulton (2017, p. 8) with sources from: http://www.nec.go.tz (various election reports), http://africanelections.tripod.com/tz.html (both accessed 16 November 2022). * Poulton noted that different sources give different figures for the total number of seats during the various parliaments, so there could be a small margin of error in the figures in this column.

children. As a result, in the Kilombero Valley, cases of dropping out of school and teenage pregnancies have been reported (Smalley et al., 2014; Dancer and Sulle, 2015; Bilinga, 2019).

4.3   The Politics of Outgrowers' Partnership and Land Acquisition

From 1995 to 2015, the Kilombero Valley recorded an increasing political shift towards the opposition party Chadema. For example, in the 2015 general election, all the wards in the Kilombero Valley, where sugarcane plantations are located, went to the opposition party because of local dissatisfaction with the ruling party and the local elites (Blache, 2019). The ongoing political trans-formation in the country and the expected benefits from government shifted the political dynamics on the ground. The decline in the votes for the ruling party in the rural areas of Kilombero District are not unique. The broader outlook of the election results, recently collected by Colin Poulton, further shows similar trends in other parts of the country (Table 5.3).

Nonetheless, for years, despite a hostile policy environment, smallhold-ers have remained resilient and absorbed shocks, even after the disastrous implementation of structural adjustment programmes, which rolled back state provision of inputs and extension services. Policy reforms carried out from the early 2000s, which include reducing heavy taxes on agricultural produce and encouraging private investments and innovation (Wiggins and Keats, 2014), have boosted farmers' outputs and incomes. SAGCOT may be changing its still contradictory narratives. For example, during one of our interviews, an official at the SAGCOT Secretariat claimed that the current SAGCOT leader-ship did not establish SAGCOT. The official explained that, unlike previous leaders, the current leadership is pro-smallholder. A SAGCOT senior executive confirmed this change, stating that '[s]mall-scale farmers/smallholders can surpass large-scale farmers in some high-value crops because smallholders not only put [in] knowledge but love … they feel farming is part of their life'.[15] However, SAGCOT's blueprint and other documents issued by its proponents do not fully emphasize that growth in Tanzania's agricultural sector is driven by its smallholders, who contribute more than 90 per cent of the country's total production (Yvonne et al., 2014).

Even though the KSCL stands out as a success story of good relations between outgrowers and the company, the fact that outgrowers' trust in the company's staff has been volatile since the 1980s has been documented (Smalley et al., 2014). Interviewed farmers and leaders observed that outgrowers feel a lack of transparency in respect of KSCL's honesty in exchange deals, as well as among the Tanzanian company's staff who determine sucrose levels and the weight of cane outgrowers deliver to the processing mills. This is known from other contexts (see Buur et al., 2020) as there is no independent authority to regulate and monitor company data regarding production, sucrose levels (a key determinant for payment) or efficiency (overall profit from the industry). Outgrowers and state agencies simply rely on the trustworthiness of the companies.

It is therefore not surprising that, while the sugar industry in Tanzania has created opportunities for outgrowers, the sugar industry and its involvement in the national economy remains subject to contested debate. Land disputes have been on the rise and will continue to do so due to the continuing claiming of lands for large-scale agricultural investments (Smalley, 2013). In terms of sugarcane production, smallholders are being pushed off their land by more successful farmers and have to search for farmland in distant areas (Smalley, 2013).

5.   CONCLUSION

This chapter has argued that the current relationship between smallholders and investors is changing over time and that the politics of resource ownership, including the ongoing political transformation of the country, are shaping this relationship. The case of KSCL and its partnership with its outgrowers suggests that the reciprocal exchange deal, that at first seemed ideal, has had a mixed effect since different parties have different outcomes, and more importantly have different expectations. Although the relationship is not static, it has changed and will continue to change over time. The relationship provides benefits to many households, mostly medium- and large-scale farmers, but the impact of the relationship between small-scale producers and sugar producers is highly differentiated. Along gender lines, there are huge differences: only a few low-quality jobs are created on plantations, few of which go to women. Given the poor policy, legal and institutional frameworks that govern nucleus-outgrower schemes and large-scale land-based investments, even those who partner with small-scale producers are not well supported.

For KSCL, its engagement with outgrowers needs to be viewed against its attempt to build its reputation as a model for how to organize the relationship between itself and the cane-producers. This model has largely been adopted by various development partners. The KSCL has, in past years, managed to secure funding to support the rehabilitation of its infrastructure and those of its outgrowers not only for its operations in Tanzania but also in Mozambique (Paradza and Sulle, 2015) as part of the EU's accompanying measures. As such, although the company's direct financial support, apart from its payments for outgrowers' produce, is limited, private development partners have contributed to improving outgrowers' conditions in the area. Support for outgrowers is deemed necessary by the company in order to increase outgrowers' share of cane production to meet the demands of the mill.

Yet, the growing interest in private-sector investments that will engage smallholder farmers in various arrangements, such as contract farming or outgrowing schemes, must be viewed in broader terms. As a type of contract farming, outgrower schemes are not only preferred by Tanzanian policymakers but are also being promoted by African governments and development agencies (FAO, 2013; World Bank, 2013; Smalley et al., 2014). The interest of stakeholders in outgrower schemes and contract farming and its promotion by influential organizations such as the World Bank and the FAO need to be viewed in the context of post-structural adjustment programmes, in which governments rolled back the provision of credit, subsidies and extension services to farmers after 1980 (Oya, 2012; Key and Runsten, 1999; Dirven, 1996; Schejtman, 1996; Smalley et al., 2014). This has created a space for private investors to provide finance, market access and different types of services to support outgrower schemes and contract farming, thus filling in a space left by the retreat of the state.

This chapter has examined the relationship between investors and outgrowers (part of local populations) in Tanzania. It has highlighted the exchange relationships that centre around input and service provision, access to credit schemes, and importantly a clear, if contested, and stable market for sugarcane. The compatible interest between investors and ruling elites in the sugar industry means that the ruling elites facilitate and shield the investors from complaints from local populations. This means that power is often concentrated along the ruling elite/investor relationship axis, which at different times will support both the investors in sugar production and by implication the outgrowers by restricting sugar imports into Tanzania. In this sense, smallholder–investor relations cannot be detached from the relationship with the ruling elites, which extend to policies, politics and election promises that shape investments in land. However, as long as the institution and regulatory frameworks governing large-scale investments do not address the positions of local populations, including outgrowers, investors will continue to have the upper hand.

NOTES

1. The TNBC is an institution established under Presidential Circular No. 1 of 2001 to provide a forum for public- and private-sector dialogue for change. Since its formation the Kilimo Kwanza Initiative has enjoyed presidential support with close monitoring from the office of the prime minister.
2. TNBC, 'Ten Pillars of Kilimo Kwanza', Tanzania On-Line, Dar es Salaam (2009), http://www.tzonline.org/pdf/tenpillarsofkilimokwanza.pdf (see Sulle, 2015) (accessed 20 September 2019).
3. For more details about SAGCOT, its partners and project plans, see Southern Agricultural Growth Corridor of Tanzania, 'SAGCOT', http://www.sagcot.com/ (accessed 18 October 2019).
4. Besides SAGCOT and Kilimo Kwanza, other influential initiatives include the 'Comprehensive Africa Agriculture Development Programme (CAADP)' and the 'New Alliance for Food Security and Nutrition' initiative (New Alliance). CAADP, better known as the Maputo Declaration, is Africa's policy framework for agricultural transformation, wealth creation, food security and nutrition, economic growth and prosperity for all; it was passed by the heads of African states and governments in Maputo in 2003 (Sulle, 2015). The New Alliance launched by the heads of G8 countries in collaboration with six African heads of state and governments in Camp David in May 2012 aims to foster private-sector and development partners' investments in African agriculture and lift 50 million people out of poverty by 2022 (Sulle, 2015; Sulle and Hall, 2013).
5. One reason why the grand visions of agricultural commercialization and transformation through partnership between investors and smallholders has not yielded the expected results is that, despite the existence of policies and legislation, there is still a lack of adequate information regarding land-based investments in the country. The institution charged with collecting, monitoring and updating information on land-based investments, especially the Tanzania Investment Centre, is highly understaffed (Sulle and Hall, 2013).
6. A 'jaggery' is an unrefined sugar product that is sometimes referred to as a non-centrifugal sugar catalyst. It is not spun during processing, which would remove the nutritious molasses.
7. Through the now disbanded BRN and SAGCOT, the government aimed to conclude 25 commercial farming deals for paddy and sugarcane by 2015 (ibid.). While there is little publicly available information about BRN's progress towards meeting these goals, key informant interviews reveal that access to land has, so far, been the major hurdle in implementing large-scale deals. The Minister for Agriculture, Livestock and Fisheries conceded in Parliament that the government was still reconciling land-based conflicts in areas earmarked for BRN projects (Sulle and Hall, 2013; MALF 2016/17). Additionally, for a number of years, the EU has financed capacity development and infrastructural development for both estate and outgrower schemes in Kilombero Valley as part of the Accompanying Measures Programme (Smalley et al., 2014). Recently, the EU has also funded

a two-phase irrigation and infrastructure development project for Kilombero outgrowers (Dubb et al., 2017).
8.   See https://www.illovosugarafrica.com/about-us/tanzania (accessed 11 January 2023).
9.   URT, Development Vision (see Nshala et al., 2013).
10.   Interview with Sugar Board Official, Dar Es Salaam, 11 April 2017.
11.   'Catalytic Trust Fund: Funding Opportunity Advertisement Call for Business Concept Proposals' http://www.sagcot.com/newsdetails/article//catalytic-trust -fund-funding-opportunity-advertisement-call-for-business-concept-proposals/ (accessed 4 August 2017).
12.   See http://www.sagcot.com/newsdetails/article//new-project-to-link-farmers-to -agribusiness-in-tanzania/ (accessed 5 August 2017).
13.   'World Bank Allows Tanzania to Sidestep Rule Protecting Indigenous Groups', http://www.huffingtonpost.com/entry/world-bank-allows-tanzania-to-sidestep -rule-protecting-indigenous-groups_us_57607769e4b09c926cfd6b1c (accessed 27 August 2017). This did not go uncontested, as the United States, a key supporter of SAGCOT, immediately issued a statement through its Treasury expressing its disappointment with the Bank's decision.
14.   Providing an overall analysis of three case studies of outgrowers, commercial farming and plantations from Ghana, Kenya and Zambia, Hall et al. (2017) con-cluded that the three agricultural commercialization models affect communities differently and that the outcomes of such investments are context-specific.
15.   Interview with senior SAGCOT Secretariat staff, Dar Es Salaam, 11 August 2017.

REFERENCES

Aminzade, R. (2013) 'Race, nation, and citizenship in post-colonial Africa: The case of Tanzania.' New York: Cambridge University Press.
Baum, E. (1968) 'Land use in the Kilombero Valley: From shifting cultivation towards permanent farming', in H. Ruthenberg (ed) *Smallholder Farming and Smallholder Development in Tanzania: Ten Case Studies*, Muenchen: Weltforum Verlag, pp. 21–50.
Bilinga, M. (2019) 'Examining the influence of sexuality education programmes on Tanzanian pupils' knowledge and skills on pregnancy: A case of primary schools in Morogoro Region', *Tanzania Journal of Sociology*, 5(27), 58–71.
Blache, A. (2019) 'Grabbing land, catching votes! Land and the 2015 election cam-paign in Kilombero District, Tanzania', *Les Cahiers d'Afrique de l'Est/The East African Review*, 53. https://doi.org/10.4000/eastafrica.791.
Booth, D., Cooksey, B., Golooba-Mutabe, F. and Kanyinga, K. (2012) 'East African prospects', in A. Ronald (ed) *Race, Nation and Citizenship in Post-Colonial Africa: The Case of Tanzania*, Cambridge: Cambridge University Press, pp. 35.
Boudreaux, K. (2012) 'An assessment of concerns related to land tenure in the SAGCOT region', Unpublished report for USAID Tanzania.
Buur, L., Mondlane, C. and Baloi, O. (2011) Strategic privatisation: Rehabilitating the Mozambican sugar industry, *Review of African Political Economy*, 38(128), 235–56.
Buur, L., Nystrand, M.J. and Pedersen R.H. (2017) 'The political economy of land and natural resource investments in Africa: An analytical framework', Danish Institute for International Studies (DIIS) Working Paper, Copenhagen: DIIS.

Buur, L., Pedersen, R.H., Nystrand, M.J. and Macuane, J.J. (2019) 'Understanding the three key relationships in natural resource investments in Africa: An analytical framework', *The Extractive Industries and Society*, 6(4), 1195–204.

Buur, L., Pedersen, R.H., Nystrand, M.J., Macuane, J.J. and Jacob, T. (2020) 'The politics of natural resource investments and rights in Africa: A theoretical approach', *The Extractive Industries and Society*, 7(3), 918–30.

Chachage, C. (2012) 'Kilombero Sugar Company/Illovo: Economically sabotaged?', Udadisi blog, 24 January, http://udadisi.blogspot.com/2012/01/kilombero-sugarcompanyillovo.html (accessed 24 June 2017).

Chachage, C. and Baha, B. (2010) *Accumulation by Land Dispossession and Labour Devaluation in Tanzania: The Case of Biofuel and Forestry Investments in Kilwa and Kilolo*, Dar es Salaam: Land Rights Research and Resources Institute (LARRRI/HAKIARDHI) and Oxfam.

Chachage, C. and Mbunda, R. (2009) *The State of the then NAFCO, NARCO and Absentee Landlords, Farms/Ranches in Tanzania*, Dar es Salaam: Land Rights Research and Resource Institute (LARRRI/HAKIARDHI).

Dancer, H. and Sulle, E. (2015) 'Gender implications of agricultural commercialisation: The case of sugarcane production in Kilombero District, Tanzania', Future Agricultures Working Paper, Future Agricultures, Brighton.

Dirven, M. (1996) 'Agroindustry and small-scale agriculture: A comparative synthesis of different experiences', Report LC/R.1663, Economic Commission for Latin America and the Caribbean, Santiago, Chile.

Dubb, A., Scoones, I. and Woodhouse, P. (2017) 'The political economy of sugar in southern Africa: Introduction', *Journal of Southern African Studies*, 43(3), 447–70.

ERM (2012) *Southern Agricultural Growth Corridor of Tanzania (SAGCOT) Strategic Regional Environmental and Social Assessment*, Interim report, prepared for the Government of Tanzania, July 2012, http://www.sagcot.com/uploads/media/Interim_Report__SAGCOT_SRESA_Final_12_02.pdf (accessed 12 June 2017).

FAO (2012) *Analysis of Incentives and Disincentives for Sugar in the United Republic of Tanzania: Monitoring African Food and Agricultural Policies*, Rome: FAO.

FAO (2013) *Trends and Impacts of Foreign Investment in Developing Country Agriculture: Evidence from Case Studies*, Rome: FAO.

Gabagambi, D.M. (2013) 'Tanzania's growth experience following economic reforms: Comparative perspectives with Vietnam', *International Journal of Humanities and Social Science*, 3(9), 97–106.

Hall, R., Scoones, I. and Tsikata, D. (eds) (2015) *Africa's Land Rush: Rural Livelihoods and Agrarian Change*. Woodbridge, UK: James Currey, https://repository.uwc.ac.za/bitstream/handle/10566/2459/IntroChapLandRush_0.pdf?sequence=1& isAllowed (accessed 21 June 2017).

Hall, R., Scoones, I. and Tsikata, D. (2017) 'Plantations, outgrowers and commercial farming in Africa: Agricultural commercialisation and implications for agrarian change', *Journal of Peasant Studies*, 44(3), 515–37.

Illovo Sugar Ltd (2014) *Tanzania Socio-Economic Impact Assessment: Internal Management Report*, Durban: Illovo.

Kamanga, K.C. (2008) *The Agrofuel Industry in Tanzania: A Critical Enquiry into Challenges and Opportunities – A Research Report*, Dar es Salaam: Hakiardhi and Oxfam Livelihoods Initiative for Tanzania (JOLIT).

Key, N. and Runsten, D. (1999) 'Contract farming, smallholders, and rural development in Latin America: The organization of agroprocessing firms and the scale of outgrower production', *World Development*, 27(2), 381–401.

Lindsay, J., Deininger, K. and Hilhorst, T. (2016) 'Compulsory land acquisition in developing countries: Shifting paradigm or entrenched legacy', in *Proceedings for the Annual World Bank Conference on Land and Poverty*, Washington DC: Cambridge University Press, pp. 14–18.

Maganga, F.P., Askew, K., Odgaard, R. and Stein, H. (2016) 'Dispossession through formalization: Tanzania and the G8 Land Agenda in Africa', *Journal of Asian and African Studies*, 40, 3–49.

Majaliwa, C. (2016) 'Sugar boom as "the 2Ks" resume production', *Daily News*, 25 May, http://dailynews.co.tz/index.php/home-news/50085-sugar-boom-as-the-2ks -resume-production (accessed 25 September 2016).

Massay, G.E. and Kassile, T. (2019) 'Land-based investments in Tanzania: Legal frame- work and realities on the ground' in S. Moyo, P. Jha and P. Yeros (eds), *Reclaiming Africa: Advances in African Economic, Social and Political Development*, Singapore: Springer, pp. 163–81.

Massimba, J., Malaki, C. and Waized, B. (2013) *Consultancy Services for Collecting Policy Based Evidence for Enhancing Sugar Industry Regulatory Framework of Tanzania*, Morogoro: SUGECO.

Mbilinyi, M. and Semakafu, A.M. (1995) 'Gender and employment on sugar cane plantations in Tanzania', Sectoral and Working Discussion Papers, no. 85, Geneva: International Labour Organization.

Nshala, R., Locke, A. and Duncan, J. (2013) 'A proposed land for equity scheme in Tanzania: Issues and assistance', Discussion Paper, Overseas Development Institute, London.

Oya, C. (2012) 'Contract farming in sub-Saharan Africa: A survey of approaches, debates and issues', *Journal of Agrarian Change*, 12(1), 1–33.

Paradza, G. and Sulle, E. (2015) 'Agrarian struggles over resources: Insights from two sugarcane plantations in Mozambique' in R. Hall, I. Scoones and D. Tsikata (eds) *Africa's Land Rush: Implications for Rural Livelihoods and Agrarian Change*, Oxford: James Currey, pp. 150–61.

Pedersen, R. and Buur, L. (2016) 'Beyond land grabbing: Old morals and new perspec- tives on contemporary investments', *Geoforum*, 72(1), 77–81.

Peters, P. (2013) 'Conflicts over land and threats to customary tenure in Africa', *African Affairs*, 112(449), 543–62.

Peters, P. (2016) 'The role of the land policies, land laws and agricultural development in challenges to rural livelihoods in Africa', *Afriche e orienti (Italian Journal on African and Middle Eastern Studies)*, 17(3), 25–45.

Poulton, C. (2017) 'APRA policy processes and political economy: Tanzania country review', APRA Working Paper 05, APRA: Brighton.

Purdon, M. (2013) 'Land acquisitions in Tanzania: Strong sustainability, weak sustain- ability and the importance of comparative methods', *Journal of Agricultural and Environmental Ethics*, 26(6), 1127–56.

SAGCOT (2011a) *Investment Blueprint*, http://www.sagcot.com/uploads/media/ InvestBlueprint-SAGCOT_High_res.pdf (accessed 26 May 2017).

SAGCOT (2011b) *Southern Agricultural Corridor: Investment Blueprint*, http://www .sagcot.com/uploads/media/Invest-Blueprint- SAGCOT_High_res.pdf (accessed 26 May 2017).

SAGCOT (2012) *SAGCOT Investment Partnership Program: Opportunities for Investors in the Sugar Sector*, Dar es Salaam, Tanzania: SAGCOT Centre Limited.

Schejtman, A. (1996) 'Agroindustry and small-scale agriculture: Conceptual guidelines for a policy to encourage linkage between them', Rep. LC/R.1660, Com. Econ. Am. Lat. Caribe (CEPAL), Santiago, Chile.

Scoones, I., Mavedzenge, B., Murimbarimba, F. and Sukume, C. (2018) 'Tobacco, contract farming, and agrarian change in Zimbabwe', *Journal of Agrarian Change*, 18(1), 22–42.

Shivji, I.G. (2009) *Accumulation in an African Periphery: A Theoretical Framework*, Dar es Salaam: Mkuki na Nyota Publishers Ltd.

Smalley, R. (2013) 'Plantations, contract farming and commercial farming areas in Africa: A comparative review', FAC Working Paper 55, Future Agriculture: Brighton.

Smalley, R., Sulle, E. and Malale, L. (2014) 'The role of the state and foreign capital in agricultural commercialization: The case of sugarcane outgrowers in Kilombero District', Tanzania: Future Agricultures Working Paper, Brighton.

Sulle, E. (2015) 'Land grabbing and commercialization duality: Insights from Tanzania's agricultural transformation agenda', *Afriche e orienti (Italian Journal on African and Middle Eastern Studies)*, 17(3), 109–28.

Sulle, E. (2017a) 'Of local people and investors: The dynamics of land rights configuration in Tanzania', Working Paper, Danish Institute for International Studies (DIIS), Copenhagen.

Sulle, E. (2017b) 'Social differentiation and the politics of land: Sugar cane outgrowing in Kilombero, Tanzania', *Journal of Southern African Studies*, 43(3), 517–33.

Sulle, E. and Dancer, H. (2020) 'Gender, politics and sugarcane commercialisation in Tanzania', *Journal of Peasant Studies*, 47(5), 973–92.

Sulle, E. and Hall, R. (2013) 'Reframing the New Alliance agenda: A critical assessment based on insights from Tanzania', Policy Brief by Institute for Poverty, Land and Agrarian Studies and Future Agricultures Consortiums, Brighton.

Sulle, E. and Nelson, F. (2009) *Biofuels, Land Access and Rural Livelihoods in Tanzania*, London: International Institute for Environment and Development (IIED).

Sulle, E. and Nelson, F. (2013) 'Biofuels investment and community land tenure in Tanzania: The case of Bioshape, Kilwa District', Working Paper 73, Future Agricultures Consortium, Brighton.

Sulle, E. and Smalley, R. (2015) 'The state and foreign capital in agricultural commercialization in Tanzania: The case of Kilombero Sugar Company' in R. Hall, I. Scoones and D. Tsikata (eds), *Africa's Land Rush: Implications for Rural Livelihoods and Agrarian Change*, Oxford: James Currey, pp. 114–31.

Sulle, E., Smalley, R. and Malale, L. (2014) 'Opportunities and challenges in Tanzania's sugar industry', Lessons for SAGCOT and the New Alliance: Future Agricultures Consortium and PLAAS Policy Brief, Brighton.

Tanzania Daily News (2016a) 'Tanzania: Cuban firms invited to invest in sugar, drugs' (31 August), http://allafrica.com/stories/201608310026.html (accessed 16 June 2017).

Tanzania Daily News (2016b) 'Tanzania: Bakhresa lands sugar covenant' (7 October), http://allafrica.com/stories/201610070108.html (accessed 27 October 2016).

URT (2013) *Tanzania Development, Vision 2025, Big Results Now: National Key Result Area – Agriculture Lab*, Dar es Salaam: United Republic of Tanzania.

URT (2016) 'Hotuba ya Waziri wa Kilimo, Mifugo na Uvuvi Mheshimiwa Mwigulu Lameck Nchemba Madelu (MB)', Kuhusu Makadirio ya Mapato na Matumizi ya Fedha ya Wizara ya Kilimo, Mifugo na Uvuvi kwa Mwaka 2016/2017, Speech by the Minister for Agriculture, Livestock and Fisheries, Honorable

Mwigulu Lameck Nchemba Madelu (MP), Regarding the Estimate for Revenue and Expenditure for the Ministry of Agriculture, Livestock and Fisheries for the Year 2016/2017, https://docplayer.net/66617299-Hotuba-ya-waziri-wa-kilimo-mifugo-na -uvuvi-mheshimiwa-mwigulu-lameck-nchemba-madelu-mb-kuhusu-makadirio-ya -matumizi-ya-fedha-ya-wizara-ya-kilimo.html (accessed 20 October 2017).

URT (2017) 'Hotuba ya Waziri wa Kilimo, Mifugo na Uvuvi Mheshimiwa, Eng. Dkt. Charles John Tizeba (MB)' Kuhusu Makadirio ya Mapato na Matumizi ya Fedha ya Wizara ya Kilimo, Mifugo na Uvuvi kwa mwaka 2017/2018, https://docplayer.net/ 66617299-Hotuba-ya-waziri-wa-kilimo-mifugo-na-uvuvi-mheshimiwa-mwigulu -lameck-nchemba-madelu-mb-kuhusu-makadirio-ya-matumizi-ya-fedha-ya-wizara -ya-kilimo.html (accessed 17 June 2017).

URT (2020) 'Hotuba ya Waziri wa Kilimo, Mheshimiwa Japhet Ngailonga Hasunga (MP)', Kuhusu Makadirio ya Mapato na Matumizi ya Fedha ya Wizara ya Kilimo kwa Mwaka 2020/2021, Speech by the Minister for Agriculture, Honorable Jasephet Ngailonga Hasunga (MP), Regarding the Estimate for Revenue and Expenditure for the Ministry of Agriculture for the Year 2020/2021, https://www.kilimo .go.tz/uploads/HOTUBA_YA_WIZARA_YA_KILIMO_2020.pdf (accessed 20 November 2020).

Veit, P.G. and Larsen, G. (2013) 'Overlapping land and natural resource property rights: A comparative analysis from Africa' in *World Bank Conference on Land and Poverty*, 8–11 April 2013, Washington DC, USA: World Bank.

Wiggins, S. and Keats, S. (2014) 'Smallholder engagement with the private sector', EPS PEAKS, Department for International Development (DfID) http://www .bdsknowledge.org/dyn/bds/docs/868/TopicGuideonSmallholderEngagementwithpr ivatesecto.pdf (accessed 17 June 2018).

World Bank (2013) *Growing Africa: Unlocking the potential of agribusiness*, Washington, DC: World Bank.

Yvonne, P., Poulton, C., Frankenberger, T., Ajayi, O. and Finighan, J. (2014) 'African agriculture: Drivers of success for CAADP implementation', Synthesis report, Firetail, SOAS, Tango and CTA, http://www.firetail.co.uk/reports/Drivers%20of %20Success%20Synthesis%20Report.pdf (accessed 20 August 2017).

6. A failing local exchange deal: rights to land and resources in the WanBao rice investment in Mozambique

Lars Buur and Kathrin Beykirch

1. INTRODUCTION

Rice is a priority agricultural product for the Mozambican government, one that appears in all its agricultural policies. In both urban and rural settings, its population is dependent on this crop to cover its nutritional needs. Rice is also one of the most important basic food products in Mozambique, where the livelihoods of a large number of rural Mozambican farmers rely on it. Due to its fertile arable land and important river systems in the south, centre and north of the country, Mozambique has the capacity to produce most of what it consumes. Rice therefore matters in Mozambique: increasing rice production through both large-scale investments and smallholder production can help transform the economy by accelerating economic growth, creating jobs and strengthening the links between local economies and the global economy.

However, until now only a fraction of the increasing volumes of rice consumed in urban Mozambique has been covered by national rice production. Most of the rice consumed in the country comes instead from imports from Asian countries and is sold at a price that makes Mozambican rice uncompetitive on the national market.

Several large-scale investments in processing and rice production have been financed and implemented, such as the 60 million USD Complexo Agro-Industrial de Chókwè (Agro-Industrial Park in Chókwè or CAIC) and WanBao's 289 million USD investment in rice production and industrial plant in Xai-Xai, both located in southern Mozambique. Both investments have faced a series of problems since their implementation from flooding, failed rains and a lack of capital and supporting investments, having failed in different and spectacular ways despite some initial success.[1]

This chapter analyses the implementation of the WanBao investment by focusing on the relationship between small-scale rice producers and WanBao, a Chinese investor, as it evolved over time and exploring what types of exchange deals farmers involved in rice production established with WanBao. The chapter also analyses the relationships between WanBao, the ruling elite and local populations, as these had an important bearing on how the rice investment was implemented.

The chapter argues that, if one looks at the farmers who were trained by means of the rice investment, the WanBao initiative can to a considerable extent be considered a success, as it developed something approaching a reciprocal exchange deal, giving farmers access to training, new technologies and inputs. However, seen from a broader perspective in which farmers were excluded from the investment by the local state, while local ruling elite farmers obtained access to inputs and loans without using them productively, the picture becomes murkier. The fact that the investment failed economically is due less to relations between the investor and local farmers than to the dynamics of relations between the investor and the ruling elite, which undermined the economic feasibility of this initially promising investment in rice.

The chapter is based on research undertaken as part of the 'Hierarchies of Rights: Land and Investments in Africa' Research Programme, which studies how investments in sub-Saharan Africa affect local populations' rights based on a set of primarily qualitative comparative case studies.

The rest of the chapter proceeds as follows. Section 2 starts by giving a brief overview of the rice sector and its place in national agricultural policymaking in Mozambique. The section will also briefly analyse the national rice strategy, what it aimed to achieve and how it was conceived. Section 3 explores the implementation of the 20,000 ha Chinese WanBao investment in Xai-Xai, including the initial struggles over the land, and considers what type of local exchange deal evolved between WanBao and local rice farmers. The section also explores how the responsible state institution, Regadio de Baixo Limpopo – Empresa Pública (RBL-EP), which owned the land, acted with regard to land and procedural rights. Section 4 explores the wider relationships between RBL-EP and WanBao and between RBL-EP and local rice farmers who became part of the WanBao outgrower scheme over time. Section 5 explores why, after being implemented, the WanBao investment failed and went bankrupt in 2018, despite being recapitalized twice. The conclusion briefly summarizes the main issues emerging from the analysis.

2. MOZAMBIQUE'S RICE SECTOR

Rice production in Mozambique was introduced by the Portuguese colonial government in the 1930s and 1940s, when it began to invest in irrigation schemes. Production flourished, and because rice had not yet become one of the major food crops consumed by Mozambicans, the country became a net exporter of rice. After independence, most rice production was nationalized and administered through large-scale production on state farms, where infrastructure had already been established by the colonial regime (Mosca, 2011). This mainly happened along the Nkomati and Limpopo river systems in the south of the country. However, state-owned land was slowly abandoned due in part due to local resistance to state farming and in part to the war of destabilization that turned into a civil war after 1978 and after 1980 was extended to all parts of the national territory (Hermele, 1988; Bowen, 1989; 2000). During this period, internally displaced rural farmers started settling on these abandoned state-farm lands, cultivating them both for their own food security and for commercial purposes, and feeding the main urban centres such as Xai-Xai in the Lower Limpopo river basin and Maputo. Along the river systems in the centre and north of Mozambique, rice production was now mainly carried out by smallholders and subsistence farmers.

During the civil war between 1977 and 1992, basic food production declined dramatically. The production of maize and rice was particularly affected, as it declined by 70 per cent. Almost simultaneously, during the 1980s and 1990s, rice gained in importance as a food crop in Mozambique, as it covered people's everyday food supplies, though it could not satisfy all the demand. This widening gap between production and consumption was covered by imports and humanitarian donations, which rose by a staggering 488 per cent (EUCORD, 2012, p. 21; Kajisa and Payongyong, 2008, p. 4). Despite favourable conditions for rice production, over the past decade domestic milled rice production has met only approximately 28 per cent of national rice consumption on average.

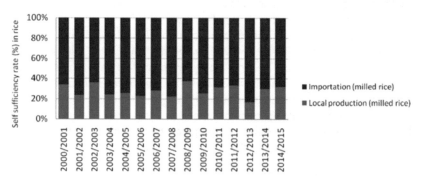

Source: NRDP (2016, p. 6). Data on imports has been sourced from FAO statistics. Local production of milled rice was calculated after adjusting for milling recovery and seed/feed losses from local paddy (rough rice) production data.

Figure 6.1   Proportion of domestic and imported rice in meeting the demand for consumption

As Figure 6.1 suggests, even through local production has indeed increased over the last decade, reliance on imported rice seems to have increased, as local production has been outstripped by the rapid increase in consumption. The widening fissure between domestic production and consumption has seen Mozambique import rice grains from rice-producing countries in Asia mainly through four trading houses. These imports are exerting a substantial strain and drain on the country's foreign exchange, trade balance and indeed food security.

Today, rice is one of the main basic food crops in Mozambique, especially for rural populations in the major river valleys (the Nkomati and Limpopo in the south; the Save and Zambezia in the central and northern regions) and an important basic food crop for the country's growing urban populations. The agricultural potential for the production of rice is estimated at 900,000 ha, with around 300,000 ha presently under cultivation (NRDP, 2016, p. 5), but it is unclear how much land is actually being utilized. It is relatively clear that land for rice is potentially available and also where the necessary infrastructure exists. More than 50 per cent of the potential area is in Zambezia and Sofala provinces, followed by 7 per cent in the provinces of Nampula and Cabo Delgado. The remaining land is to be found in the Frelimo stronghold of Gaza province, with a total of around 3 per cent (the Chókwè and Xai-Xai irrigation schemes), where paradoxically most of the irrigation infrastructure is also present (see Buur and Jacob, 2023 forthcoming). While rice production is possible in most of the country where there are major river basins, it is indicative of the consequences of the shift from the colonial to post-colonial period that the main irrigation capacity is situated in districts along the lower Limpopo basin in the south of the country. This is where the different regimes have invested in areas with settler populations and local communities that support these regimes. Potentially, however, the main rice-growing areas are in the central and northern districts of Zambezia and Sofala provinces, which are considered Renamo rebel provinces (Renamo being Frelimo's old foe from the civil war).

One consequence of this discrepancy between where the infrastructure is situated, where the investments have been made and where the main potential is located, is that productivity (yields per hectare) is extremely low, as Figure 6.2 shows.

Rice covers nutritional needs and food security, and it also represents economic survival for many rice farmers, who belong to the neglected rural population and often also to the poorest segments of society. In 2012, 80 per cent of the rural workforce in some parts in Mozambique were employed in the rice-producing sector (NRDP, 2016, p. 11). Rice farmers in Mozambique mainly belong to rural populations that are often considered poor, with 90 per cent of them working as smallholders on small plots of land (Interview:

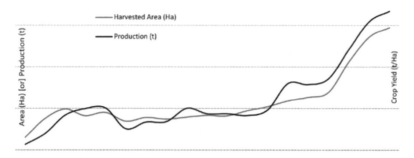

Source: Adopted from NRDP (2016, p. 5). English version: Trends in land area under rice cultivation and paddy (rough rice) production over the past two decades.[2]

Figure 6.2   Land use and rice production

MASA, Maputo, 17 November 2016). They produce up to 97.7 per cent of all rice based on subsistence rain-fed smallholder farming in what Frelimo-run governments in Mozambique since independence in 1975 have called the 'family sector'.

As rice production mainly takes place in rain-fed areas, it is highly exposed to climatic conditions. This is a paradox, given that most of the de facto irrigation capacity is located in the great river system of the Limpopo in the south of the country. Due to farmers' low-risk and low-input strategies, the average production level is 0.5–1.0 tonne/ha, which is very low and primarily consists of subsistence farming (NRDP, 2016, p. 3). In comparison, the global average for rice production is 4.3 t/ha, and the Sub-Saharan African average is 2.3 t/ha (NRDP, 2016, p. 11). A key characteristic is that Mozambican rice farmers are not well organized, unlike, for example, sugar farmers and producers of cane (see Buur et al., 2011; 2012). This makes the problem of collective action a major challenge to be overcome.

Due to an increase in the amount of land prepared for subsistence cultivation during the last ten years (see Figure 6.2), production has increased 2.83-fold according to the National Rice Development Programme (NRDP). However, the production average of 1.0 t/ha has stagnated. Due to increasing consumption, especially by growing urban populations, national production cannot provide sufficient amounts, so most of the demand must be covered by imports (see Figure 6.3). Since 2000 an average of 400,000 tonnes of rice has been imported yearly (NRDP, 2016, pp. 5–6).

Imported rice enters the country through international trading companies like Delta, ADC and Olam, who then sell it to warehouses, mainly state-owned, from which it is distributed across the country (Interviews: Olam, 25 January

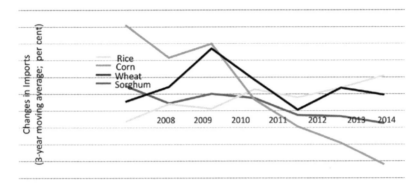

Source: NRDP (2017, p. 6). Importation data sourced from FAO statistics.

Figure 6.3   *Importation trends (three-year moving average) of major cereal grains in Mozambique*

2016; ADC, 10 January 2017, both in Maputo). Due to low import taxes, the imported rice can be sold more cheaply than the nationally produced rice, which is therefore not competitive in the domestic market.

It is commonly argued that the reasons for the low rice production are, inter alia:

• insufficient use of qualitative technologies and machinery
• low levels of access to infrastructure and support services
• weak financial services
• weak management of the water-supply systems in the fields
• a high level of post-harvest losses
• problematic climatic conditions that lead to both droughts and floods (NRDP, 2016, p. 3; MASA, 17 November 2016)

Furthermore, access to fertilizers and seeds is also problematic. According to Kajisa and Payongyong (2008, p. 5), only 2.5 per cent of rice farmers use fertilizers, while roughly 5.2 per cent use pesticides that are highly taxed and therefore expensive products that smallholders cannot afford (Interview: Japanese International Cooperation Agency (JICA), Maputo, January 2017). This means that Mozambican rice is of very low quality, and its only advantage over its Asian competitors is its relative 'freshness' (Interviews: MASA, 21 November 2016; Olam, 14 December 2016, both Maputo; NRDP, 2016, p. 4). Furthermore, as a high-level member of the Ministry of Agriculture and Food Security (MASA) (Interview: Maputo, 21 November 2016) stated, the whole rice value chain in Mozambique is incomplete due to the gap that exists between harvesting and milling.

The Mozambican government has acknowledged these problems and has mentioned increased national production as a goal in several agricultural policies and strategies over the last ten years. MASA (Interview, Maputo, 17 November 2016) states that rice is now the ministry's priority concern on a list of seven main basic food crops. The most important strategy in addressing the low level of rice production and productivity is the NRDP, which suggests that Mozambique has a high potential for increasing production in a relative short time span.

2.1   The Rice Strategy[3]

The National Rice Development Programme (NRDP) was first elaborated in 2009 as a response to the Japanese International Cooperation Agency's (JICA's) Coalition for African Rice Development programme (CARD),[4] but it was not approved for eight years. Parts of the programme have since been implemented, but inconsistently. We examine the aims of the policy programme, including how it was expected to benefit the rice sector and how and by whom the rice strategy was developed.

The NRDP's main goal was to increase national rice production in order to decrease rice imports (NRDP, 2016, p. 18). The strategy aimed to do this by increasing inputs to the sector, which was supposed to foster an increase in the average farm's productivity from roughly 1.0 t/ha to 1.8 t/ha by 2019 (NRDP, 2016, pp. 3–19) and total production from 357,305 t in 2015 to 624,177.5 t by 2018 (NRDP, 2016, p. 19). The 'inputs' were better rice production technologies for smallholders and improvements in the effectiveness of their use. This was expected to be achieved by, inter alia, capacity-building for rice producers; aligning value chain actors and supporters;[5] strengthening the links to other sectors; decreasing post-harvest losses in the field and in industry; and stabilizing the price in the main rice markets. As a first step before 2019, the strategy was planned to improve the quality, access and effective use of seeds and fertilizers, as well as to support improvements in rice-crop management and water management to cope with droughts and floods (NRDP, 2016, pp. 20–22). It also suggested promoting a reduction in the costs of using machinery in the sector, as well as making improvements to the quality of the rice and its handling post-harvest. This was to be achieved by improving market access and access to finances, as well as increasing research and extension services (NRDP, 2016, pp. 22–5).

The rise in local rice production was expected to increase the incomes of rice farmers in the six Mozambican provinces where the implementation was to take place, namely Maputo, Gaza, Sofala, Zambezia, Nampula and Cabo

Delgado (NRDP, 2016, p. 26). The aim was that implementation should take place in cooperation with provincial and district agricultural offices, public institutions and private companies. The National Directorate of Agriculture and Silviculture (DINAS) has been appointed to implement and monitor the programme and its production (NRDP, 2016, p. 27).

As envisaged, the rice strategy was to be funded by the Mozambican government at 50 per cent, with another 50 per cent coming from private investors and key international aid donors. The estimated cost was set at 120 million USD. MASA also planned to set up a Consultative Group on Rice (GCA), including representatives from the public and private sectors, to be responsible for monitoring and evaluating the implementation process (NRDP, 2016, pp. 26–30).

Even though the rice strategy places the onus on the Mozambican state as the financer and active player, the commercial sector was considered an essential partner in reaching the targets for increasing rice production in Mozambique. By 2016 commercial production accounted for only 2.3 per cent of production and was taking place mainly in irrigated areas. However, the fertility of irrigated land has decreased over time, and in the past, post-independence state-owned companies have gone bankrupt (NRDP, 2016, p. 11). Nonetheless, with irrigation, the productivity of commercial enterprises was expected to reach between 2.8 and 3.5 t/ha, which was significantly higher than the productivity of the smallholders. Through land reforms in key river valleys, the NRDP planned to attract public-private partnership investments in commercial rice production. Through the reforms, the land itself will still be 'owned' by the state and administered by the government, but production from the land would belong to the private sector (NRDP, 2016, p. 7).

This last aspect, which is designed to attract investors, was the part of the strategy that has been implemented without the overall programme being approved, given that there were already investments producing rice commercially in Mozambique. The Chinese company WanBao in Xai-Xai (see Chichava, 2010; Chuanhong et al., 2015), in partnership with the public enterprise RBL-EP and the public-private industrial complex CAIC in Chóckwè, another Mozambican-Chinese partnership, were both mentioned in the strategy paper. The aim was to identify more investors who could contribute to national production with advanced farming technologies and the ability to process and market their products further. By making rice production in Mozambique economically viable, it was hoped that this would make the country less dependent on rice imports.

The national rice strategy was not a stand-alone policy. As is often the case with policy formulation in developing countries, strategies were linked to and aligned with other main agricultural policy plans, which in Mozambique all have the overall goal of securing food supplies and reducing *pobreza absoluta* (absolute poverty) in the country. The NRDP was aligned with all important strategy papers: (1) PARPA[6] aimed to transform the agricultural sector from subsistence farming into competitive and sustainable farming and mentioned rice development as one of its eight priority commodities; (2) PNISA[7] was an investment framework for PEDSA,[8] which promoted private and public agricultural investments, with rice featuring prominently; and (3) the NRDP was also aligned with the PAPA,[9] which aimed at securing food security in Mozambique in the fight against absolute poverty. Another project to which the rice strategy was linked was the World Bank-funded PROIRRI[10] (2011–16), which was working to increase the productivity of small-scale rice farms by improving the irrigation infrastructure in rural areas. The key actors that were part of the PROIRRI implementation process were the government, public-private partnerships and development organizations, the most important actor being JICA and the CARD programme, which led to Mozambique drawing up a national rice strategy in the first instance (NRDP, 2016, pp. 8–10).

In principle, the strategy itself was well aligned with a whole set of agricultural policy papers, which all focused on or made rice a priority commodity and promoted it as one of the most important food crops for the development of Mozambique's agricultural sector. One could therefore expect considerable political support for the NRDP and rice investments at all levels of the ruling elite, state and government.

However, the rice strategy was not formally approved by the responsible minister until May 2017, even though the CARD secretariat and MASA staff considered it "'a state-of-art strategy" that was much better elaborated than strategies for other countries that got their strategies approved very quickly' and therefore had access to funding from CARD (Interviews: MASA, November 2017). We will shortly return to why the approval took so long, in Section 5. Here it is sufficient to point out that rent-seeking interests by ruling elite groups in cahoots with rice importers delayed formal approval. Despite the delay, however, parts of the strategy were implemented in the form of investments related to WanBao rice production and processing plants in Xai-Xai and CAIC in Chóckwè, which operated some of it until it went bankrupt in July 2017 due to a lack of rice for processing (see Buur and Jacob, 2023 forthcoming). These investments have therefore been implemented in order to suit the interests of the ruling elite that approved them. In the next section, we will explore how WanBao's 289 million USD investment was implemented and what kinds of exchange relations evolved over time between WanBao and local populations.

3. CONFLICT OVER LAND IN XAI-XAI

We will start this section by elaborating on the background to the Chinese WanBao Grain and Oil Investment Company[11] (hereafter WanBao) in Xai-Xai in the southern Mozambican province of Gaza before exploring how the relationship between the investment and the local populations evolved over time, including an initial phase of violent conflict and the infringement of rights. This will be followed by an analysis of the political economy of the investment, where the shifting relationship between investor, local elites and state institutions and the different interests they represent influenced the rice investment.

The 2012 WanBao investment is located next to the city of Xai-Xai, the capital of Gaza province situated at the end of the lower Limpopo river basin.[12] WanBao's investment is still the biggest rice investment in Mozambique (despite later bankruptcies), with around 289 million USD in total being envisaged for reclaiming the irrigation scheme, dike protection, land preparation, dam construction, smallholder production and the installation of a rice-cleaning and production unit in Xai-Xai (Interview: WanBao, October 2016; see also Chuanhong et al., 2015; Chichava, 2014a; 2014b). The fertile Limpopo valley, where the lower Limpopo basin or the Regadio do Baixo Limpopo is located, has approximately 70,000 ha of land suitable for irrigation. The Limpopo river feeds the two main irrigation schemes used for watering the rice fields in Chóckwè and Xai-Xai (Alba et al., 2016, p. 575). These irrigation schemes were originally planned and initiated by the colonial regime for rice production (Hermele, 1988). WanBao's reclamation of one of the largest rice projects in the Regadio do Baixo Limpopo was intended to place an additional 20,000 ha under rice cultivation as part of a concession granted to it (Interview: WanBao, October 2016; Porsani et al., 2017).

The 289 million USD WanBao investment was substantial: once the irrigation schemes had become fully operational with dam and dike protection, it was expected not only to create jobs and increase productivity for smallholders from 0.5–1.0 t/ha to 4.0–6.0 t/ha, but also to reduce the area's vulnerability to drought and flooding (Interview: WanBao, October 2016; Porsani et al., 2017). In partnership with the state-owned enterprise RBL-EP, WanBao was named owners of the land, because they were expected to maintain the irrigation schemes, which require a high level of maintenance and management.

The Regadio do Baixo Limpopo was established by the Portuguese in the 1950s (Alba et al., 2016, p. 575). After independence, it was nationalized and turned into a state farm to make Chóckwè the 'grain basket of Mozambique' (Mosca, 2011). During the civil war, the government effectively abandoned the state farm in the Limpopo basin, which local peasants and internally displaced people (IDPs) started to cultivate to feed themselves and the provincial city of Xai-Xai. When the war ended, the government formally reclaimed the land in the Limpopo valley, around 70,000 ha in Xai-Xai and 30,000 ha in Chóckwè further up the river system. However, not much happened with regard to formal investments in the irrigation scheme except for different small and medium-scale farm-investment projects, as well as many national and provincial ruling elite groups securing land in the basin. Until the predecessor to WanBao, the Hubei-Gaza rice project, arrived in 2007 (Chichava, 2014b, p. 1), production in the irrigation scheme was dominated by small-scale and/or family-based production of rice, horticulture and cattle.

Land ownership was nonetheless not straightforward. According to the Mozambican Land Law of 1997, farmers living and working the land in the formerly state-owned Regadio had user rights to the land. This was nonetheless nullified in 2010 when the state created two public enterprises, the RBL-EP[13] in Xai-Xai and HICEP[14] in the upper part of the valley around Chóckwè, which took formal charge of all the land in the Limpopo valley. The formal task of the two enterprises was to manage the land, distribute concessions like WanBao and distribute DUATs (user rights) in the areas under their jurisdiction. The provincial government or the Council of Ministers decided to concede formal DUATs to RBL-EP. The DUAT system stands formally for Direito de Uso e Aproveitamento da Terra ('Right to Use and Benefit/Profit from the Land' in English) and is the Mozambican user rights system that came into effect with the 1997 land law.[15]

Formally, after 2010 all the 70,000 ha in the Regadio do Baixo Limpopo belonged to the RBL-EP in Xai-Xai, making it the largest, most important and most powerful state institution in Xai-Xai next to the provincial government. In order to differentiate it, a new modern headquarters was built 20 kilometres to the north of Xai-Xai in order to broadcast to the public and investors alike that the RBL-EP is not a Xai-Xai institution, but stands above the local politics of the provincial capital.

According to RBL-EP (Interview: Xai-Xai, 3 November 2016) and interviews in the provincial office in charge of the land register (November 2016), in contrast to public perceptions, all 70,000 ha of the land around Xai-Xai in the Limpopo delta are owned by RBL-EP through a state decree creating it as a public enterprise. Of this land, WanBao had 'Concession Rights' for 20,000 ha and a much smaller DUAT (roughly 1000 ha) for the land where an industrial plant is under construction within the Regadio. The prevailing public perception is nonetheless (see Porsani et al., 2017) that the owner of the land in the Regadio do Baixo Limpopo, at least of the 20,000 ha, is WanBao. The confusion regarding ownership related to WanBao is in part due to the circumstance that, while all land in Mozambique is formally owned by the state, the latter can give a DUAT holder (for example, an investor) the right to use the land for up to 50 years.[16] Formally, DUAT title-holders can only 'own' what is constructed or placed on the land, but this has de facto ended up as a system of 'ownership' of the land itself so it can be transferred. Formal state ownership of the land and the ownership of what is constructed or placed on it has, as Porsani et al. (2017) suggest,

> contributed to blurring the public/private ownership divide, as in practice, it has allowed land titles to be transferred/sold between individuals. The semi-privatiza-tion of land is an attempt to reconcile the neo-liberal market economy of free circulation and the accumulation of capital (reliant on a *de facto* system of property rights) with the protection of Mozambicans from landlessness. (Porsani et al., 2017, p. 1148, note 48)[17]

Furthermore, the Land Law of 1997 included a 'protection' clause recognizing the special 'rights' of those who had worked the land before a DUAT or con-cession was granted. Those who had worked on a parcel of land for more than ten years before an investment was made had legitimate claims related to the customary norms governing access to land. The ten-year customary protection of land rights meant that many of the small and/or family-based peasants who worked in the Limpopo delta as individuals and/or communities were holders of a DUAT or legitimate 'users' due to the time they had farmed the land in the delta. On top of this, the Land Law stipulated that any investor, or if it was the state that took control of land then the state itself, was required to hold consultations with the communities affected by their land being targeted. As such, land could not be formally acquired without due 'consultation' with the affected communities. This did not mean that communities could block investments, only that, for an investment to be 'legitimately' implemented in accordance with the right procedures, the state and/or the investor had to 'consult' the community.[18]

As a public enterprise, RBL-EP was therefore the formal DUAT holder of all the land WanBao received as a concession in the Regadio and was also responsible for maintaining the main infrastructure of the river irrigation system: water, canals, dikes, dams, feeder systems and so on. The most comprehensive irrigation scheme in Mozambique, which covered 70,000 ha, was in this way 'owned' by the state through RBL-EP as the public enterprise formally managing both the land and the water. Questions related to com-pensation for displacement and resettlement, and the formal rules regarding Environmental Impact Assessments (EIAs), therefore rest firmly with public state enterprises.

3.1   WanBao and Conflict over Resettlement

WanBao started operating in Mozambique in 2011 (Chichava, 2014b, p. 2). Following in the footsteps of the predecessor it replaced – the Hubei-Gaza friendship farm, which had started to test varieties of rice and maize in the lower Limpopo on a demonstration farm (Porsani and Lalander, 2018) – meant it inherited a series of problems related to expectations emanating from the local population and local ruling elite groups. WanBao's plan was to produce rice on the 20,000 ha concession and to set up and run two industrial units. Part of the business model was teaching and employing local farmers on their fields as outgrowers. It would also set up its own production with Chinese producers, who would also function as 'trainers' in order to source rice for the industrial unit (Chichava, 2015, p. 3). The Chinese Development Bank (CDB) initially granted WanBao a loan of 20 million USD (Amanor and Chichava, 2016). Over a period of three to five years, the WanBao project planned to spend 289 million USD on the industrial unit, training, farming and infrastructure. This mostly seems to have happened, even though WanBao ran into financial problems for the first time in 2016 and needed to be recapitalized.

Even though the WanBao concession was granted by RBL-EP and was within the Regadio, where after 2010 all the land belonged to the state, WanBao was faced with a series of local protests that acquired an international audience when it emerged on the scene in 2011. In part, this was because the project was fast-tracked by RBL-EP and the provincial government, or, as Porsani et al. call it, by 'quick implementation [where] regulations were overlooked' (Porsani et al., 2017, p. 1189). WanBao's concession was on both sides of the Limpopo river and ran down through the basin, but on the east side of the river cultivation was restricted, while cultivation on the west was left in abeyance till a later date. When WanBao arrived on both sides of the river, there was therefore virtually no 'empty land'. All land was being used for either family or small-scale farming or animal husbandry (Porsani and Lalander, 2018; Interview by authors, March 2017). This reflected the historical mixture of land uses that emerged after independence in 1975 and the subsequent civil war that ended in 1992, leaving extensive user rights to the land in the hands of local populations. Despite the state formally owning the land in the Regadio, local populations felt entitled to the land they had acquired by having followed the customary norms for generations, though they were aware that at some point in time, before independence, Portuguese private companies and/or the state had controlled the land.

The state could technically bypass the Land Law of 1997 when the land in question was classified to be of 'national interest', for example, when an investment was considered to be of great importance to the country according to the Law of Territorial Planning, the Regulation of Relocation Process due to Economic Activities, and their related regulations and directives. In such cases, even though the involuntary expropriation of land is legally recognized and local populations do not have the right to reject the project or to refuse to cede their land, they still have the right to consultation and after 2014 also the right to information and fair compensation sufficient to enable the establishment of living standards equal to or better than previously (Mozambican Republic, 2014).

When WanBao obtained access to the land, neither the state (central or provincial) nor its public company, RBL-EP, had settled the issue of land transfers with local populations or had even tried to do so. As Porsani (2020) clearly shows, inadequate or non-existent consultations with local populations in the Regadio affected by the WanBao investment was the norm:

> In some areas, information about the land concession reached land users, and some individuals were partially compensated with fields elsewhere, whereas in other areas farmers found out about the land concession first when they saw Chinese tractors entering their fields ('machambas') and received no compensation. In none of the affected communities were land users consulted on whether they accepted to cede the land and under which conditions. (Quoted from Porsani and Lalander, 2018, p. 8, pre-published version)

The broader issue was that local populations affected by the emergence of the WanBao had not been informed, consulted or compensated except for a few who had close relations with local Frelimo party elites. Furthermore, it was unclear if WanBao had acquired the DUAT for their concession, and if so from whom. There are rumours that when RBL-EP was created it was granted all the DUAT for the zone under its administration. Thus, RBL-EP may have transferred the DUAT to WanBao, thus exempting the Chinese company from applying for the title from the Mozambican government. If that was indeed the case, the law was broken not by WanBao, but by the government when it granted RBL-EP a DUAT with reference to land already being used without consulting its existing users. In any case, since a large part of the targeted land was under customary use, whereas other parts had been occupied for more than ten years, the affected land users had the legal right at least to be informed and fairly compensated prior to the confiscation of their land (and thus to participate in consultations in which what was 'fair' was to be discussed).

4. WHAT KIND OF RELATIONSHIP EMERGED FROM THE RICE INVESTMENT?

During the first year, 1800 ha of land were developed for rice production, followed by another 8800 ha during the second year (Fieldwork by the author, November 2016). Next to growing rice, facilitating rice growing and working with local farmers, the company also planned to market rice in Mozambique and to export rice over time. For marketing purposes, the company constructed two rice-processing units and built a huge warehouse. Until these units were functioning, the company used the machinery of the agro-processing firm CAIC in Chóckwè (Chichava, 2015, p. 3; Interview: CAIC, Chóckwè, 1 November 2016). During the next two years from 2017–18, another 10,000 ha of land was planned to be cultivated (Interview: WanBao, Xai-Xai, 5 October 2016).

4.1   WanBao and Outgrower Producers

The farmers working for WanBao can be divided into three groups. The first group are the Chinese farmers who were brought from China to start up the production. Due to financial problems, in 2015 they were reduced in number from 50 to 30, even though each of them cultivated 40–50 ha of land with a high level of productivity (Interview: WanBao, Xai-Xai, 5 October 2016) and thus produced much more than a Mozambican farmer. This made the company dependent on them for bringing rice to market (Chichava, 2014b).[19] In 2017 the Mozambican state decided to expel 20 WanBao 'employees' because they were considered 'illegal workers' (Club of Mozambique, 13 June 2017).[20] Members of this Chinese farmer group are also used as trainers when WanBao wants to train Mozambican farmers in hands-on practical knowledge.

The second group of farmers that can be identified are members of ARPONE, an association of the larger local farmers in Xai-Xai created mainly by high-level members of Frelimo and state/government employees. Of the 150 ARPONE members, 46 were chosen to participate in the WanBao project (Chichava, 2015). This meant that they were initially also entitled to receive loans from the Agricultural Development Fund (FDA), a state-organized credit facility, and similar credit providers funding agricultural production. These farmers farm their own land but are able to make use of WanBao's services and inputs, including machinery and technology. Furthermore, they also sell their harvested rice to WanBao. A few still produce for WanBao, but most of the farmers in this group have been blacklisted by credit providers for not paying back loans. This is something they strongly contest, as they see it as their privilege as the vanguard of small and medium-scale farmers in the province. Seen from the perspective of WanBao, it was considered a mistake that they bowed to pressure and trained members of this group, as they were considered or came to be considered 'free riders', mainly participating in order to access machinery, inputs and cheap loan options, money they used for construction and other non-agricultural projects. Despite the problems with ARPONE, several members have continued to produce for WanBao, thus living up to the criteria established by WanBao and credit organizations.

The third group of farmers are the local smallholders who are trained by and work on WanBao land, land adjacent to WanBao land or land controlled by RBL-EP. These farmers can again be divided into three different groups, depending on the year they started receiving training (Interview: farmer A, Xai-Xai, 5 October 2016), as described above. According to WanBao (Interview: Xai-Xai, 5 October 2016), there are currently almost 300 Mozambican farmers working for or being deployed by WanBao. It is this large group of farmers we focus on, as it is them who initially lost land to RBL-EP and by implication to WanBao. However, not all of those who lost land to RBL-EP have been included so far and have received training by WanBao. Few from this group have stopped farming: they are generally very positive about the project, and all seem to have gained considerably from being part of WanBao's training, input and state-driven credit facilities.

Thus, despite the negative public perceptions of the WanBao investment that initially soured the relationship between WanBao and farmers in Xai-Xai, their business concept rapidly gained momentum and praise from those who were included in the company's hands-on training. Key here was the concrete exchanges between WanBao and local farmers embedded in the business or outgrower model. WanBao based this policy on its willingness to teach and treat 'ordinary' local rice farmers in a professional manner. This does not apply to all farmers, only to those who have been selected and are considered ready to receive training by RBL-EP and the local Frelimo state (initially not necessarily by WanBao). The aim was to increase the average rice production of smallholders from 1 ha to 4–5 ha or even higher (Interview: WanBao, Xai-Xai, 5 October 2016). The training programme for local farmers, some of whom were moved from the land by the state, that is, after WanBao received the concession, works roughly in the following manner. Local rice farmers are trained onsite, on parts of the land given over to the company. Ten thousand ha of the land is supposed to be cultivated by Mozambican rice farmers by the end of the training programme. The individual farmers start out with 1 ha of land, but each year the amount of land cultivated by each farmer increases, depending on their capacity and ability to increase productivity.

While the farmers are able to produce 2–3 t/ha of rice at the beginning of the training, they are expected to increase production to reach up to 6–7 t/ha after the training has been terminated. The plan was to train a new group of farmers every year so that in the end hundreds of local farmers would be able to cultivate between 5–10 ha of land after a couple of years' experience. The company accordingly trained 22 farmers in 2013/14, 38 in 2014/15 and 130 in 2015/16 (Interview: RBL-EP, Xai-Xai, 3 November 2016; fieldwork notes from farmer interviews).

After two years of training and monitoring, local farmers are expected to work independently. This is also when they are supposed to start investing by themselves in seeds, tools and labour, so that over time they become less dependent on WanBao and state-guaranteed credit lines. The farmers we interviewed were largely content with this plan, as they experienced increased productivity and were more able to handle more land.

Through approval by WanBao, farmers are able to obtain credits through the FDA for their investments. The (s)election of farmers to access the WanBao training programme, and through it the FDA's credits, is formally carried out by RBL-EP, which, using (Frelimo) secretaries at lower levels of the state governance system, identifies the most 'capable farmers'. These are usually trusted members (*pessoas de confiança*) of the party who have been working with agriculture and have shown an interest in rice production (Chichava, 2015, p. 4; Interviews: farmer A, 5 June 2016; farmer B, 6 October 2016; RBL-EP, 3 November 2016; FDA, 3 November 2016, all Xai-Xai).

WanBao was clearly suspicious of RBL-EP's selection of farmers and complained, even though it could do little to change it, as not all farmers entered the scheme with the aim of producing rice paddy, as indicated by ARPONE (see above). However, the farmers who entered the training and production scheme, who aimed to learn to work with new seeds, fertilizers and techniques of production, clearly increased their production levels dramatically.

Farmers generally managed to increase the land they produced year on year. They invested their surpluses not only in more land but also in their own machinery, animals, motorcycles, tractors and pick-ups so they could work the land and move workers, inputs and surplus production themselves. They also showed with pride how they had invested in their estates and storage facilities with zinc roofs, increased house sizes, and electricity and water supplies, besides schooling for their children.

In this sense, the relationship between WanBao and the farmers who were increasingly included in the rice production scheme resembled a reciprocal exchange deal with various (unequal) exchanges that were appreciated on both sides and increased trust in a deeper relationship of exchange. Farmers queued up to join the next batch of trainees, not only because of access to inputs and credit, but also because of the training, the access to new technology and the visible improvements to the living conditions of the scheme's graduates. However, with access being screened by RBL-EP and the local Frelimo state officials, there were conditions for accessing these opportunities that were only articulated on the side and on conditions of anonymity. Loyalty to Frelimo and avoiding being a troublemaker for RBL-EP and the local state officials were preconditions for access.

4.2 Marketing a Field of Contestation

Although much suggests that the WanBao investment somewhat approximated to a reciprocal exchange deal, there was nonetheless one major contentious issue related to the relationship that generated complaints and insecurity. While the WanBao rice investment and the training of local farmers, with all that implied, was relatively uncontroversial, the marketing of the rice in terms of pricing and payment was heavily criticized. One reason for the controversy was related to the involvement of other actors – principally RBL-EP – in making price-setting decisions.

The farmers generally complained about the prices paid for paddy (just as any other outgrower of sugarcane, banana or tobacco would do), for which they criticized WanBao: 'Wanbao don't want to pay the full price for paddy'; 'Wanbao deduct too much'; 'Wanbao cannot be trusted, they are in cahoots with the RBL', and so on. However, in interviews farmers interestingly ended up showing more mistrust of RBL-EP than Wanbao. Let us explore why this was the case.

As described by various farmers, WanBao and RBL-EP officials, with some notable exceptions, the process seems to give RBL-EP considerable control, as RBL-EP apparently oversees and has control of the flow of payments and deductions related to the marketing of the rice. Even though farmers 'sell' their paddy to 'Wanbao', they are not paid directly by WanBao, but through a complicated and, it seems, not fully transparent system by RBL-EP, which works in the following way:

- After the harvest, the rice is bought by WanBao at a fixed price set by RBL-EP and WanBao, decided for each year
- WanBao transfers the farmer's payments after subtracting the costs of the inputs it provided, such as training, fertilizers, use of machinery, to RBL-EP's account
- RBL-EP subtracts the costs it has incurred related to training and the use of machinery, including fees for the use of the irrigation scheme (water and infrastructure) controlled by RBL-EP
- RBL-EP then repays FDA for any credits that have been advanced
- The surpluses left after various deductions are then paid out to the farmers

Farmers who were interviewed and took part in the surveys were all highly positive and quite happy about the money they earned from their rice production (Tembe field report, 2017). They were nonetheless also highly critical of the deductions made in the payment system because, from their perspective, this was less than transparent. Their anger was directed less at WanBao (even though they would like to have a higher reference price, which is set by RBL-EP and WanBao) than at RBL-EP, which they felt was withhold-ing money and making greater deductions than it was entitled to. RBL-EP deducted payments for the services it provided and the training of farmers after the first years, as it wanted to take over from WanBao, but the farmers gener-ally complained that this was a 'waste of time' and much preferred to obtain assistance from WanBao. Key here was that RBL-EP's training was general, whereas WanBao provided specific and specialized training that could be used concretely in improving production.

In contrast to RBL-EP, FDA, the credit-granting authority, was generally considered a trusted partner, and it in return was proud of the 100 per cent repayment of credits by all WanBao-trained farmers, something it had not experienced before in Xai-Xai. In contrast, the group of farmers mentioned above who belonged to ARPONE, consisting mainly of high-level members of Frelimo and state/government employees who also farmed, did not pay back loans with the same frequency, as rice farming was rarely their first occupa-tion. This contrast in loyalty to the rice scheme was clearly acknowledged by WanBao and the local provincial authorities, but they had no real ability to sanction or outlaw ARPONE's activities, as the latter were well connected and protected by powerful ruling elite networks at the provincial and national levels.

5.   TRACES OF THE PARTIALLY IMPLEMENTED NRDP

Given top-level government support to the WanBao rice investment, the latter approximates to something resembling a compatible exchange deal between the investors and the ruling elites, combined with what clearly looks like a reciprocal exchange deal between the investors and the local populations included in the rice production scheme. Furthermore, WanBao's investment seems to fulfil all the requirements formulated in the rice strategy about what kinds of investments should be supported in order to increase rice production, reduce food insecurity and contribute to poverty reduction in Mozambique. WanBao is a public-private partnership where the state owns the land, while the company has the concession (user) rights to the land and owns the production facilities. Furthermore, the investment contributes to the aim of generating spill-over effects for local farmers in obtaining access to new technologies, irrigation and inputs. Farmers are trained and supported and are able to increase their production by 3–5 to 6–7 t/ha, while the national average is 1 t/ha or below. WanBao also provides new technologies and machinery, seeds and fertilizers, and creates links to marketing and industry by setting up rice-processing units and warehouses. Therefore, the government and local institutions should be in favour of the investment project and support it, since it covers their expectations as set out in the NRDP. With such policy links and formal government support, one can wonder why WanBao went bankrupt and why the rice production scheme felt apart?

When one zooms in on how regional and national elite groups reacted to and, we suggest, undermined the investment over time, the emerging picture seems less rosy. The first season was hit by floods, which led to a major loss of production. In the following seasons (the harvests of 2014 to 2017), WanBao restricted cultivation to the east of the river. Cultivation on the west bank was put on hold until at least mid-2017. Therefore, WanBao faced financial and technological difficulties stemming from difficult climatic conditions and what we suggest was uneven support from the Mozambican state and ruling elite, or maybe more precisely because of the delicate interplay between formal support and informal undermining: that is, support by some part of the state/government, and ignorance or direct undermining by other parts. While the government was interested in the Chinese investment and arranged high-level visits to the Xai-Xai site by the provincial governor, minister of agriculture and president, and therefore formally supported it, other state/ government public institutions like RBL-EP and the ministry of agriculture had, we suggest, a more complex way of operating that, when combined, undermined the investment.

First, RBL-EP did not carry out all its duties related to the maintenance of the infrastructure around the rice investment, and there was no pressure from the central state to make sure RBL-EP honoured its part of the deal. RBL-EP is formally the public enterprise in charge of the irrigation scheme in Xai-Xai and the owner of the land, as it holds the DUATs for the land on behalf of the state. It is its obligation to secure the provision of infrastructure, such as water, dikes, roads, transport lines and electricity. Since the institution has the official DUAT for the land, it is RBL-EP that granted the concession to WanBao. But while RBL-EP is actively taking on its formal task, interviews (including with lower level RBL-EP cadres) suggest that WanBao often paid for the rehabilitation of the infrastructure itself. RBL-EP did not initially provide or maintain the protective dikes, so the devastating flooding in 2013/14 destroyed most of the irrigation system WanBao had rehabilitated, and thus the first season of production that WanBao had paid for. The losses amounted to more 200 million USD. The floods literally drained WanBao's capital, which increased its need for external funds.

As a result, during 2016 WanBao went through a second round of recapital-ization with a new leadership despatched from China. However, the Chinese banks initially held off giving further funds to the company due to what they deemed the insecurity of the investment (Interview: WanBao, Xai-Xai, 5 October 2016). This is why the company was not able to cultivate more than one-third of its land. According to Sergio Chichava (2015, pp. 3–4), WanBao was only able to cultivate 700 ha after working the land for three years.[21] In sum, as the state entity managing the irrigation scheme, RBL-EP did not invest properly in rehabilitation and maintenance work, undermining WanBao and therefore also the investments of the smallholders.

Second, it is not only WanBao that loses out when, through RBL-EP, the state does not fulfil its obligations. The extra costs passed on to WanBao were, in the end, carried by the farmers, since there was less profit to share. As explained above, and as stated by WanBao and the FDA (Interview: Xai-Xai, 5 October 2016; 3 November 2016), RBL-EP was in charge of choosing local farmers to participate in the training provided by WanBao (they did so by relying on the local Frelimo secretaries), and RBL-EP also decided who would be given access to loans and credits. RBL-EP in turn states that the local leaders (Frelimo secretaries at the lower level) were those who choose who is given contracts with WanBao (Interview: RBL-EP, Xai-Xai, 3 November 2016). The Agricultural Development Fund (FDA) gives loans to the 'farmers' who work for WanBao. That means that they then rely on WanBao to train those farmers so they can pay the money back and pay WanBao for the service it provides.

Therefore non-payment, for example, by members of ARPONE, in the end undermines the FDA's funds, with implications for all farmers and WanBao, which does not receive its payment for service provision, leaving it with fewer funds the following year (Interview; FDA, Xai-Xai, 3 November 2016). Furthermore, the farmers are used to receiving the FDA loans every year. This means that they do not have to save money to pay the expenses for the next harvest themselves. That is also difficult because of the high inflation rate. Farmers' surpluses are immediately invested in material assets so that they do not depreciate too much. Furthermore, the FDA's funds are attractive because it charges a far lower interest rate than the commercial banks (during fieldwork, this was above 18 per cent). Several informants from the state and workers from WanBao also hinted that WanBao had to provide special credits for high-level Frelimo members and RBL-EP employees to make sure it was not 'harassed'. All in all, this undermined the FDA as well as WanBao, as they had to absorb extra costs related to production, as well as maintain good relations with the local and national ruling elites.

Third, WanBao's marketing of the processed rice on the regional (Xai-Xai) and national markets at a relative high reference price issued by the government after negotiations between the two parties required the government to stick to its promises to protect the industry from unfair competition from rice imports. Local farmers are not included in the discussions related to price setting but are formally represented by the RBL-EP. According to WanBao (Interview: Xai-Xai, 5 October 2016) its quality rice brand, called 'Bom Gosto' (after a phase used by the former President Guebuza during a visit), is only sold locally, while rice of other qualities entered the national market. The high-quality 'Bom Gusto' rice gains its competitiveness from being 'fresher' and more 'natural' than the rice imported from Asia and is less affected by the cheaper foreign imports from the big national or multi-national rice traders, as it is a niche market. However, one informant in the company (Interview: Xai-Xai, 5 October 2016) did acknowledge that the imports of cheap rice by 'Maputo-based rice traders' are outcompeting the local rice on the national market. The problem lies in the high costs for a relatively low level of production, as RBL-EP does not provide the services that were promised, and the state does not provide protection for imported rice as stipulated by the NRDP.

Fourth, a new field of conflict has emerged that has the potential to further undermine the local exchange deal. This new conflict is related to training, inputs, advice and the marketing of the rice. From 2016, as the economic crisis following in the slipstream of the government's secret loans (see Macuane et al., 2018) began taking its toll on the Mozambican state's ability to finance itself, the budgets of public enterprises were severely cut. This saw state enterprises quickly having to find ways of financing their own expenses, as the state could no longer cover defaults. Suddenly RBL-EP, for example, began deducting increasing amounts of money from small-scale farmers' transfers of profit after deductions for training and inputs (WanBao), water and irrigation (RBL-EP) and credits (FDA). But besides taking control of all cash flows, which is exactly where rents can be deducted, RBL-EP also insisted on taking over the training and advising of farmers in order to use its workforce.

New local farmers who entered the scheme were highly critical of RBL-EP taking over tasks that had formerly been carried out by WanBao. On top of taking over the training of new farmers as part of the WanBao rice scheme, RBL-EP announced that it would begin rice and bean production using 'surplus' land in order to generate its own funds. This had been stipulated by government intervention during the autumn of 2016, as the financial crisis began to bite seriously, and at the end of 2016 the government formally went bankrupt. The farmers considered this an inferior arrangement, as the machine park was now increasingly being mobilized for RBL-EP's own production, and its training, inputs and advice were considered inadequate compared to the input and service provided by WanBao. Added to this, all RBL-EP leaders and higher-level functionaries had their own rice paddy fields, which were serviced first according to local farmers. In many ways, the crisis and the need for public enterprises to finance themselves after being milked for years (see Macuane et al., 2018) by the ruling elite have changed what in some ways looked like a favourable arrangement and was experienced as such by local farmers trained by WanBao.

6.   TOWARDS A CONCLUSION

In this chapter, we have argued that, after the initial high-level ruling elite aid to the WanBao rice investments that resembled compatible exchange relations, as well as the reciprocal exchange deal between the included farmers and WanBao, the investment still failed and went bankrupt several times, having had to be recapitalized several times in order to survive. Through the ruling elite, WanBao had easy access to fertile land and water in exchange for investing heavily in irrigation and rice production along with the training of farmers, input provision and marketing. This created the foundations for developing productive relations with the farmers included in the rice scheme over time. As discussed above, WanBao's rice investments also suited the national rice strategy, the NRDP, well from 2017.

However, despite the many positive outcomes of the investment for local farmers included in the rice production scheme, the latter was based on initially violating the rights of smallholders living in the river basin, as the rights of the local populations were not protected by the local and national Frelimo state (see Porsani, 2020). The rights entrenched in the Land Law of 1997 were undermined, with only some of those who lost their access to livelihoods gaining from the rice investment, as they became part of the WanBao rice scheme or were given limited compensation. But also, despite initial support to it, WanBao was undermined by the provincial and national ruling elites. Firstly, it had to pay the reputational costs of the initial conflicts over land, even though it was clearly the national and provincial governments that were not adhering to the rules for land compensation and dialogue. Secondly, WanBao also had to accept a large group of unproductive local and national Frelimo actors as part of the rice scheme, even though only a few actively produced rice. Thirdly, RBL-EP, the state representative that controlled the DUAT and river basin, did not follow through on its obligation to protect the dikes and infrastructure. This had dire consequences when the river basin was flooded, as it has been several times in the last ten years. Fourthly, when it ran into economic problems after 2016, RBL-EP itself began to use the rice scheme for rent extraction related to loan-taking through the FDA's micro-credits for agricultural production, for rent extraction related to rice payments of producers by producers, and for taking over much of the service and input scheme for its own profit after 2016. This had grave consequences for the local farmers, who clearly felt that the inputs and services were of lower quality. Finally, the rice investment was not protected from unfair rice imports and the dumping of rice donations, as stipulated by the NRDP of 2017.[22]

In many ways, this analytical tale speaks to the wider political economy and history of productive sector development in Mozambique. Here the interests of the power-holding ruling elites in Mozambique, as in most developing countries, have their interests firmly anchored in short-term political survival strategies (Whitfield and Buur, 2014) instead of long-term policy ideas for transforming production (Whitfield et al., 2015). We now know from the political settlement literature that, in order to stay in power, ruling political elites, underpinned by weak formal economies, develop in such a way that benefits are exchanged for political and economic support (Khan, 2010; Behuria et al., 2017).[23] Within the Mozambican rice sector, huge rents are generated through inflows of different types of rice. Rice is imported by trading companies that have to pay the ruling elite in exchange for import licences, while import tariffs are kept extremely low to meet the interests of the trading companies. Keeping prices low also functions for the regime by counteracting rising urban food prices in order to avoid food riots that could challenge the political legitimacy of the ruling elite coalition (see Buur and Salimo, 2018). Such strategies are pursued instead of longer-term productive strategies that could have extensively transformed the livelihoods of thousands of farmers.

NOTES

1. The CAIC investment went bankrupt in 2017. See http://clubofmozambique .com/news/us60-million-gaza-industrial-complex-ceases-production/ (accessed 17 November 2022).
2. Data for the years 1994–95 to 2006–07 were sourced from MASA Aviso Previo, and data for the years 2008–09 to 2013–14 from Grupo Consultivo de Arroz (Memorias da v reunião de arroz – 2013).
3. The programme was originally written and called the National Rice Strategy, but the minister of agriculture did not like it being called a strategy, as there were already various national strategies and agricultural strategies in existence, such as the Action Plan for the Reduction of Absolute Poverty (PARPA), the Strategic Plan for Agricultural Development (PEDSA) and the National Agriculture Investment Plan (PNISA), as well as a sub-programme under PNISA (Sub-program to Support the Production of Rice 2014–2018), all referring to rice. It was therefore renamed a programme, but internally in the ministry and among stakeholders it was referred to as a strategy. On JICA's CARD website the most recent version from 2018 (stated as referring to a meeting in Benin on 9 February 2009, which seems a mistake) refers to it as a 'National Rice Development Strategy'. We refer to it interchangeably as a programme or a strategy in this chapter.
4. See Jica's programme website: https://www.jica.go.jp/english/our_work/ thematic_issues/agricultural/card.html (accessed 17 November 2022).
5. The strategy aims at enhancing and strengthening the different components of the value chain and reinforcing the links between smallholder producers and other actors in the value chain who cater for inputs, transport, agro-processing and marketing.
6. Action Plan for the Reduction of Absolute Poverty.
7. National Agricultural Investment Plan.

8.   Strategic Plan for Agricultural Development.
9.   Action Plan for the Production of Food.
10.   Sustainable Irrigation Development Project.
11.   WanBao was earlier known as the Hubei-Gaza rice project (see Chuanhong et al., 2015; Ganho, 2013, 2015; Chichava et al., 2013).
12.   The Limpopo river flows through Botswana, South Africa and Zimbabwe, before reaching Mozambique.
13.   Regadio de Baixo Limpopo – Empresa Pública (RBL-EP).
14.   Hidráulica de Chokwe – Empresa Pública (HICEP).
15.   Lei de Terras [Land Law] 19/97. For the most comprehensive discussion of the Land Law and its further developments, see Serra, 2013.
16.   See Porsani et al., 2017; Tanner, 2010; Lunstrum, 2008.
17.   See in particular Tanner, 2010.
18.   The stipulations regarding 'consultation' are widespread and are written into investment promotional material. See, for example, Investment Promotion Centre (CPI) 2012, as well as Government of Mozambique (2012).
19.   However, other sources state that WanBao was still employing 162 Chinese farmers in 2015, and would continue to do so until the Mozambican farmers had acquired enough training to replace them (Brautigam, 2015, p. 145).
20.   Club of Mozambique: http://clubofmozambique.com/news/labour-inspectorate -suspends-20-workers-at-wanbao-gaza-mozambique/?utm_source=The+ Mozambican+Investor_&utm_campaign=7be65bc7cf-EMAIL_CAMPAIGN _2017_05_25&utm_medium=email&utm_term=0_d3b369a42d-7be65bc7cf -206604773 (accessed 19 June 2017).
21.   In an interview (Xai-Xai, 5 October 2016), a representative of WanBao stated that 4000 ha were being cultivated at the moment, after five years of operations, but this was probably the amount of land it had prepared for cultivation, now largely lost.
22.   An important unexplored type of rice inflow are rice donations, which are imported as emergency or humanitarian aid. These donations often end up being sold on the formal market by rice importers on behalf of the government, thus generating huge and easy rents for both the ruling elite groups and the rice traders.
23.   The financial means to support the political survival of regimes in many low-income countries are derived from rents and active rent-seeking, since the formal state budget cannot pay for the maintenance of the regime (Khan, 2010).

REFERENCES

Alba, R., Bolding, A. and Ducrot, R. (2016) 'The Politics of Water Payments and Stakeholder Participation in the Limpopo River Basin, Mozambique', *Water Alternatives*, 9(3), 569–87.
Amanor, K.S. and Chichava, S. (2016) 'South–South Cooperation, Agribusiness, and African Agricultural Development: Brazil and China in Ghana and Mozambique', *World Development*, 81(C), 13–23.
Behuria P., Buur, L. and Gray, H. (2017) 'Research Note: Studying Political Settlements in Africa', *African Affairs*, 116(464), 508–25.
Bowen, L.M. (1989) 'Peasant Agriculture in Mozambique: The Case of Chokwe, Gaza Province', *Canadian Journal of African Studies*, 23(3), 355–79.

Bowen, L.M. (2000) 'The State against the Peasantry: Rural Struggles', *Colonial and Postcolonial Mozambique*, Charlottesville and London: University Press of Virginia.

Brautigam, D. (2015) *Will Africa Feed China?* New York: Oxford University Press.

Buur, L. and Jacob, T. (2023 forthcoming) 'Echoes from Mozambique: Did the Idea of High Modernism ever Vanish?', SECO Working Paper Series, Roskilde University.

Buur, L. and Salimo, P. (2018) 'The Political Economy of Social Protection in Mozambique', ESID Working Paper no 103, Manchester University.

Buur, L., Mondlane, C. and Baloi, O. (2011) 'Strategic Privatisation: Rehabilitating the Mozambican Sugar Industry', *Review of African Political Economy*, 38(128), 235–56.

Buur, L., Mondlane, C. and Baloi, O. (2012) 'The White Gold: The Role of Government and State in Rehabilitating the Sugar Industry in Mozambique', *Journal of Development Studies*, 48(3), 349–62.

Chichava, S. (2010) 'China in Mozambique's Agriculture Sector: Implications and Challenges', Paper presented at 'Celebrating the 10th Anniversary of the Establishment of the Forum on China-Africa Co-operation' (FOCAC), Johannesburg, 18–19 November 2010.

Chichava, S. (2014a) 'Acumulação num context de lógicas e dinâmicas neo-patrimoniais: O caso da ARPONE em Xai-Xai' in de Brito, L. 'Desafios para Moçambique', Maputo: IESE, pp. 413–25.

Chichava, S. (2014b) 'Assessing Chinese Investment', in Alden, C. and Chichava, S. (eds), *China and Mozambique: From Comrades to Capitalists*, Johannesburg: Jacana, pp. 24–37.

Chichava, S. (2015) 'Mozambican Elite in a Chinese Rice "Friendship": An Ethnographic Study of the Xai-Xai Irrigation', Working Paper 111, Future Agriculture, pp. 1–10.

Chichava, S., Duran, J., Cabral, L., Shankland, A., Buckley, L., Lixia, T. and Yue, Z. (2013) 'Chinese and Brazilian Cooperation with African Agriculture: The Case of Mozambique', FAC Working Paper 049, Future Agricultures Consortium CINDES, Brighton.

Chuanhong, Z., Xiaoyun, L., Gubo, Q. and Yanlei, W. (2015) 'Interpreting China-Africa Agricultural Encounters: Rhetoric and Reality in a Large Scale Rice Project in Mozambique', FAC Working Paper 126, pp. 1–18.

EUCORD – European Cooperative for Rural Development (2012) 'Rice Sector Development in East Africa', A desk study prepared for the Common Fund for Commodities by the European Cooperative for Rural Development, https://eucord.org/wp-content/uploads/2018/01/CFC__Rice_Sector_Development_in_East_Africa_2012.pdf (accessed on 19 November 2022).

Ganho, A.S. (2013) 'Agro-investimentos Privados e os seus Reflexos na Regulamentação Fundiária e Hídrica em dois Regadios Estatais em Gaza', in de Brito, L., Castel-Branco, C.N., Chichava, S. and Francisco, A., *Desafios para Moçambique*, Instituto de Estudos Sociais e Económicos (IESE), pp. 281–303), Maputo, Mozambique.

Ganho, A.S. (2015) 'Regadio do Baixo Limpopo (Xai-Xai, Gaza): Awakening a 'Sleeping Giant'?' in Castel-Branco, C.N., Massingue, N. and Muianga, C., *Questions on Productive Development in Mozambique*, Maputo, Mozambique: Instituto de Estudos Sociais e Económicos (IESE), pp. 148–72.

Government of Mozambique (2012) *Stimulating Private-Sector Agribusiness Investment in Mozambique: Multi-Stakeholder Action Plan*, http://pdf.usaid.gov/pdf_docs/PA00JZ7F.pdf (accessed 17 November 2022).

Hermele, K. (1988) 'Land Struggles and Social Differentiation in Southern Mozambique', Working Paper, The Scandinavian Institute of African Studies, Uppsala, Sweden.

Investment Promotion Centre (CPI) (2012) *The Investors Guide: Mozambique*, http://www.plmj.com/xms/files/Guias_Investimento/2012/Guia_de_Investimento_em_Mocambique_final.pdf (accessed 12 May 2016).

Kajisa, K. and Payongyong, E. (2008) 'Is Mozambique on the Eve of a Rice Green Revolution? A Case Study of the Chokwe Irrigation Scheme', FASID Discussion Paper.

Khan, M. (2010) 'Political Settlements and the Governance of Growth-Enhancing Institutions', Research Paper Series on Governance for Growth, School of Oriental and African Studies, London, available at http://mercury.soas.ac.uk (accessed on 1 January 2015).

Lei de Terras [Land Law] (1997) '19/97 Mozambican Republic. Mozambique's Land Law', Law 19/97 of 1 October, Maputo.

Lunstrum, E. (2008) 'Mozambique, Neoliberal Land Reform, and the Limpopo National Park', *Geographical Review*, 98(3), 339–55.

Macuane, J.J., Buur, L. and Monjane, C.M. (2018) 'Power, Conflict and Natural Resources: The Mozambican Crisis Revisited', *African Affairs*, 117(468), 415–38.

Mosca, J. (2011) *Políticas Agrárias De (em) Moçambique (1975–2009)*, Maputo: Escolar Editora.

Mozambican Republic (2014) 'Constitution of the Republic', Maputo.

NRDP (2016) 'National Rice Development Programme of Mozambique', República de Moçambique: Ministério da Agricultura e Seguranza Alimentar, Maputo, Mozambique.

Porsani, J. (2020) 'Livelihood Implications of Large-Scale Land Concessions in Mozambique: A Case of Family Farmers' Endurance', Södertörns högskola, Södertörn Doctoral Dissertations, Sweden, SE-141 89 Huddinge.

Porsani, J. and Lalander, R. (2018) 'Why Does Deliberative Community Consultation in Large-Scale Land Acquisitions Fail? A Critical Analysis of Mozambican Experiences', *Iberoamerican Journal of Development Studies*, 7(2), 164–93.

Porsani, J., Börjeson, L. and Lehtilä, K. (2017) 'Land Concessions and Rural Livelihoods in Mozambique: The Gap between Anticipated and Real Benefits of a Chinese Investment in the Limpopo Valley', *Journal of Southern African Studies*, 43(6), 1181–98.

Serra, C.M. (2013) *Estado, Pluralismo Jurídico e Recursos Naturais*, Maputo: Escolar Editora.

Tanner, C. (2010) 'Land Rights and Enclosures: Implementing the Mozambican Land Law in Practice', in Anseeuw, W. and Alden, C. (eds), *The Struggle over Land in Africa: Conflicts, Politics and Change*, Cape Town: HSRC Press, pp. 105–30.

Whitfield, L. and Buur, L. (2014) 'The Politics of Industrial Policy: Ruling Elites and their Alliances', *Third World Quarterly*, 35(1), 126–44.

Whitfield, L., Therkildsen, L., Buur, L. and Kjær, M. (2015) *The Politics of African Industrial Policy: A Comparative Perspective*, New York: Cambridge University Press.

7. Exchange relations in rice contract farming schemes in Tanzania

Eileen Dyer Jarnholt, Faustin Maganga and George Schoneveld

1. INTRODUCTION

This chapter analyses exchange relations in rice contract farming schemes in Mbeya, Tanzania. Rice is an important food crop for the Tanzanian economy, as well as for the livelihoods of smallholders and their families. This chapter examines two rice-producing companies: Kapunga Rice Plantation Limited and Mtibwa Sugar Estates. The chapter analyses what characterizes the exchange relationships between contract farmers and investors by identifying what is exchanged in the different relationships and what the outcomes are. The empirical data in this chapter were gathered using household surveys and interviews in 2015 (Jarnholt, 2020). Using the analytical framework on triangular relations between investors, local populations and ruling elites developed by Buur et al. (2017; 2019; 2020), the chapter focuses on the relationship between contract farmers (or the included local population) and investors.

Here this relational model is used to discuss the different exchanges and outcomes, as well as to understand how these exchanges happen and what drives the contract farming schemes. Specifically, this chapter is guided by the following questions: what is exchanged in rice contract farming schemes in Tanzania, and how do these exchanges influence the schemes' outcomes? The chapter argues that the relationship between the included local population and investors can best be described as one of reciprocal exchange deals, as both parties benefit in different ways from the contract farming relationship. However, far from all farmers in the local area are included in these schemes, and struggles over land have intensified over time.

This chapter consists of the following sections. The first section presents a brief review of rice in Tanzania and an introduction to the two cases. The second section presents the contract farmers surveyed in the two cases, and the exchanges between the investors and the contract farmers are analysed and discussed. The next section explores the outcomes of the contract farming schemes and how the contract farmers entered the scheme: the latter being an important factor for understanding more successful outcomes. This will be followed by an analytical section that explores what characterizes the exchange relationships themselves.

2.   RICE IN TANZANIA

Rice is a staple food crop across the world. In Tanzania, it is the third most important food crop after maize and cassava (Wilson and Lewis, 2015). Approximately 20 per cent of farmers in Tanzania produce rice (ibid.), which is cultivated on more than 1.25 million ha of land (Wrobel and Mtaki, 2021). National rice production in 2021 was 2.1 million tonnes (Wrobel and Mtaki, 2021). Smallholders rely on rice as both a food source and for income by selling it to local traders and other farmers. Rice production has increased over the past decade. In 2009, there was a 15 per cent rice deficit of around 150,000 tonnes (RLDC, 2009), meaning that the national demand could not be met. In 2014, however, there was a rice surplus, estimated to be 700,000 tonnes (RCT, 2015). More recently, the surplus was estimated to be 1.3 million tonnes (Joseph, 2018), with the government expecting to decrease imports again in 2022 (Wrobel and Mtaki, 2021). Most rice is grown on small-scale farms, although recent promotions by the Food and Agriculture Organization (FAO) and others (Wilson and Lewis, 2015) have led to a greater focus on improving the rice sector's productivity. Rice also has a central role in the policies and agricultural initiatives established by the Tanzanian government. Like sugar, rice has been associated with conflicts over importation as reflected in specific policies and strategies, which include the rice sector as a major target for agricultural and economic development. One of the key issues and increasingly important motivations for improving the rice sector's productivity is its value as a food crop and concerns regarding food security, most recently following the 2007–08 food crisis. In a self-assessment, Tanzania ranked itself as having comparatively high food insecurity relative to other Sub-Saharan African countries (Headey, 2013, p. 22). The perception that food insecurity is increasing has been a motivating factor behind policies and movements to increase Tanzania's rice output. Furthermore, climate change may negatively affect Tanzania's food security over time (Arndt et al., 2012), in part due to its heavy reliance on rain-fed agriculture. Policies and strategies, including the National Rice Development Strategy, Southern Agricultural Growth Corridor of Tanzania, and Feed the Future, all include a focus on the rice sector (URT, 2009; Wilson and Lewis, 2015; SAGCOT, 2011; URT, 2017). The main focuses in these policies and initiatives are promoting the development of the rice sector as a way of combating food security by increasing rice production and addressing failures in the rice markets. The specific market failures in the

rice sector in Tanzania are related to input provision, access to and maintenance of irrigation systems, storage, transportation and market access.

2.1   Rice Production

Rice in Tanzania is produced primarily by smallholders, who account for
about 90 per cent of production, while the remaining 10 per cent is produced
by larger and/or more commercial farms (URT, 2019). About 5 per cent of the
rice produced in Tanzania is exported; the rest is sold on the national market
(Wilson and Lewis, 2015). The average rice yield for smallholder farmers
is estimated at 2.4 metric tonnes (mt) per ha, whereas it is much higher for
larger-scale farms, at around 12 mt/ha (URT, 2012). However, despite the high
yields of the large-scale farmers, smallholder rice production still accounts for
the majority of rice production. According to the Rice Council of Tanzania,
two major issues faced by these farmers are that: (1) they struggle to market
their production; and (2) access to inputs is difficult (RCT interview, 2015;
Wilson and Lewis, 2015). While voucher programmes providing access to,
for example, fertilizers have been available in Tanzania, they have not been
deemed very successful, producing mixed results for farmers (Kato and
Greeley, 2016). In their survey of the National Agricultural Input Voucher
Scheme (NAIVS), Kato and Greeley found that the better-off farmers benefited
the most from such schemes, as opposed to the poorer farmers, probably due
to better access to state services. They therefore argued that the programme's
implementation was weak. Following market liberalization from the 1990s on,
the effective dismantling of the National Agriculture and Food Corporation
(NAFCO) and the National Milling Corporation, which controlled marketing
and regulation of the grain markets, Tanzania has faced disorganization and
confusion in its marketing management. The National Rice Development
Strategy does not emphasize better access to markets but rather preparation for
the market. The Agricultural Sector Development Program II (2016) aims to
improve rural market infrastructure and access, although it is vague regarding
its methods of implementation.

The use of yield-improving inputs for rice production is still limited among
smallholders in Tanzania. The Agricultural Sector Development Programme
(ASDP)[1] 2009/10 report (URT, 2011) showed that around 2 per cent of smallholders use improved seeds. A baseline study (Nkuba et al., 2016) indicated
that about 50 per cent of the farmers surveyed used fertilizers and about 40
per cent used pesticides. Many factors impede the procurement of inputs like
fertilizers, including availability, distribution, cost and a lack of knowledge
about new inputs (Wilson and Lewis, 2015).

2.2   Import-Export Issues in the Rice Sector

Because Tanzania's rice sector has historically been unable to produce enough to meet national demand, imports of rice have been allowed; however, there has been a certain trade in illegal and/or smuggled rice, driven by price differentials rather than consumer demand (Therkildsen, 2011; Andreoni et al., 2021). Before 2005, imported rice accounted for up to 50 per cent of all rice on the market in Tanzania (Nyange and Morrison, 2005). Thus, rice imports in Tanzania have been complicated by the illegal smuggling of rice, which has increased the challenges to Tanzanian rice producers in selling their rice. In 2018, the government stopped rice imports because of a surplus from national rice production (Joseph, 2018), however, rice is being imported again (Wrobel and Mtaki, 2021). Given that some of the weakest elements of the rice sector in Tanzania are the lack of affordable inputs and problems accessing markets and technical knowledge, contract farming could be a viable option since these elements are often provided through the contract. The promotion of contract farming as a viable intervention is further supported by the fact that recent policies aim to address some of these issues by encouraging private-sector development and contract farming (URT, 2016; SAGCOT, 2011). Where government provision and infrastructure are limited, contract farming can provide legitimate pathways to increasing yields and welfare. Since these conditions apply to the rice sector in Tanzania, this study is critical because it examines what contract farming has provided in a sector that needs improvement in order to reach its full potential. Rice farmers have reported that well-functioning and accessible markets continue to be paramount in the rice sector, given the current surplus (Joseph, 2018).

3.   THE CASES

The two cases included in this chapter are the Mtenda Kyela Rice Supply Company Ltd (MKRS) and Kapunga Rice Plantation Ltd (Kapunga) – two of the 'big four' large-scale rice processors in Tanzania (Wilson and Lewis, 2015). Located in the Mbeya region, they represent 21.57 per cent and 5.57 per cent of national rice production, respectively (Chauvin et al., 2017). The two cases differ in that MKRS is under the sole proprietorship of a single family, whereas Kapunga is owned by the multinational Export Trading Group (ETG).[2] A processor of rice without its own plantation, MKRS sources rice from more than 10,000 farmers (Chauvin et al., 2017; Wilson and Lewis, 2015; Interview, 2015) and has formal contracts with a small group of these farmers. Kapunga in contrast has its own plantation, but only sources from a small group of contract farmers. Thus, the two cases differ in that MKRS does not have land and processes rice outside the communities where it buys the rice, while Kapunga has a plantation and processing mill in the same location where its contract farmers are located and where it rents land to the latter.

3.1   Kapunga Rice Plantation Ltd

Kapunga Rice Plantation Ltd (Kapunga) has a long and somewhat tumultuous history in the region. This formerly state-owned farm was bought by ETG during the era of liberalization and privatization in the 1990s. ETG is associated with the Asian-African Patel family, who are known to have influential political contacts and as rice traders (Africa Confidential, 2013; Therkildsen, 2011). There have been claims that the state farm's privatization involved corruption, with accusations of selling Tanzanian state property cheaply to 'foreigners' (Therkildsen, 2011, p. 40) in exchange for benefits for political leaders and the then ruling Chama Cha Mapinduzi (CCM or the 'Party of the Revolution'). The ETG Kapunga Rice Plantation Ltd inherited about 7,370 ha of land from the NAFCO project at the time of privatization in 2005. While apparently state-owned, this land emerged from a 1995 transfer whereby villagers in Kapunga village, Mbarali district, 'gave' (i.e. were forced to give by the state) 5,500 ha to NAFCO for a rice production project with no compensation in return. When NAFCO was dismantled in 2005, the state offered a title deed for the 7,370 ha to the Kapunga Rice Plantation Ltd, including around 2,000 ha of land in Kapunga village. More recently, in 2015, 1,870 ha of the land owned by the farm were repossessed by authorities and given back to the community due to the company not using it (Kahango, 2015) and village hostility towards the original deal (see below).

Kapunga Rice Plantation Ltd has about 200 employees and owns a rice mill for processing and packaging rice before it is sent to retailers for the domestic market. Up until 2015, the total capital investment was about 8.85 million USD. The plantation yields on average 7 mt/ha of rice annually. Each hectare of land requires 2.5 million Tanzanian shillings (TZS) to operate per year, and around 3,500 ha are currently being cultivated. Kapunga Rice Plantation Ltd cultivates the majority of the land, but it also leases out some land to tenants operating as contract farmers, although they are labelled outgrowers. One group of contract farmers operates as traditional tenants with simple lease contracts. Another group of contract farmers has a more detailed contract than traditional tenants, with the Kapunga investor providing various services, inputs and benefits as part of the contract. Kapunga has contracts with about 60 farmers, although more recent media reports indicate that this number has reached 98 (Citizen Reporter, 16 February 2018). Kapunga produces about 10,000 mt of processed rice per year, making it one of the largest producers in the country. It employs about 2,000 seasonal workers to work on its rice fields. It targets domestic retailers and traders, and its main market is the Mbeya region.[3]

Land conflict

As mentioned, Kapunga has a history of conflict over land which provides an important context for understanding its local investments and its power. Studies from the last two decades provide a context for understanding the history of Kapunga contract farming in Mbarali district (see AFDB, 1995; Chachage and Mbunda, 2009; Greco, 2010; 2015a; 2015b). The Kapunga rice farm was originally a parastatal, and its privatization created a situation ripe for conflict in the 1990s after liberalization policies were implemented (Greco, 2015b). Chachage and Mbunda (2009 discuss privatization of farms owned by the then NAFCO, the ranches under of the National Ranching Company (NARCO) and land belonging to absentee landlords. These researchers observed that the process was 'marred by controversies that have elicited animosities between investors and small-scale producers on the one hand, and between small-scale farmers and pastoralists on the other hand' (Chachage and Mbunda, 2009, p. viii). Experience shows that investors and/or parastatals that have transferred their title deeds to new investors have sometimes infringed on local populations' rights to compensation and consultation (Greco, 2015a). Studies show that up until the late 1950s, until it was transformed into an important commercial rice farming area, Mbarali, where Kapunga is located, was a pastoral grazing area (Hazelwood and Livingstone, 1978; Walsh, 1984).

The Kapunga rice farm was planned in 1979 as an irrigation scheme to be paid for by the Tanzanian government through an African Development Bank (AFDB) loan co-financed by the Nigerian government, and was finally established in the late 1980s after expropriating village land (Greco, 2015b). The state farm, whose land had been levelled for the construction of water canals, had two components: the large-scale estate (3,015 ha) and a smallholder scheme (800 ha). These components were interdependent, as they both relied on a single, shared water canal, and they had a shared title deed, which was a source of conflict when the farm was finally privatized in 2005. The estate was originally composed of 6-ha rice plots, pooled together for mechanized production, plus the estate headquarters, the workers' compounds, a large rice mill, a warehouse and other undeveloped areas (AFDB, 1995). The smallholder scheme was subdivided into 1-ha plots, which the state allocated to farmers from the Chimala Ward. To acquire the land for the state farm, the state moved and resettled several farmers. As Sulle (2017) observed, the compulsory acquisition of village land by the government 'for public interest' purposes was enabled by the Land Acquisition Act of 1967, which gave the president extensive discretionary powers as the trustee of public land. A small group of residents belonging to the area's early settler families and recognized as the village's founders opposed the resettlement, but their resistance was unsuccessful. The farm started operating in 1991 under the management of

NAFCO, which managed it until privatization in 2005. The state farm turned out to be unfeasible and was sold to ETG during the liberalization process. According to Therkildsen (2011), the state farm's privatization was 'shrouded in controversy' involving corruption and accusations of selling Tanzanian state property cheaply to 'foreigners' in exchange for benefits for the ruling CCM-aligned elite, which gave access to land to contract farmers (Therkildsen, 2011, p. 40). The company was founded in Kenya and is a multinational company with corporate offices in Tanzania. One aspect of the controversy was that the company obtained not only state land but additional land during the privatization process. The offer of around 2,000 ha of Kapunga village land created tensions between the investor and more than 4,000 villagers who felt the state had transferred 'their' land to a private property holder for the second time without due compensation (the first time being when the state farm was originally established). To solve this problem, in September 2015 the Ministry of Lands revoked the ownership of 1,870 of the original 7,370 ha of land and returned it to Kapunga village (Kahango, 2015). Although the Minister of Agriculture, Food Security and Cooperatives made statements promising that this land would be returned in 2009 and 2011, the process from the statement of initial intention until final implementation took six years.

3.2   Mtenda Kyela Rice Supply

The Mtenda Kyela Rice Supply Company Ltd (MKRS) was established in 2006, is privately owned by a Tanzanian businessman, George Mtenda, and has its headquarters in Mbeya, the largest city in the Mbeya region. MKRS has only a handful of permanent employees; at the time of fieldwork in 2015, there were only 13 fully employed workers and officials.[4] The company has a main office and a rice mill in Mbeya, where rice sourced from small- and medium-scale farmers is processed. The company sells most of its rice to wholesalers in Dar es Salaam (Wilson and Lewis, 2015). MKRS does not own land for rice production, but instead works with a small but growing number of contract farmers. The town of Mbeya is situated quite high up in terms of elevation; therefore, there is a significant distance (up to 100–200 km) between the mill and the districts where the company sources the rice, depending on which district they source from, because rice is grown at lower altitudes. According to a Bill & Melinda Gates Foundation (BMGF) report from 2012, in its existence thus far, MKRS had received several grants and loans for its smallholder programme and for scaling up its production. The total capital investment at the time of fieldwork was reported to be 1.6 million USD. The Tanzanian Private Sector Foundation provided a training grant, the Agricultural Council of Tanzania (ACT) co-financed the development of demonstration plots, and Oikocredit extended MKRS a loan for 2012–14

(BMGF, 2012; Interview with MKRS, 2015). MKRS also received funds from the Southern Agricultural Growth Corridor of Tanzania's (SAGCOT's) catalytic fund and is a strategic partner within SAGCOT in aiming to improve the rice sector (SAGCOT, 2016).

The BMGF data (2012) show that farmers who participated in MKRS's scheme had significant benefits from doing so, increasing yields and profits through a combination of training and inputs. MKRS has been hailed as promoting a rice-processor scheme that provides opportunities to transform the work of smallholders (Wilson and Lewis, 2015). The ability of MKRS to produce increased yields (claiming 6.8 mt/ha for those smallholders it has trained (BMGF, 2012) with higher profits for farmers) has enhanced its position as a strategic partner in SAGCOT, perhaps triggering some of the grants and loans. This study focuses on MKRS's new contract farming scheme.

MKRS acquires rice in three ways: by buying it at local markets, by buying it from individuals, and more recently through contract farming (Interview, 2015). The company annually targets the same communities in three districts of Kyela, Momba and Mbarali. MKRS's agricultural officers estimate that they source approximately 10,000 to 15,000 smallholders annually (Interview, 2014; SAGCOT, 2016; Wilson and Lewis, 2015; Chauvin et al., 2017). In 2014, MKRS started offering formal contracts to farmers in selected communities to increase the productivity of the farmers from whom they source rice; it is these farmers that are the primary focus of this study.

MKRS's employees conduct agricultural field days in the various districts in which they operate to educate the local sourcing communities on farming techniques, inputs and best practice. Additionally, the company supplements fuel costs for 'state' extension officers who travel far into the various districts. For the input schemes, MKRS used approximately 3.4 billion TZS ($150,000) a year to procure various inputs and training in 2014 alone. Plans to expand include building a mill closer to where the rice is sourced. In 2014, the profit was 1.9 million TZS and the company purchased 10,000 mt of rice. But numbers seem to vary considerably, as MKRS purchased 6,000 mt of rice in 2017 for processing (Interview, 2018). The company produces between 3,500 and 4,000 mt of processed rice per year for the market and targets domestic markets through retail shops primarily in Mbeya and Dar es Salaam.

3.3   Key Differences between the Cases

In this chapter, the two cases of Kapunga Rice Plantation Ltd and Mtenda Kyela Rice Supply Company Ltd are being examined in order to explore what characterizes the exchange relationships between investors and contract farmers, thus allowing for an understanding of what drives contract farming schemes. Based on identifying the exchange relations and outcomes of these

Table 7.1   Household characteristics of the contract farmers

Contract farming group	Average household size	Education household head	Average number of livelihood activities per household	% of female-headed household	Average land-holding per household (ha)
Kapunga contract farmers (n = 49)	3.5	35% secondary school 16% university	3.8	2	27.7
MKRS contract farmers (n = 46)	5.4	62% primary school	3.5	10	3.6

Source: Household surveys of Kapunga and MKRS contract farmers.

contract schemes, which include inputs, credits, extension services and land, it is argued that, despite differences in the structure of the schemes and the attributes of the main actors, significant exchanges come close to resembling reciprocal exchange deals in the relationship between the investors and the contract farmers in these two cases.

However, despite the similarities, it is important to point out that the Kapunga scheme contracts a small group of contract farmers and rents its land out to them, whereas the MKRS investors have no land themselves and rely on purchasing from farmers who do have it. This difference is relevant when it comes to outcomes, as discussed at the end of the chapter. The key household characteristics are depicted in Table 7.1, where the most important difference is the average area of land among the contract farmers.

From Table 7.1, it can be seen that the Kapunga and MKRS contract farmers are similar in their average number of livelihood activities. The average household size is much higher for the MKRS contract farmers, while the Kapunga contract farmers have a higher level of education as a group among household heads. It is not common for women to head the MKRS contract farming households. From Table 7.1, it is clear that the Kapunga contract farming scheme is unique in comparison to the MKRS farming scheme, as the 49 farmers from the Kapunga tenants surveyed in this study have access to much more land. This is because they rent the land they use for rice production from the Kapunga Rice Plantation Ltd investment project, which owns the land. These farmers have on average access to 27.7 ha of land each, of which on average 27.4 ha are rented from the Kapunga investor, on whom they depend for access to the contract farming scheme.

This group of contract farmers is unique geographically in that the majority of them are domiciled somewhere other than on their farm leases. Thus, they are not in regular contact with the rice fields. Only 24 Kapunga contract farmers are located in the actual village of Kapunga. Of the total number of Kapunga farmers, 16 per cent are located in larger cities at least 70 km away from Kapunga, including Mbeya, Makambako and Dar es Salaam. The locations of the Kapunga contract farmers are relevant in light of the long-term conflict between the investor and the local population over the land. Local farmers were dispossessed of the land when the state gave it to the investor, and the conflicts that arose because of this continue today (Greco, 2015b; Kahango, 2015).

As Table 7.1 also suggests, the Kapunga contract farmers have an average of 3.8 livelihood activities per household, and 71 per cent of them pursued at least one off-farm activity.[5] Livelihood activities (see Scoones, 1998; Ellis, 1998; de Haan and Zoomers, 2005) include anything that supports a household's income or provision. The number of livelihood activities a household has can indicate its ability to withstand risk (Scoones, 1998; Ellis, 1998). A higher number of livelihood activities indicates that a household is less susceptible to crises. In short, the Kapunga contract farmers have a number of livelihood opportunities and often follow an off-farm activity based geographically outside the investment site. This suggests they are better able to stand up to risks.

In contrast to the Kapunga case, the group surveyed from the MKRS contract farming scheme consists of 46 households, representing close to the entire population of households engaged in formal contracts with MKRS, around 50 at the time of the fieldwork. However, according to recent contact with an MKRS employee, this has risen to 200 with the contracts including improved seedlings, fertilizer, training and credit.[6] These farmers use land they own or have acquired through other sources; thus, in contrast to Kapunga, MKRS as investor does not own the land the contract farmers use. MKRS contract farmers have on average 3.25 ha of land per household, substantially less than the Kapunga farmers. The MKRS contract farmers have an average of 3.5 livelihood activities per household, and 52 per cent are engaged in off-farm activities, suggesting some diversification (Scoones, 1998). Unlike Kapunga, MKRS does not have a history of conflict, perhaps because the contract farming scheme is still relatively new and/or MKRS has acquired land from local populations using the state as a broker.

4.   CONCRETE EXCHANGES

Concrete transactions in the form of inputs, grouped together here as access to irrigation, fertilizers, pesticides, seedlings, machinery credits, and extension services, in exchange for rice, underpin the foundation of the relationship

Table 7.2   *Usage and access to inputs for contract farmers as a percentage of the entire group of farmers*

Input table	Fertilizer	Improved seedlings	Pesticides	Tractor	Irrigation
Mtenda n = 46					
Used input	46	9	36	29	11
Accessed through company	23	1	0	0	0
Accessed through shops	23	8	36	29	0
Irrigation only: accessed through government or scheme					11
Kapunga n = 49					
Used input	48	47	48	41	40
Accessed through company	24	43	3	19	3
Accessed through other means	24	0	0	20	23
Irrigation only: accessed through government or scheme					14

Note: n = number of respondents.
Source: Household surveys of contract farmers in MKRS and Kapunga.

that developed between investors and the included contract farmers. It is known from the literature that these forms of exchange often lead to changes in productivity, as well as possible welfare improvements (Bellemare, 2012; Kirsten and Sartorius, 2002). According to the literature on contract farming (Key and Runsten, 1999; Dixie et al., 2014), inputs, exposure to learning and technology, and access to markets, are among the main benefits of, and thus motivators for, farmers' joining contract farming. Additionally, the provision of these inputs and services helps the company secure access to higher quality paddy and rice, a key reason companies establish contract farming schemes (Kirsten and Sartorius, 2002; Bolwig et al., 2009).

In the households surveyed during fieldwork, respondents identified their use of inputs as indicative of some of the concrete exchanges. Access to and use of inputs provided by investing companies are separated here into a series of concrete inputs for production, and the inputs exchanged in the contract farming relationship are shown in the row labelled 'accessed through company' in Table 7.2.

As suggested by the data presented in Table 7.2, almost all the respondents within the two contract farming schemes use fertilizer regularly, and most also use tractors and pesticides. The vast majority of Kapunga respondents use improved seeds provided by the company, while only a small percentage of MKRS respondents do so. This difference is due in part to the contracts' content: improved seedlings are a regular part of Kapunga contracts, unlike the MKRS contracts. For both companies, fertilizer is sourced from the company and other suppliers, indicating that while fertilizer is a main exchange item from company to farmer within the contract, farmers also obtain additional inputs. While the Kapunga contract provides more types of input, both groups state that they purchase additional inputs outside the contract farming schemes. This could indicate that either the companies do not offer enough affordable inputs within the contract to satisfy production needs, or that the contracted farmers have additional resources with which to purchase additional inputs. Table 7.2 also suggests that the contract itself matters because the Kapunga farmers receive more inputs than the MKRS farmers – that is, the Kapunga contract offers more concrete inputs. The MKRS contract does not provide for pesticides, which are sourced from local shops. It is important to note that, while these inputs were not exclusively accessed through the contract farming schemes, the schemes' ability to provide a pathway to inputs, even if not the only one, was important (Interviews, 2018).

Access to irrigation is primarily provided through irrigation schemes, although according to the survey only about 25 per cent of MKRS farmers claimed to use irrigation. However, according to the survey responses, 41 households out of the 46 farmers in the MKRS contract farmers group are members of an irrigation scheme. Thus, there is a mismatch between the number of farmers claiming membership of an irrigation scheme and the number of farmers who use irrigation. Unlike the MKRS farmers, the majority of Kapunga farmers indicated they used irrigation, in contrast to the low percentage of MKRS farmers.

Access to extension services means access to technical knowledge and opportunities to increase yields, as well as improved farming techniques. MKRS offers some services provided by the company and supports state-driven extension services in the area, but to our knowledge, Kapunga does not (based on fieldwork from 2014–15). About 20 per cent of the MKRS farmers report receiving extension services from the company and 50 per cent from the government extension officers. In contrast, fewer than 20 per cent of the Kapunga farmers reported gaining access to the company through either government extension officers or the company. Compared to the Kapunga farmers, the MKRS respondents were far more likely to receive extension services, primarily through government extension officers. The irrigation scheme and rice associations provided little access to extension services. Therefore, while the contracts with both MKRS and Kapunga allowed for exchanges of extension services, government extension officers were the primary contributors of training for these farmers. The BMGF (2012) report indicated that MKRS trained smallholders in order to increase yields; while this information seems to be correct, the data suggest that only a limited number of farmers have received training in farming methods through MKRS. Based on information gained during fieldwork, it is clear that MKRS pays for state extension officers' transportation costs, bolstering the state's acceptance of the investment and ensuring that farmers get training and information which will potentially lead to higher quality paddy and greater yields (Interview with MKRS, 2015).

4.1   Motivations for Entering into a Contract

Examining the motivations for entering into a contract sheds more light on what contract farmers expect to gain from doing so. Farmers joined contract schemes largely due to market-related issues such as access to a market and marketing guarantees related to having a secure buyer for their rice. MKRS employees stated that they targeted a few select communities of smallholders who were already organized into irrigation schemes when looking for contracts (interview with MKRS, 2015). Access to irrigation was therefore not the first priority for farmers.

Farmers from both contract schemes stated in surveys that they signed the contract to access market opportunities they would not otherwise have had, for example, though the state. Over 60 per cent of the MKRS farmers and 92 per cent of the Kapunga contract farmers cited this as a reason for joining the contract farming scheme. Market access for rice is problematic in the Mbeya region, and many farmers must resort to selling through a middleman at a low price (Interview with Raphael, 2015; Rice Council of Tanzania interview, 2015; Wilson and Lewis, 2015). Also, access to fertilizer is beneficial for farmers in order to access affordable agricultural inputs, as well as being important in light of problems in implementing input voucher schemes in Tanzania (Kato and Greeley, 2016). Eighteen farmers who joined the MKRS contract scheme mentioned in interviews that this scheme was the only opportunity they had to access inputs and a stable market, further underscoring the lack of sufficient market access for farmers in this area, as well as for 12 of the Kapunga contract farmers.

5.   RELATIONSHIPS BETWEEN CONTRACT FARMERS AND INVESTORS

This section focuses on the outcomes of relationships between the contract farmers and the investors in the two rice investment cases, Kapunga and

MKRS. By examining the two surveyed groups of contract farmers from MKRS and Kapunga, this section explores the exchanges between the contract farmer and the investors, the different outcomes and finally how farmers accessed the schemes.

5.1   Land and Conflict

The Kapunga contract farmers had significantly more land than excluded members of the local population (Jarnholt, 2020). The contracts offered by the investor facilitated access to land for a select and exclusive group of contract farmers. Kapunga's contract farmers gain access to a substantial share of land through the contract without necessarily being embedded in the local communities. Out of the Kapunga group of contract farmers, 46 plots were reported, all varying in size from a few hectares up to hundreds of hectares, with an average of 27.7 ha. Many of the Kapunga contract farmers had access to other forms of livelihood elsewhere that offer a secure income. For example, 25 of the farmers had at least one shop or restaurant in addition to their rice production, and 12 were government employees (e.g. nurse, teacher, government official).

In contrast to the Kapunga case, for MKRS farmers, the average land holdings are 3.25 ha per household. The Kapunga contract farmers therefore have on average access to eight times more land than MKRS. MKRS land tenure is mostly in the form of individual deeds. Because most smallholders own the deeds to the land on which they grow rice, they have security of land ownership as opposed to most of the Kapunga outgrowers, who do not own the land they farm. In contrast, only three of the MKRS farmers had service employment, and only 11 had a shop or restaurant. A major difference therefore is that MKRS does not have its own farmland, nor is it located where the rice is sourced. The geographical separation between the company's headquarters and the rice production in which it has an interest was reflected in the comments of several farmers who have a contract with MKRS. They complained that MKRS did not show up to collect the rice as agreed in the contracts (Focus group, 2015). Because MKRS sources rice from three different districts and has only a small number of full-time employees, the lack of geographical proximity could have implications for the type of relationship it can establish with contract and other rice farmers in the sourcing villages. However, as stipulated in the contract, MKRS targets farmers with approximately 0.1 to 0.8 ha of land available for rice and reserves the right to inspect that land, which could be described as giving it indirect access to land as stipulated in the contract. Despite the criticisms over a lack of availability, MKRS generally had considerable legitimacy in the three districts it sources rice from.

This is in clear contrast to Kapunga's limited acceptance by the surrounding local community, which was characterized by conflict over land and the company's proximity to the CCM government. At the core of the conflict is the state's privatization of a state farm, with the state taking land from local populations that was given to the investing company. This gave the company authority over several thousand hectares of land. At the core of the conflict is the fact that the main beneficiaries were a small group of local elite power-brokers with links to the CCM ruling party, many of whom do not actually live in Kapunga, yet gained access to land as part of the contract farming scheme. In contrast, land is not exchanged between the MKRS rice investor and the local populations. This may be because land has not played a significant role in the outcomes of the relationship between the contract farmers and the investor and has therefore actually strengthened the relationship.

In summary, for MKRS contract farmers, the contract provided fertilizer and some access to extension services. Access to other inputs, such as credits, pesticides and irrigation, was gained through shops or irrigation schemes because these were not offered in the MKRS contract. For Kapunga contract farmers, fertilizer, improved seedlings and tractors were the inputs they received as part of the contract.[7] Thus, the Kapunga contract was more comprehensive than the MKRS contract in offering more services to the farmers, and land was exchanged through the Kapunga scheme.

5.2   Outcomes and Reciprocity in Contract Farming Relationships

Both groups of contract farmers perceived themselves as benefiting from the schemes. Even though Kapunga farmers were better off from the outset than MKRS farmers (due to their diverse livelihoods, having more off-farm employment and being from different locations), both groups gained from the contract farming schemes. For Kapunga, 90 per cent of the contract farmers responded that they have been better off since joining the contract farming scheme. For MKRS, 61 per cent of the farmers who responded said they were better off, but 37 per cent did not respond to the question. Because the scheme was still new in 2015, they stated it was too early to tell if it had any differences.

In their survey responses, the farmers explained that, due to the higher incomes, they could buy material items like bicycles, motorbikes, cars and radios, and could afford to spend more money on health and education. Two-thirds of the MKRS farmers stated that their status had improved since starting the contract farming scheme. However, given that it had only been running for a year, certainty about absolute gains is difficult. On the other hand, given the reasons for joining the contract schemes, farmers could have seen improvements in areas that were previously problematic, for example, in

accessing inputs and markets. Thus, farmers clearly indicated that they benefited from contract farming investments.

When asked whether or not engaging in contract farming with rice allowed
investment in other livelihood activities, 85 per cent of the MKRS farmers
and 94 per cent of the Kapunga farmers responded positively. The types of
activities farmers invested in varied, but the most common ones for the MKRS
farmers were investing in a small business such as a restaurant or retail shop,
purchasing more land or building more sturdy houses. Many MKRS farmers
also attributed the ability to cover basic needs (e.g. housing, school fees, access
to healthcare) to the profits they gained from rice farming (Household surveys
of MKRS farmers, 2015). For the Kapunga farmers the results were similar,
although owning more land was also a common outcome of rice farming,
and there was more investment in additional farming than among the MKRS
farmers.

For the MKRS farmers their sense of having profited from the contract
farming scheme was related to their gaining access to inputs, markets and
extension services. Farmers reported that the contract farming scheme met
their need to find a place to sell their rice and allowed them to reinvest in
other livelihood activities. The ability to gain access to inputs like fertilizers
is important in that the contract provided concrete exchanges that otherwise
might not have been available to the farmers. The investor also provided the
contract farmers with exchanges in the form of establishing agricultural field
days and helping extension officers get to the villages where the contract
farmers were located.

On the other hand, the company received paddy from identified and secure
sellers through the contracts. In addition to the secure access to rice, MKRS
also received indirect access to land in accordance with the contract stipu-
lating that they could inspect the land and pay for extension officers to visit
the farmers. Thus, reciprocity occurred because both sides contributed to
and received something out of the relationship. By identifying these specific
exchanges and outcomes, the analysis has shown what potentially compels the
contract farming scheme to continue. The exchanges and outcomes the MKRS
contract farmers and investors experience are the driving forces behind the
scheme. Similarly, the Kapunga farmers were motivated by access to market
opportunities when joining the scheme but stressed that they saw access as
providing special opportunities for profit due to the relatively large amounts of
land they could access and the stable access to inputs. The Kapunga contract
farmers not only gained access to large plots of land, but also to inputs and
were guaranteed access to a market. They clearly perceived themselves to be
better off after entering the scheme and reinvested profits from rice contract
farming in other activities. The Kapunga investors, in turn, received high
quality rice that they could process at their mill (Interview with Kapunga

employee, 2015). They outsourced production on their fields to other farmers, potentially reducing some of their transaction costs. They also determined that each contract should cover fairly large plots of land to be leased to the farmer, thus reducing their transaction costs by having fewer farmers who were well connected with the state administration, with which they could negotiate. The investor, in turn, has recruited farmers to work their land and provide high quality product, meaning they can standardize their production, spreading the risks of production and managing their labour costs. These characteristics of the contract farmer-investor relationship at Kapunga show what drives the contract farming scheme.

This chapter's empirical findings contribute to the literature on contract farming schemes and increase our knowledge of how such schemes function, particularly in Tanzania. Contract farming is said to be beneficial when it can address market failures (service provision, inputs, access to markets) and can provide benefits to the contract farmers (Grosh, 1994; Bellemare, 2012; Maertens and Swinnen, 2009; Miyata et al., 2009; Warning and Key, 2002). According to Tanzanian policies and reviews of the rice sector (Wilson and Lewis, 2015; BMGF, 2012; Kato and Greeley, 2016), access to such inputs, services and markets is important in resolving the absence of such inputs (Buur et al., 2017). While the schemes are still small, they may affect how the local rice markets function in these geographical locations, which is important when considering contract farming's potential role in terms of larger community or sector impacts. For MKRS, land tenure is in the hands of the farmers, reducing the farmers' levels of risk when engaging in contract farming. The company also avoids potentially volatile conflicts which have caused major issues among large-scale investments in Tanzania, including Kapunga, because it does not control the farmland itself. This finding is also consistent with the literature on the advantages of farmers' engaging in contract farming as a way to access land without having formal ownership (Oya, 2012; Minot, 2009).

The Kapunga farmers who joined the contract schemes were motivated by access to precious land that gave them opportunities for profit, as well as access to inputs and markets. Through their own relationships, the investors sought out contract farmers who could meet the standards of cultivating large tracts of rented land. Seeking out farmers for whom the profits can be the greatest is considered a strategic move that companies employ (Barrett et al., 2012). For the majority of the 95 contract farmers in these cases (Household surveys, 2015), contract farming enriches their lives and livelihoods.

6. CONCLUSION

This chapter has addressed the following research question: *What is exchanged in rice contract farming schemes in Tanzania, and how do these exchanges influence the contract farming schemes' outcomes?* In both cases (Kapunga and MKRS), significant exchanges are made between investors and contract farmers. Specifically, contract farmers receive exchanges in the form of access to inputs, markets and credits, while investors receive access to a higher quality product from a stable source. Land is exchanged in the Kapunga case because the contract farmers lease land from the investor. In the MKRS case the contract farmers own the land themselves, although the investor is contractually allowed to inspect the land on which rice is grown for sale. The outcomes for the contract farmers include their becoming better off and being able to invest their profits from rice farming in other activities, indicating a largely favourable experience for most of the contract farmers in these two cases. The exchanges and the positive outcomes that both sets of actors subsequently experience are enough to maintain the scheme in being, indicating that reciprocal exchanges characterize these relationships and encourage the scheme to continue. These results also resonate with the literature on contract farming showing how contract farmers benefit from participating in the contract farming scheme.

NOTES

1. The ASDP is a framework used to guide agricultural policy in Tanzania and to commercialize the agricultural sector. The ASDP programme has involved two phases thus far (URT, 2016).
2. The Export Trading Group is a large agricultural conglomerate focusing mainly on African countries for procurement, but it also spans several continents. See http://www.etgworld.com/ (accessed 15 January 2020).
3. Information from company survey and interviews (2014, 2015).
4. Company survey and interviews (2014 and 2015).
5. An off-farm activity was considered to be anything not related to the growing and selling of produce and food (e.g. selling vegetables was not considered off-farm, but having a small shop was). Studies show that diversifying to off-farm activities can increase households' ability to withstand risk (de Haan and Zoomers, 2005).
6. Interview, September 2018.
7. Irrigation was also described as being mainly sourced outside the companies, although the patterns, at least for Kapunga, are unclear.

REFERENCES

Africa Confidential (2013) 'Tanzania: Concern over Contract Farming', *Africa Confidential*, 54(24), 6–7.
African Development Bank (AFDB) (1995) *Project Completion Report: Kapunga Rice Irrigation Project*, Tanzania: African Development Bank.
Andreoni, A., Mushi, D. and Therkildsen, O. (2021) 'Tanzania's 'Rice Bowl': Production Success, Scarcity Persistence and Rent Seeking in the East African

Community', ACE (Anti-Corruption Evidence) SOAS University of London Working Paper, 034, pp. 1–45.

Arndt, C., Farmer, W., Strzepek, K. and Thurlow, J. (2012) 'Climate Change, Agriculture and Food Security in Tanzania', *Review of Development Economics*, 16(3), 378–93.

Barrett, C.B., Bachke, M.E., Bellemare, M.F., Michelson, H.C., Narayanan, S. and Walker, T.F. (2012) 'Smallholder Participation in Contract Farming: Comparative Evidence from Five Countries', *World Development*, 40(4), 715–30.

Bellemare, M.F. (2012) 'As You Sow, so Shall You Reap: The Welfare Impacts of Contract Farming', *World Development*, 40(7), 1418–34.

Bill & Melinda Gates Foundation (BMGF) (2012) *Developing the Rice Industry in Africa: Tanzania Assessment*, accessed 18 November 2022 at http://www.inter -reseaux.org/IMG/pdf/20120803_Tanzania_rice_value_chain_analysis_external_ .pdf.

Bolwig, S., Gibbon, P. and Jones, S. (2009) 'The Economics of Smallholder Organic Contract Farming in Tropical Africa', *World Development*, 37(6), 1094–104.

Buur, L., Nystrand, M. and Pedersen, R.H. (2017) 'The Political Economy of Land and Natural Resource Investments in Africa: An Analytical Framework', DIIS Working Paper, no. 2, vol. 2017, Danish Institute for International Studies (DIIS), Copenhagen.

Buur, L., Pedersen, R.H., Nystrand, M. and Macuane, J. (2019) 'Understanding the Three Key Relationships in Natural Resource Investments in Africa: An Analytical Framework', *The Extractive Industries and Society*, 6(4), 1195–204.

Buur, L., Pedersen, R.H., Nystrand, M., Macuane, J. and Jacob, T. (2020) 'The Politics of Natural Resource Investments and Rights in Africa: A Theoretical Approach', *The Extractive Industries and Society*, 7(3), 918–30.

Chachage, C. and Mbunda, R. (2009) 'The State of the then NAFCO, NARCO and Absentee Landlords' Farms/Ranches in Tanzania', Report prepared for the Land Rights and Resources Institute, Haki Ardhi, Dar es Salaam.

Chauvin, N.D., Porto, G. and Mulangu, F. (2017) *Agricultural Supply Chains, Growth and Poverty in Sub-Saharan Africa: Market Structure, Farm Constraints and Grass-Root Institutions*, Berlin, Heidelberg: Springer.

Citizen Reporter (2018) 'How Modern Farming Practices Helped Triple Production of Rice', *The Citizen* (16 February 2016), accessed 18 November 2022 at https:// www.thecitizen.co.tz/News/Business/How-modern-farming-practices-helped-triple -production-of-rice/1840414-4307252-gj4pw0z/index.html.

De Haan, L. and Zoomers, A. (2005) 'Exploring the Frontier of Livelihoods Research', *Development and Change*, 36(1), 27–47.

Dixie, G., Jaeger, P., Jonasova, M., Ronchi, L., Sergeant, A. and Yap, J. (2014) 'An Analytical Toolkit for Support to Contract Farming (English)', Agriculture and Environmental Services, Washington, DC: World Bank Group, accessed 18 November 2022 at http://documents.worldbank.org/curated/en/575871468204575206/An -analytical-toolkit-for-support-to-contract-farming.

Ellis, F. (1998) 'Household Strategies and Rural Livelihood Diversification', *Journal of Development Studies*, 35(1), 1–38.

Greco, E. (2010) 'The Land Question Revisited: Tanzania 1987–2007', PhD thesis, L'Orientale, University of Naples, unpublished.

Greco, E. (2015a) 'Local Politics of Land: The Restructuring of Rice Farming Areas', LCSV Working Paper Series, University of Manchester, no. 12.

Greco, E. (2015b) 'Landlords in the Making: Class Dynamics of the Land Grab in Mbarali, Tanzania', *Review of African Political Economy*, 42(144), 225–44.

Grosh, B. (1994) 'Contract Farming in Africa: An Application of the New Institutional Economics', *Journal of African Economies*, 3(2), 231–61.

Hazelwood, A. and Livingstone, I. (1978) *The Development Potential of the Usangu Plains*, London: Commonwealth Fund for Technical Cooperation.

Headey, D. (2013) 'The Impact of the Global Food Crisis on Self-Assessed Food Security', *The World Bank Economic Review*, 27(1), 1–27.

Jarnholt, E.D. (2020) 'Contract Farming Schemes in Rice and Sugar in Tanzania: Assessing the Implications of Exchange, Power and Differentiation', Double Degree PhD dissertation, Roskilde University and University of Utrecht.

Joseph, J. (2018) 'Rice Importation Suspended as Local Production Doubles', *The Citizen* (13 September 2018), accessed 18 November 2022 at https://www.thecitizen.co.tz/News/Rice-importation-suspended-aslocal-production-doubles/1840340-4757084-xxfedb/index.html.

Kahango, G. (2015) 'Ownership of 1,870 ha of Rice Fields Revoked', *The Citizen* (26 September 2015), accessed 15 January 2020 at https://www.thecitizen.co.tz/News/Ownership-of-1-870ha-of-rice-fields-revoked/1840340-2886448-10c9eo9z/index.html.

Kato, T. and Greeley, M. (2016) 'Agricultural Input Subsidies in Sub-Saharan Africa', *IDS Bulletin*, 47(4), 33–48.

Key, N. and Runsten, D. (1999) 'Contract Farming, Smallholders, and Rural Development in Latin America: The Organization of Agroprocessing Firms and the Scale of Outgrower Production', *World Development*, 27(2), 381–401.

Kirsten, J. and Sartorius, K. (2002) 'Linking Agribusiness and Small-Scale Farmers in Developing Countries: Is there a New Role for Contract Farming?', *Development in Southern Africa*, 19(4), 503–29.

Maertens, M. and Swinnen, J. (2009) 'Trade, Standards, and Poverty: Evidence from Senegal', *World Development*, 37(1), 161–78.

Minot, N. (2009) 'Contract Farming in Developing Countries: Patterns, Impact, and Policy Implications' in P. Pinstrup-Andersen and F. Cheng (eds) *Case Studies in Food Policy for Developing Countries, Volume II: Domestic Policies for Markets Production, and Environment*, Ithaca, NY: Cornell University Press, pp. 36–49.

Miyata, S., Minot, N. and Hu, D. (2009) 'Impact of Contract Farming on Income: Linking Small Farmers, Packers, and Supermarkets in China', *World Development*, 37(11), 1781–90.

Nkuba, J., Ndunguru, A., Madulu, R., Lwezaura, D., Kajiru, G., Babu, A., Chalamila, B. and Ley, G. (2016) 'Rice Value Chain Analysis in Tanzania: Identification of Constraints, Opportunities and Upgrading Strategies', *African Crop Science Journal*, 24(Issue Supplement 1), 73–87.

Nyange, D. and Morrison, J. (2005) 'Extent and Impact of Food Import Surges: The Case of Tanzania', Final Report, FAO, Rome.

Oya, C. (2012) 'Contract Farming in Sub-Saharan Africa: A Survey of Approaches, Debates and Issues', *Journal of Agrarian Change*, 12(1), 1–33.

Rice Council of Tanzania (RCT) (2015) 'Tanzania's Rice Industry is under Threat', Position paper, Dar es Salaam.

Rural Livelihood Development Company (RLDC) (2009) 'Rice Sector Strategy: Improving Rice Profitability through Increased Productivity and Better Marketing Focusing on Tanzania's Central Corridor', Board version, Dar es Salaam.

SAGCOT (2011) 'Southern Agricultural Growth Corridor of Tanzania: Investment Blueprint', Dar es Salaam.

SAGCOT (2016) *2016 Annual Report*, Dar es Salaam: SAGCOT Centre Ltd.

Scoones, I. (1998) 'Sustainable Rural Livelihoods: A Framework for Analysis', IDS Working Paper, Institute of Development Studies, University of Sussex.

Sulle, E. (2017) 'Social Differentiation and the Politics of Land: Sugarcane Outgrowing in Kilombero, Tanzania', *Journal of Southern African Studies*, 43(3), 517–33.

Therkildsen, O. (2011) 'Policy Making and Implementation in Agriculture: Tanzania's Push for Irrigated Rice', DIIS Working Paper, no. 26, DIIS, Copenhagen.

The United Republic of Tanzania (2009) 'National Rice Development Strategy', Dar es Salaam.

The United Republic of Tanzania (2011) 'Agricultural Sector Development Programme (ASDP)', *ASDP Performance Report 2009–2010*, ASDP M&E Working Group, Dar es Salaam.

The United Republic of Tanzania (2012) 'National Sample Census of Agriculture 2007/2008, Large Scale Farms Volume IV', Zanzibar.

The United Republic of Tanzania (2016) 'Agricultural Sector Development Programme Phase II', Government Programme Document, Dar es Salaam.

The United Republic of Tanzania (2017) 'Agricultural Sector Development Programme Phase II', Ministry of Agriculture, Dar es Salaam.

The United Republic of Tanzania (2019) 'National Rice Development Strategy Phase II', Ministry of Agriculture, Dar es Salaam.

Walsh, M. (1984) 'The Misinterpretation of Chiefly Power in Usangu, South-West Tanzania', PhD Thesis, University of Cambridge.

Warning, M. and Key, N. (2002) 'The Social Performance and Distributional Consequences of Contract Farming: An Equilibrium Analysis of the Arachide de bouche program in Senegal', *World Development*, 30(2), 255–63.

Wilson, R.T. and Lewis, I. (2015) 'The Rice Value Chain in Tanzania: A Report from the Southern Highlands Food Systems Programme', FAO, Rome.

Wrobel, J. and Mtaki, B. (2021) 'Grain and Feed Annual Report: Tanzania', United States Department of Agriculture, Foreign Agricultural Service, Washington DC.

8. Conclusion

Lars Buur and Rasmus H. Pedersen

While we were in the final stages of preparing this manuscript for submission, the war between Russia and Ukraine blew up. It had been coming for months, but the shock among chapter contributors and editors was apparent. Immediately it became clear that the threat to European energy security and the rise in energy prices opened up new possibilities for stalled investments in a number of African countries. Whereas a number of Western countries and institutions at the COP26 climate change conference in Glasgow, UK, at the end of 2021 had pledged to cut their funding for fossil-fuel projects in developing countries, European governments and oil and gas companies now started scrambling for alternatives to Russian gas in, for instance, Algeria, Senegal, Tanzania and Mozambique.

These events have also upended international political relations in many ways, most conspicuously demonstrated in Mozambique, where Western donors have agreed to fund Mozambique again after pulling out over a debt scandal in 2016. The scandal has not been resolved, but the new urgency in stabilising Mozambique and securing strategic gas and mineral reserves in the re-emergence of geopolitical competition between Russia, China, the European Union and the USA has had important consequences for extractive investments in southern and eastern Africa. The US and the European Union have also increased support for Mozambican efforts to quell 'Shabaab' youth rebelling in the northern regions of Cabo Delgado that threatened the gas investments. The French government appears to be paying for a military intervention by Rwanda to facilitate the French oil company Total returning to its gas investments in Cabo Delgado after they pulled out in 2021.

Investments in the 'green transition' – wind and solar power – and strategic minerals and graphite (used for lubricants, batteries and fuel cells) have also started flying off the ground, with investment approvals coming thick and fast. Stalled wind and solar power projects have begun moving[1] and gas and mining investments are being fast-tracked with the European Union launching its Repower plan to fix its reliance on Russian oil.[2] In other words, the fact that what was earlier impossible even to consider could now happen so suddenly has, in just the last three months, been made possible by global and regional socio-political developments.

To a large extent, the dramatic developments triggered by the war between Russia and Ukraine make this volume's findings even more important. Whereas approvals and investment decisions are now moving ahead thick and fast, it is an open question whether these new investments will be implemented, whether the rights of local populations will be upheld, or whether they will trigger new conflicts. We can, however, learn from the experience of past resource booms. This requires a focus on the relations of key groups of actors and on investment processes in both the short and longer terms, which is exactly what the volume is about.

In all our cases, sectors' and countries' extractive investments are ongoing, changing, stalling and moving in new directions due to changes in the organisation of political settlements, local resistance to investments and/or the foreign investors and their insertion into global value chains and the world economy. The order is constant chance, sometimes incremental, at other times ruptures, rarely stability, even if this is the order we would like to have. The cases discussed and analysed in this book clearly suggest that it is rather difficult to implement investments while accommodating the different rights of local populations. Extractive investment processes are inherently complex and latently conflictual. Every time one thinks some stability has been achieved with an investment or other, and now all the actors are somehow aligned, world market prices, international political dynamics, internal political dynamics or social cleavages disrupt the picture, whether separately or together. Analysing large-scale investments in natural resources therefore entails a careful unpacking of the underlying processes, histories of the investments and outcomes. This involves accepting that change is the order of the day. Still, it is possible to identify patterns in the sample of cases from Mozambique, Tanzania and Uganda discussed in this book.

We have argued in favour of a critical unpacking of these issues by focusing on each of the three-way key relationships between ruling elites, investors and local populations, and what characterises these relationships in the different cases of investment. Our analysis of the relationships between these actors points to the inherently tension-ridden and conflictual relationships between the different parties. This triangular relationship that is characterised by the mutual exchange relations depicted in the relational model presented in the introduction thus represents an ideal and to some extent idealised situation. In practice, the compositions of ruling elites, investors and local populations and the exchange relations between them will vary and will inevitably lead to differences in outcomes. This is clearly suggested by the case of gas pipeline development in Tanzania, gas in Mozambique, coal in Tanzania, sugar in Uganda and Tanzania and rice in Mozambique and Tanzania.

What seems clear from the seven cases discussed in this book is that processes related to investments in natural resources, ranging from oil/gas and coal to agriculture, are often more contingent than some of the recent literature on natural resource extraction suggests. In exploring why this is the case, we have tried to move beyond simplistic notions of who seems most powerful from the outset where foreign investors have been given privileged positions by different bodies of literature. While foreign investors may appear to be the most important actors due to their economic, technical and market capital, our analyses demonstrate that the relationships between all the actors are important and evolving. This allows us to understand in new ways why investments are implemented and whether rights are promoted.

1.   RESTATING THE VENTURE

The work underlying this edited book was grounded on two main challenges that extractive resource investments are presently confronted with. First, many natural resource investments fail to become implemented or end up in ongoing conflict scenarios that undermine their potential to underpin the processes of economic transformation that are needed for Sub-Saharan African economies to live up to the expectations of their diverse socio-political populations. Second, our focus has been on whether and how the rights of local populations can be accommodated by being established in and through investments, as a proxy for achieving some kind of justice and benefits when they are affected by large-scale extractive investments.

In this final chapter, we summarise what our analyses of the Ugandan, Tanzanian and Mozambican case studies have contributed to addressing these two main challenges. We do this by first going through the lessons that can be drawn from our focus on the three main relationships between (various) investors, ruling elites and local populations and their outcomes. Second, we relate this to what it can contribute to our focus on rights as the outcomes of evolving relations and why this is important at this particular moment in time, when the green transition has put even more pressure on extractivism.

2.   RELATIONSHIPS

2.1   Ruling Elites-Investors

The new literature on the effects of the resource curse (Ovadia, 2016), mining (Kirsch, 2014) and agricultural investments suggests that different types of investment play different roles in the survival and reproduction of the ruling elites. For example, when we revisit the analysis of the Tanzania pipeline and the analytical model, it becomes clear that large-scale investments in gas play a different role for ruling elites than agricultural investments. One key reason for this difference is how important the investments are for the economic and political survival of the ruling elites and the more or less democratic regimes that underpin them (Whitfield et al., 2015). The ability to extract rents, whether legally or illicitly, as suggested for Mozambique (Salimo et al., 2020; Salimo, 2022; Macuane et al., 2018) may also be important for why ruling elites are ready to push through investments despite strong local resistance and heavy transaction costs.

These differences have implications when it comes to the de facto implementation of investments and how rights are engaged. Whereas, for example, oil investments are nearly always implemented because they are important for the survival of ruling elites, as we argue in this book, investments in agribusinesses often fail to materialise altogether or break down during implementation because they take much longer to mature and their benefits are only long term. This was the case for rice in Mozambique, particularly when the regime does not need the investments for its own survival, in which case they do not have a strong interest in protecting them. In contrast, as Jacob's text in this volume shows, mining in Tanzania can see very intimate relations between investors and ruling elites emerge, but these are subject to change if they undermine the ruling elite's relations with important electoral constituencies. Much the same can be said about the Tanzanian and Ugandan sugar sector when the ruling parties have an interest in pleasing key constituencies and still base their rule in some form or idea about being 'legitimate'.

The broader point is that, even though ruling elites, and the state apparatus they control, have approved a particular investment, there is no guarantee that they will not be undermined by electoral constituencies or other ruling elite factions, as the case of rice in Mozambique shows in several examples. Alternatively, that support might be shallow from the outset, as 'support' is aimed more at getting the investment approved so that they, as the rulers, can demonstrate their success and ability to attract resources rather than seeing it implemented. Implementation often requires a strong commitment and an ability to absorb transaction costs, for example, by going against key electoral constituencies or other interest groups.

Another reason for these differences in alignment between investor and ruling elite interests and their role in the reproduction and survival of ruling elites is that, for very large investments, the investors often have considerable 'holding power'. As we have explained in the introduction to this volume, investors have technical know-how, access to market and marketing and strong backing from bilateral and multilateral organisations, on top of financial power that few developing countries could dream about. This can be further complicated as illustrated by the case of the Tanzanian gas pipeline, where the investor was a state-owned enterprise (see Kweka and Pedersen, this volume), as was the case for the example of Tanzanian coal, where it was a matter of a public-private partnership involving an international mining company (see Jacob, this volume).

Even though the relationship between capital and ruling elites can be intimate, over time they can still develop their own distinct interests when the initial investments are implemented. The level and form of compatible interest can therefore differ over time, and a new modus operandi must be established for the investment to be implemented or to continue being supported. Much the same can be said about coal in Mozambique, where the Brazilian giant Vale dominated the coal industry with very tight links to the governing Frelimo ruling elite (Monjane, 2019). However, this did not mean that Vale did not, in the end, decide to pull out when the ruling Frelimo elite's interest waned and gas in Cabo Delgado became more important for its survival.

In conclusion, the fact that public-private companies are involved in gas, coal and agricultural businesses in many Sub-Saharan African countries has consequences for how rights are promoted, implemented and actually adhered to, a topic to which we shall return at the end of this conclusion. Here it is sufficient to say that the double role of the state as both investor and formal, ultimate arbiter in relation to investments and *de jure* protector as the custodian of the law of a given state's citizens' rights, does have consequences. These consequences can be both positive and negative in claiming compensation and due process when extractive natural resources are approved and attempts are made to implement them.

2.2   Investors-Local Populations

This is without a doubt the relationship that has received most of the attention in the extractive literature on land-grabbing and the broad critical social-science literature emanating from political geography, anthropology and critical investment studies. The chapters in this edited volume make it clear that, because of the uncertain role of the state and ruling elites with regard to whom they choose to support and protect and what their actual interests are, extractive investments often end up having to compensate for the loss of substantial rights and poorly executed processes related to procedural rights that, formally and technically, should have been dealt with by the state when approving the investments.

One important implication is that, at the beginning of an investment, the often insecure exchange relations between local populations and investors become more important than is often anticipated and realised in the literature. In our framework, we have emphasised the concept of the 'reciprocal' when the relationship evolves in a productive and more positive way. This is important because natural resource investments are often framed as either accommodating or infringing local rights to land, due process and compensation. From the local population's point of view, it may make more sense to see exchange deals as involving what Sahlins famously called 'balanced reciprocity' (Sahlins, 1972, pp. 194–5), where both parties 'feel obliged to deal with each other on a moral basis' (Graeber, 2001, p. 219).

However, as we have made amply clear in this edited volume, this does not in any way imply that local populations and investors are entering relations on an equal footing or that they will necessarily develop what we call 'reciprocal exchange deals', that is, where what is exchanged is considered sufficient by both parties to accept from each other and continue working together. Rather, as should be clear, the exchange relations will normally be more or less unequal (and often unfair) because the actors' respective 'holding powers' can be quite different. Due to their different economic resources and interests, their different abilities to activate external actors for support and their different links to governments, power differences play an important role. The exchange may be informal, ad hoc and based on patron-client relations, but it may also become more stable, touching on broader processes of the institutionalisation of contracts and private property over time. Importantly, different forms and types of rights become important in and through the investments. Where much of the literature on land-grabbing and extractive investments tends to emphasise that rights are trampled on (and often they are), ignored or undermined, this is far from always being the case.

Often procedural rights involving rights, due process, consultation and compensation are first articulated, formulated and fought over when a particular investment emerges as a prospect (see, for example, Salimo, 2022; Jacob, 2020), begins to be developed and is implemented. As we have seen in the case of the gas investments in the north of Mozambique, it was actually only when big multinational investors became involved and the prospect of concessions became serious, that demands by investors, financers and multilateral institutions underwriting, the investments made rights to due compensation pertinent and put them into law. This is where the Mozambican government, like most Sub-Saharan governments, was initially hesitant and probably still is to a very high degree, as international standards of compensation for the loss of livelihoods and land are much more generous than most national standards written into law.

This is obviously quite at variance with many of the post-structural adjustment and neoliberal criticisms of foreign investment, and it poses certain problems for those assisting the post-colonial state to act in support of its own population. It is not a given that the Sub-Saharan state per se will be on the side of its population, though it is often taken for granted that it will be. Instead, due and proper compensation, as discussed by Salimo, Jacobs, and Kweka and Pedersen in this volume, can indeed be seen as 'excessive' by ruling elites or as taking away important rents that they see as 'their right'. For example, it is increasingly clear that the ruling Frelimo elites, in and from Cabo Delgado, see the northern Mozambique gas investments and their future endowments as giving them the 'right' to decide on these investments, and even as their 'entitlement' as custodians of independence from colonialism.

Here one can wonder, as many now do, whether the potential for the present youth revolt to become an Al-Shabaab insurgency, given the massive displacement of local populations in and around the areas of the key liquefied natural gas (LNG) investments, is not playing into key ruling elite factions' interests, and might even have been instigated for these reasons before spinning out of their control. The point is that, when the land is emptied of displaced people and international donors intervene and pay for resettlement and the re-establishment of livelihoods elsewhere, then the 'cake' or share for the ruling elites vis-à-vis the international investors increases. The $100 million plus initially agreed to be paid to roughly 6000 households in Palma, which was based on the new international and progressive legislation described by Salimo in this volume but which has not really reached the intended populations, seems to have had effects that went far beyond their initial goals.

2.3   Ruling Elites-Local Populations

This is without doubt the relationship that has received the least attention in the major debates related to extractive investments. Where most of the literature on land-grabbing, the resource curse, Corporate Social Responsibility (CSR) and so forth tends to focus more on the intimate relationship between ruling elites and investors or foreign investors and local populations, the important relation between ruling elites, the states they manage and local populations is usually not analysed. As we have shown throughout the volume, the relationships between local populations, ruling elites and the state may be just as important or even the most important relationships when and if we want to understand why extractive investments and the rights of local populations are promoted and adhered to. The examples of sugar in Uganda and of gas, coal and rice in Tanzania and Mozambique clearly suggest that this relationship and its longer history of what we call mutual recognition – or as is often the case misrecognition – is important for understanding how and why conflicts arise. One can therefore wonder why the relationships between the ruling elites and local populations involving large-scale natural resource investments have have received limited attention in the literature on extractives.[3]

In Uganda the intimate relations between President Museveni, the state and investors, while allowing for the approval of the sugar investments in Amuru in northern Uganda, encountered strong opposition based on the longer history of National Resistance Movement (NRM) state intervention in the area of the sugar investment that undermined further development (Buur et al., 2019).

The case of Tanzanian gas clearly shows the importance of including a longer engagement in state formation, suggesting that it is important to pay more attention to historical patterns of relations between elites and local populations, as they open windows not only into why investments are resisted, but also into how government responses can engage with long-established local resistance positively.

This becomes even clearer when one first considers the agribusiness examples. Even though they are supported by presidents and ruling coalitions, as with sugar in Uganda or rice in Mozambique, agricultural investments will often see local resistance materialise due to encroachments on land and key resources, such as water, that are important for the livelihoods of thousands of peasants or local residents. We know from the second wave of work on land-grabbing that most investments in agriculture either do not get beyond the agreement stage (Cotula and Oya, 2014; Locher and Sulle, 2014; Hall, 2013) or fall through shortly after being implemented but before the investments mature due to local resistance. Furthermore, as noted above, agricultural investments need a long time to mature, usually between six and ten years (Ouma, 2014), when few investors have the economic resources to stave off natural hazards, like flooding and drought and conflicts over land and water, or have the ability to wait so long before the investment matures.

The relationships between the ruling elites, the states they manage and local populations are therefore not just externalities related to extractive investments, but lie at the very heart of engaging with and understanding any extractive investment. The analytical bias towards not focusing on the relationships between local populations and ruling elites and their state histories in studies of extractive investments is a major problem because these relationships often have a long history that is important. Exactly how extractive investments intersect with, for example electoral cycles, is largely unresearched territory. What this volume suggests is that electoral cycles increasingly matter, despite the populist and authoritarian turn of many Sub-Saharan regimes.

The relationship between ruling elites and local populations also influences these actor group's relations with investors. Access to multilateral institutions' generous lending facilities, low interest International Finance Corporation (IFC) and World Bank loans, as well as loans from the various Asian, Latin American and African development banks and competitive commercial loans, often hinges on certain indicators of good governance and particular ideas about the stability or equilibrium of the socio-economic order. This stability is often imagined and has rarely been experienced by most African states during the relatively short period of post-independence state formation that has been the order of the day thus far. This clearly contrasts with the Latin American experience, where independence was achieved a century earlier and with a much stronger civil society being developed (Donaghy, 2018; Bebbington et al., 2018), thus allowing for very different state-society dynamics to emerge.

3.   RIGHTS AS RELATIONS

This volume clearly suggests that it is very difficult to implement extractive investments, and even more difficult to do so if the rights of local populations are not accommodated. Several of our case studies illustrate how the lack of accommodation of rights creates conflicts that may undermine investments. We have argued that, in order to analyse whether and how rights are accommodated during implementation, all three relationships between investors, ruling elites and local populations have to be taken into account. This constitutes a contribution to the different bodies of literature pertaining to CSR, the resource curse and land-grabbing in at least two ways. First, it emphasises that the underexplored relationship between ruling elites and local populations might be at least as important as the other two relationships. Secondly, it shows that the three relationships are themselves interrelated and affect each other, as well as the success of implementation and the accommodation of rights. This suggests that, besides the importance of taking into account all three relationships, the quality of all three and what characterises them is important.

Emphasising this for some possibly trivial reason at the present moment, when attention has turned towards the green transition, which has put even more pressure on the extraction of minerals, might be less trivial than it first appears. As some newly emerging literature[4] suggests, there is absolutely no guarantee that the extraction of minerals needed for the green transition will offset strategies for greening 'dirty' industries in the form of conservation and forest development and wind and solar projects, nor that it will treat local populations and their rights any better than former cycles of extractive industries have done.

NOTES

1.   See, for example, for Tanzania: https://www.africa-energy.com/news -centre/article/tanzania-negotiations-under-way-solar-and-wind-ipps;   and for   Mozambique: https://energy-utilities.com/totalenergies-selected-for -mozambique-solar-news117155.html. Both accessed on 28 June 2022.
2.   For the European Union's Repower plan see: https://ec.europa.eu/commission/ presscorner/detail/en/IP_22_3131, and for a discussion of it see: https://www .theguardian.com/environment/2022/may/18/eu-plans-massive-increase-in -green-energy-to-rid-itself-of-reliance-on-russia. Both accessed on 28 June 2022.
3.   This is even more intriguing considering that the Free Prior and Informed Consent (FPIC) that is today widely accepted is principally concerned with the role of the state as the responsible party that should secure FPIC on behalf of the

implicated populations. In practice this often ends up becoming the investor's responsibility when the state is not proactive.

4. See, for example, Fletcher and Cortes-Vazquez (2020); Hanaček et al. (2022); and for a more positive impression see Krane and Idel (2021).

REFERENCES

Bebbington, A., Abdulai, A.G., Bebbington, D.H., Hinfelaar, M. and Sanborn, C.S. (2018) *Governing Extractive Industries: Politics, Histories and Ideas*, Oxford: Oxford University Press.

Cotula, L. and Oya, C. (2014) 'Testing claims about large land deals in Africa: findings from a multi-country study', *Journal of Development Studies*, 50(7), 903–25.

Donaghy, M. (2018) 'Reforming the relationship between the state and civil society in Latin America', *Latin American Research Review*, 53(2), 388–93.

Fletcher, R. and Cortes-Vazquez, J.A. (2020) 'Beyond the green panopticon: new directions in research exploring environmental governmentality', *Environment and Planning E: Nature and Space*, 3(2), 289–99.

Graeber, D. (2001) *Towards an Anthropological Theory of Value: The False Coin of Our Own Dreams*, New York (US) and Houndmills (UK): Palgrave.

Hall, D. (2013) 'Primitive accumulation, accumulation by dispossession and the global land grab', *Third World Quarterly*, 34(9), 1582–604.

Hanaček, K., Kröger, M., Scheidel, A. and Rojas, F. (2022) 'On thin ice: the Arctic commodity extraction frontier and environmental conflicts', *Ecological Economics*, 191(January), 107247.

Jacob, T. (2020) 'The return of the state: a political economy of resource nationalism and revived state-owned enterprises in Tanzania's coal sector', Thesis, Roskilde University, https://forskning.ruc.dk/en/publications/the-return-of-the-state-a-political-economy-of-resource-nationali. Accessed 21 November 2022.

Kirsch, S. (2014) *Mining Capitalism: The Relationship between Corporations and Their Critics*, Oakland: University of California Press.

Krane, J. and Idel, R. (2021) 'More transitions, less risk: how renewable energy reduces risks from mining, trade and political dependence', *Energy Research & Social Science*, 82(December), 102311.

Locher, M. and Sulle, E. (2014) 'Challenges and methodological flaws in reporting the global land rush: observations from Tanzania', *Journal of Peasant Studies*, 41(4), 569–92.

Macuane, J.J., Buur, L. and Monjane, C.M. (2018) 'Power, conflict and natural resources: the Mozambican crisis revisited', *African Affairs*, 117(468), 415–38.

Monjane, C.C. (2019) 'Rethinking the political economy of commodity-based linkages: insights from the coal sector in Mozambique', Roskilde University Doctoral Thesis, Doctoral School of Social Sciences and Business, Roskilde University and The Institute of Resource Assessment, University of Dar es Salaam, https://rucforsk.ruc.dk/ws/files/67091435/PHD_DISSERTATION_CELSO_MONJANE.pdf. Accessed 21 November 2022.

Ouma, S. (2014) 'Situating global finance in the land rush debate: a critical review', *Geoforum*, 57(November), 162–6.

Ovadia, J. (2016) *The Petro-Developmental State in Africa: Making Oil Work in Angola, Nigeria and the Gulf of Guinea*, London: Hurst & Company.

Sahlins, M. (1972) *Stone Age Economics*, Chicago: Aldine Publishing Company.

Salimo, P. (2022) 'Governing petroleum in Mozambique: contentious governance reforms and deal-making', PhD thesis, Roskilde University, https://forskning.ruc .dk/en/publications/governing-petroleum-in-mozambique-contentious-governance -reforms-. Accessed 21 November 2022.

Salimo, P., Buur, L. and Macuane, J.J. (2020) 'The politics of domestic gas: the Sasol natural gas deals in Mozambique', *The Extractive Industries and Society*, 7(4), 1219–29.

Whitfield, L., Therkildsen, O., Buur, L. and Kjær, A.M. (2015) *The Politics of African Industrial Policy: A Comparative Perspective*, New York: Cambridge University Press.

Index

'national interest' land classification
158–9
National Rice Development Programme
(NRDP), Mozambique 152–4,
164–7, 169
national unity 6, 22
nationalization 129, 148
natural gas investments 61, 64, 72
see also liquified natural gas
NGOs *see* non-governmental
organisations
Nigerian Dangote Industries 54
'noise buffer zones' 64
non-governmental organisations (NGOs)
5
NRDP *see* National Rice Development
Programme
nucleus-outgrower model 132, 133, 135
Nugent, P. 19
Nyerere, Julius 41, 80–81, 83
Nystrand, Malin J. 26
Nyusi, President of Mozambique 74

off-farm activities 182, 190
oil companies
electoral competition 38
local populations relations 43
political economy 52
resistance to 44
ruling elites' interests 70
Russia–Ukraine war and 194
oil investments 51, 58, 60, 63, 66–7, 197
oil prices, COVID-19 effects 58
outgrowers
rice sector 160–164, 186, 189
sugar industry 104–5, 107–11, 117,
132–7
'ownership' of land 156–7
Oya, Carlos 3

parastatals 178
pastoral grazing land 178
payment system, rice production 163–4
Pedersen, Rasmus H. 12, 25, 69
pesticide use 151, 175, 184
Petroleum Act of 2015, Tanzania 51–3
petroleum sector 37–57, 60–61, 64
political alliances, Uganda 113–15
political economy 21–3, 51–3, 62, 69

political relations
local communities-oil companies
66–7
local state 67–9, 88–92
political settlement approach 3, 11–12,
21–3, 113
pollution 87–9
Porsani, J. 157, 159
postcolonial era 2, 19–20, 199
poverty reduction 153–4
price levels
rice sector 163, 166
sugar sector 100, 110–13, 117
private investments
rice sector 153
SLO links 94–5
privatization 128, 129, 177–9, 187
procedural rights 3, 8–9, 12
extractive investments 198–9
legalism from below 45
long-term rights regime 29
reciprocal exchange deals 16, 18
proceeds-sharing arrangements 133
procurement services 91–3, 131, 190
productive contract 19
productivity, rice production 149, 152–3,
161, 174, 180
profit margins, petroleum sector 47
profit reinvestment 188
property-formalization 127
protests, gas pipeline projects 49
public enterprises, rice sector 156–7
public-private partnerships 153, 154,
164, 198
Purdon, M. 126

RBLL *see* Rovuma Basin LNG Land
reciprocal exchange deals 4, 12–13,
15–18, 199
coal sector 89–92
rice production 147, 162, 164, 173,
181
sugar sector 99–100, 109
reciprocity 187–9, 198–9
regulatory framework, sugar industry
130–131
relational approach 4, 7–12, 173, 195,
202
rents
LNG investments 67